Tanzania in Transition:
From Nyerere to Mkapa

Tanzania in Transition: From Nyerere to Mkapa

Edited by
Kjell Havnevik and Aida C. Isinika

MKUKI NA NYOTA
DAR — ES — SALAAM

Published by
Mkuki na Nyota Publishers Ltd
Nyerere Road, Quality Plaza Building
P. O. Box 4246
Dar es Salaam, Tanzania
www.mkukinanyota.com

In association with
The Nordic Africa Institute,
Uppsala, Sweden

and
Sokoine University of Agriculture,
Morogoro, Tanzania

First Edition, 2010

© Contributors 2010

ISBN 978-9987-08-086-1

Contents

Chapter 1

Tanzania in Transition – To What?

Chapter 2

A Historical Framework For Analysing Current Tanzanian
Transitions: The Post-Independence Model, Nyerere's Ideas
and Some Interpretations

Chapter 3

The Norwegian-Tanzanian Aid Relationship: A Historical Perspective

Chapter 4

Agrarian Fundamentalism or Foresight? Revisiting Nyerere's
Vision for Rural Tanzania

Chapter 5

Smallholder Agriculture in Tanzania:
Can Economic Liberalisation Keep its Promises?

Chapter 6

Gender Dimensions of Land Conflicts:
Examples from Njombe and Maswa Districts in Tanzania

Chapter 7

Dynamism of Natural Resource Policies and Impact on
Forestry in Tanzania

List of Tables

List of Figures

List of Boxes and Annex/Appendices

Acronyms

AFRITAC	African Technical Assistance Committee
AIT	Agency Implementation Team (leading Tanzania Forest Service, TFS)
ASU	Agricultural Statistics Unit, of Ministry of Agriculture, Dar es Salaam
BA	Business Analysis
BOS	Bureau of Statistics, Dar es Salaam
BOT	Bank of Tanzania
CAG	Controller and Auditor General
CBFM	Community Based Forest Management
CBO	Civil Based Organisation
CCM	Chama cha Mapinduzi, the major Tanzania political party, established in 1977 through the joining of TANU and the Afro-Shirazi Party of Zanzibar
CHADEMA	The Party for Democracy and Development (Chama cha Demokrasia na Maendelo)
CIFOR	Centre for International Forestry Research, (headquarter in Indonesia, regional office in Harare until the end of the 1990s)
CMEW	Crop Monitoring and Early Warning Unit
CPI	Consumer Price Index
CSO	Civil Society Organisations
CUF	Civic United Front (political party)
CV	Coefficients of Variation
DAC	Development Assistance Committee (of OECD)
DANIDA	Danish International Development Agency
DFO	District Forest Officer
DGP	Development Partner Group
DP	Development Partners
DSM	Dar es Salaam
EA	Executive Agencies
EIU	Economic Intelligence Unit
ERP	Economic Recovery Programme, implemented in

	Tanzania 1986 – 1989
ESAP	Economic and Social Action Programme, part of ERP II, implemented in Tanzania from 1989-1992.
ESRF	Economic and Social Research Foundation, Dar es Salaam
EU	European Union
FAO	Food and Agriculture Organisation, Rome, special agency of the UN
FD	Framework Document
FDB	Forest and Beekeeping Division (of MNRT)
FRMP	Forest Resources Management Programme (from 1992 to 1999)
FY	Fiscal Year
GBS	General Budget Support
GDI	Gross Domestic Income
GDP	Gross Domestic Product
GEF	Global Environmental Facility
GoT	Government of Tanzania
Ha	hectare
HASHI	Hifadhi Ardhi Shinyanga (project for support of agroforestry methods in Shinyanga region)
HIPC	Highly Indebted Poor Countries
IFIs	International Financial Institutions
ILO	International Labour Union, Geneva
IMF	International Monetary Fund
IMG	Independent Monitoring Group
IPTL	Independent Power Tanzania Limited
JAS	Joint Assistance Strategy
JFM	Joint Forest Management
KVTC	Kilombero Valley Teak Company
LAMP	Land Management Programme (located in Babati, Kiteto, Simanjiro and Singida districts – supported by SIDA, from 1994 – 2008).
LARRI	Land Rights Research Institute (HAKIARDHI, Swahili acronym)
LGA	Local Government Authority

MAC	Ministry of Agriculture and Cooperatives, Dar es Salaam
MDB	Marketing Development Bureau, presently part of MAC, Dar es Salaam
MDGs	Millennium Development Goals
MKUKUTA	Swahili acronym for NSGPR
MLH	Ministry of Land, Housing and Urban Development (presently Ministry of Land and Human Settlement), Dar es Salaam
MNRT	Ministry of Natural Resources and Tourism
MoF	Ministry of Finance
MP	Member of Parliament
MTB	Ministerial Tender Board
MTEF	Medium Term Expenditure Framework
NACSAP	National Anti-Corruption Strategy and Action Plans
NAFCO	National Agricultural Farming Corporation
NBS	National Bureau of Statistics, Dar es Salaam (new name of BOT)
NCCR	Mageuzi – National Convention for Construction and Reform (political party)
NEC	National Election Commission
NEC	National Executive Committee (of CCM)
NESP	National Economic Survival Programme (implemented in Tanzania 1981-1982)
NFP	National Forestry Programme (implemented from 2001)
NGO	Non Governmental Organisation
NMC	National Milling Corporation
NORAD	Norwegian Agency for Development Cooperation
NPES	National Poverty Eradication Strategy
NSGPR	National Strategy for Growth and Poverty Reduction
NUTA	National Union of Tanzania, labour union established in the 1964
OAU	Organisation of African Unity (presently AU – African Union)
ODI	Overseas Development Institute, London

OECD	Organisation for Economic Cooperation and Development
PAC	Public Accountants Committee
PAF	Performance Assistance Framework
PCB	Public Corruption Bureau
PER	Public Expenditure Review
PFM	Participatory Forest Management
PO	President's Office
PORALG	Prime Minister's Office - Regional Administration and Local Government, Dodoma
PPW	Poverty Policy Week
PRGF	Poverty Reduction and Growth Facility
PRS	Poverty Reduction Strategy
PRSC	Poverty Reduction Strategy Credit
PRSP	Poverty Reduction Strategy Paper
PSM	Public Service Management
RDA	Ruvuma Development Association
REPOA	Research on Poverty Alleviation, Dar es Salaam
SADC	Southern Africa Development Coordination
Sida	Swedish International Development Agency
SAP	Structural Adjustment Programme
SGR	Strategic Grain Reserve
SP	Strategic Plan
SSA	Sub-Saharan Africa
SWAP	Sector Wide Approach
TA	Technical Assistance
TAKWIMU	National Bureau of Statistics (in Swahili)
TAMWA	Tanzania Media Women Association
TANESCO	Tanzania Electricity Supply Company
TANU	Tanganyika African National Union, the political party that was forerunner to CCM
TAS	Tanzania Assistance Strategy
TASAF	Tanzania Assistance Strategy Aid Facility
TAWLA	Tanzania Women Lawyers' Association
TEMCO	Tazania Election Monitoring Committee

TFS	Tanzania Forest Service
TGNP	Tanzania Gender Network Project
TI	Transparency International (headquarter in Berlin)
TLP	Tanzania Labour Party
TMC	Tanzania Media Council
TPC	Tanganyika Plantation Company
TShs	Tanzanian Shillings
UDP	United Democratic Party
Ujamaa	a Swahili word meaning family of communalism
Ujamaa vijijini	Swahili, meaning communalism or socialism in villages
UK	United Kingdom
UN	United Nations
URT	United Republic of Tanzania
VC	Village Council
VLFR	Village Land Forest Reserve
VLUM	Village Land Management Programme
WBI	World Bank Institute
WMA	Wildlife Management Areas
ZEC	Zanzibari Election Commission

Acknowledgements

This book is inspired by an international conference organised by the Nordic Africa Institute (NAI) in cooperation with the Swedish University of Agricultural Sciences, Department for Rural Development and Agroecology, in September 2005 (currently Urban and Rural Studies). The book also includes some of the findings from the first stage of a research project inquiring into rural and societal development in Tanzania in the post-independence period.

Many researchers and colleagues have supported the conference and the subsequent work on the book. We are grateful to Carin Jämtin, the then Swedish minister for development co-operation, who contributed her reflections to the conference on the Swedish/Tanzanian development assistance relationship over time. Special thanks go to the Tanzanian researchers and conference participants and contributors Gerald Monela, Samuel Wangwe, Brian Cooksey and Mohammed Bakari. We would also like to thank Rune Skarstein, Deborah Bryceson, Jonas Ewald and Jarle Simensen who have contributed important findings from their long-term Tanzania related research.

Our thanks also go to Jannik Boesen and Esbern Friis Hansen, Danish Institute of International Development (DIIS), Copenhagen, Just Faaland, Chr. Michelsen Institute, Bergen, Bertil Odén, Stockholm, Åsa Bjällås, Sida, Henning Melber, the Hammarskjöld Foundation, Uppsala, Sten Rylander, Swedish Ambassador to Zimbabwe (formerly Tanzania) and Lennart Wohlgemuth, the School of Global Studies, University of Gothenburg for their prepared comments to the presentations of the conference that have been valuable for the subsequent work to develop this book. We are also grateful to Jonathan Baker, the University of Agder (UiA), Norway, for constructive comments to the final review of the manuscript and inputs from colleagues at the Center of Development Studies, UiA.

Special thanks also go to Karolina Winbo, the Nordic Africa Institute, and other colleagues at NAI and the University of Agricultural Sciences, Uppsala, for their support. Lennart Wohlgemuth, former director of NAI, strongly supported the research leading up to the conference and the subsequent work on the book, as did Carin Norberg, the current director of NAI. All other participants of the conference contributed from their vast Tanzania related research and work experience and inspired the subsequent work, additions and modifications, of the book (a list of conference participants can be found as an annex).

At critical moments in the editing and publication process important contributions emerged from Walter Bgoya, Mkuki na Nyota Publishers,

Dar es Salaam, Birgitta Hellmark-Lindgren and Sonja Johansson, both NAI, and Elaine Almén who contributed her excellent language editing. In order to update the trends of Tanzanian development beyond Mkapa's presidency, empirical data and assessments of the years 2005-2010 are presented in a postscript, chapter 11.

The conference, the subsequent work and the publication of the book have been made possible by financial support from Sida, Stockholm and the Nordic Africa Institute. For this we are particularly grateful. This book is dedicated to the youth - the hope - of Tanzania.

Uppsala and Dar es Salaam in December 2009

Kjell Havnevik and Aida C. Isinika

To the youth - the hope - of Tanzania

CHAPTER ONE

TANZANIA IN TRANSITION – TO WHAT?

Kjell Havnevik and Aida C. Isinika[1]

Background

During recent years Tanzania has been held up as a champion of structural reforms from whom other countries should learn. This is being reflected in relatively high growth rates and stabilization of macro-economic parameters. The praise comes from various stakeholders such as the World Bank and IMF, donors and numerous consultants, domestic and international, who have assisted the process. Key elements that have emerged as critical for the reforms, seen as absent in most countries in the region, include; a stable political regime since 1995, high-level support for structural reforms and continuously good macroeconomic management promoted by a strong finance ministry.[2] These outcomes differ, it is claimed, from the phase of economic reform that coincided with the last stage of one-party rule from 1985 to 1995. In this period fiscal discipline was weak and many government institutions and their representatives were exposed for lack of efficiency, for not taking responsibility and for corruption. In general there was disappointment with what the government had achieved and a considerable degree of "aid-fatigue" emerged, including withdrawal of assistance by some donors. By the early 1990s relations between the Tanzanian government and donors had deteriorated to such a low level that an independent group of experts was commissioned to look into the matter.[3] Economic reforms during the period were not translated into change in economic structures that could underpin economic growth and reduce the high incidence of poverty in particular in the rural areas.

Hence the praise of recent Tanzanian development implies that the positive shift in the economic and broader development trajectory emerged with the presidency of Benjamin Mkapa from 1995. This, it is argued, is the

---

[1] Kjell Havnevik is senior researcher at the Nordic Africa Institute, Uppsala and adjunct professor at the University of Agder, Norway. Aida C. Isinika is professor at Sokoine University of Agriculture, Morogoro, Tanzania, presently on leave to work with Oxfam, Tanzania.

[2] Lawson, A. et al, "Does General Budget Support Work? Evidence from Tanzania". ODI, London, 2005.

[3] Helleiner, G. K., T. Killick, N. Lipumba, B. J. Ndulu and K. Svendsen, *Report of the Group of Independent Advisors on Development Co-operation Issues between Tanzania and Its Donors.* Copenhagen: Royal Danish Ministry of Foreign Affairs.

period that should be evaluated and assessed in a forward looking analysis of Tanzanian development and not so much what happened in the early post-colonial period and during the presidency of Mwinyi (1985-1995). In order to distance his government from the former, Mkapa, immediately upon his appointment established a presidential commission of which Joseph Warioba, a former Prime Minister was chairman, to address the corruption issue.[4]

However, most assessments of recent Tanzanian developments tend to be biased or focused on parts of the whole, for instance either on economic reforms or parts of it, or on democratic system change or on more narrow aspects of governance issues including corruption and development cooperation. The tendency has also been to focus on the post-1995 period, but even more so on the post year 2000 developments when growth figures and macro-economic parameters have improved markedly. However, such an approach tends to overlook the fact that the problem is not that poor African countries are unable to grow, "but that their growth spurts eventually fizzle out".[5] Hence economic growth and its contribution to long-term development should rather be analysed in a longer term perspective and in a broader context.[6]

Contribution of The Book

This book is a contribution to understanding the trajectory of Tanzanian development in a broader perspective by marrying the analysis of historical developments with insights from more recent transitions and in particular those related to the years of Benjamin Mkapa's two presidential periods from 1995 to 2005. Another important objective is to understand the character of the development outcomes emerging from transitions, whether they have a transformational character or not. This period is important also because it represents the first phase of the Tanzanian multiparty system. The contributions come primarily from Tanzanian, Nordic

---

[4] The Presidential Commission Against Corruption, 1996, "The Report of the Presidential Commission of Inquiry Against Corruption." ("The Warioba Commission" was formed by then president Benjamin Mkapa on the 17th of January 1996 as a way of fulfilling his election pledge to fight corruption in the country. The Commission was chaired by former prime minister Joseph Warioba). December 1996.

[5] Rodrik, D., "Goodbye Washington Consensus, Hello Washington Confusion?". Paper presented for the *Journal of Economic Literature*, January 2006, p. 16. See also Rodrik, D., "Where did all the growth go? External shocks, social conflict and growth collapses, "Journal of Economic Growth", December 1999.

[6] Arguments for a broad approach to development are also supported by Amartya Sen, "The case for taking a broad and many-sided approach to development has become clearer in recent years, partly as a result of the difficulties faced as well as successes achieved by different countries over the recent decades". Amartya Sen, 1999, "Development as Freedom", Oxford University Press, p. 126-127.

and other European researchers and institutions with a long-term commitment to Tanzanian development research.

The historical perspective has two major contributions. On the one hand it aims to identify and provide an understanding of development aspects that show continuity over time - across development strategies and models. Such aspects relate to culture and societal organization that have developed through generations and may not easily be changed by short-term interventions. Instead such continuities have to be understood in terms of the way they influence societal change and facilitate or hinder policy and strategy implementations. On the other hand the historical contribution aims to provide better insights into the pre-conditions in various areas on which the transitions sparked by policy reform and strategy change rest.

A broader perspective on transitions may inform whether a transition occurring in one area is representative for broader development processes or specific to that area/sector or alternatively may undercut or make more difficult transformational outcomes. Major complementary or competitive areas relating to Tanzanian transitions include e.g. economic vs political reforms, formal vs indigenous institutions, agricultural vs industrial development and inequality vs redistribution and well-being vs agency.[7]

Our argument is that such an approach will provide an informed point of departure for understanding whether transitions contribute to transformational outcomes or not. The distinction between transition and transformation is important. We define transitions as conscious policies and strategies and their implementation towards certain transformational outcomes in society. Such outcomes may include a change within and in the relative importance of economic sectors, poverty reduction, democratization, participation and agency or responses to the conditionalities of international financial institutions or donors. However, policies and strategies associated with transitional objectives may not necessarily bring about desired transformations.

A forward looking analysis of Tanzanian development needs to investigate whether current transitions have potential transformational outcomes. We define such outcomes in the institutional and governance sphere as those that lead to genuine participation, including gender equality, and including strengthening of the influence of citizens in development. In the broader sense they relate to creation of space for human agency so that people can influence their livelihoods. By institutions we understand rules, norms or enduring practices that are social in character in that they guide the behaviour of people and human interactions. Institutions are both of

---

[7] See for instance World Bank, *Economic Growth in the 1990s. Learning from a Decade of Reform.* Washington D.C and A. Sen op. cit., pp. 190-192.

formal and informal character, where the former include, laws or contracts while the latter evolve spontaneously and unintentionally over time out of human interaction taking forms such as codes of conduct, conventions or norms.[8]

As to governance there are different forms. The "old" or "state centric" type relates to the political and institutional capacity of the state to establish and maintain an enabling framework and guide its relationships with actors and stakeholders involved in development at transnational, national and local levels. This can be seen as a parallel and co-ordinated movement of political power to transnational levels of government and down to local levels. The state plays the leading role with capacity to guide development at critical levels. We call this state centric multi-level governance. This type of governance has gradually been complemented by a "new" concept of governance since the early 1990s. This saw a change in the role of the state that made room for governance that incorporated democracy, decentralisation, participation and empowerment at all levels. This process opened for space or agency through a horizontal shift of responsibilities from government administration and authorities towards non-governmental or civil society actors at all societal levels.[9]

Agency relates both to individuals and institutions. We do not see enhancement of agency as a means for development, but as an important part of development itself. Amartya Sen refers to development as freedom where freedom is central for evaluative and effectiveness reasons. The evaluative reason relates to assessment of progress in terms of enhanced freedoms for people while the effective reason is connected with the achievement of development being dependent on the free agency of people. Free and sustainable agency is seen as a constitutive part of development, but as

---

[8] A. Schotter. *The Economic Theory of Social Institutions*. Cambridge University Press, Cambridge and New York 1981, G. Eriksson Skoog, *The Soft Budget Constraint – The Emergence, Persistence and Logic of Institutions*. Stockholm School of Economics, Stockholm. 1998, A. Blom, "The Exogeneous – Traditional Institutions and Their Ownership", in Neil Webster (ed), *In Search of Alternatives, Poverty, the Poor and Local Organisations*. DCR Working Papers 98, 10, Copenhagen and K.J. Havnevik and M. Hårsmar, The Diversified Future – An Institutional Approach to Rural Development in Tanzania. Expert Group on Development Issues, EGDI, Swedish Ministry for Foreign Affairs, Stockholm. 1999.

[9] J. Pierre (ed). *Debating Governance Authority, Steering and Democracy*. Oxford University Press, Oxford, 2000, L. Hooghe and G. Marks, "Unravelling the central state, but how? Types of multi-level governance". In *American Political Science Review*, 97 (2), pp. 223-243, K. Eckerberg, and M. Joas, "Multi-level Environmental Governance: A concept under stress? In *Local Environment* , Vol. 9, No. 5, pp. 405-412, October 2004 and K. Havnevik, Tekeste Negash and Atakilte Beyene, "Introduction to Rural Livelihood and Governance Issues" in Havnevik et al. (eds), *Of Global Concern – rural livelihood dynamics and natural resource governance*. Sida studies no. 16, Sida, Stockholm, pp. 14-18.

well as a major engine of development. Free agency also, according to Sen, contributes to the strengthening of free agencies of other kind:[10]

> What people can positively achieve is influenced by economic opportunities, political liberties, social powers, and the enabling conditions of good health, basic education, and the encouragement and cultivation of initiatives. The institutional arrangements for these opportunities are also influenced by the exercise of people's freedoms, through the liberty to participate in the social choice and in the making of public decisions that impel the progress of these opportunities.[11]

It seems particularly relevant to inquire as to how far Tanzanian transitions under the multi-party party political system, from 1995 onwards, have moved in direction of creating space for people to exercise their freedoms.

The second type of transformational outcomes that we define as critical are those connected with structural change and the relative strength of economic sectors in generating an economic surplus over time. Such changes related to economic sectors have historically been intimately connected with productivity gains and broad based material improvements. Evidently Tanzanian industrial growth on the line of European or East Asian models cannot be replicated. But historical experiences clearly show that the question of expansion of economic activities beyond the agricultural sector is critical for broad based development. This is required for the creation of exit options from agriculture in rural and urban areas, to capture the value added from processing of agricultural and primary commodities, to ensure technological development and to make the nation address the constraints and opportunities of globalization.

Transitions that result in such outcomes and/or are able to marry them we define as transformational. Since we are not able to address all aspects of societal change in Tanzania, we have identified a number of critical transitions that historically have shown to be of particular relevance for transformational outcomes in many societies.

The framework of this book is thus to analyse contents of and interrelationships between pre-conditions for development (the historical perspective embodied in the post-independence model and long term continuities), the current processes of critical transitions (the major thrust of the book) and development outcomes (more precisely whether and to what extent transformational outcomes have been attained). The objective is primarily to analyse the period of Benjamin Mkapa's presidency. He was

---

[10] A. Sen, op. cit., p. 4.
[11] Ibid., p. 5.

elected the first democratic president of Tanzania in 1995 and won his second five year presidential term in 2000 taking 70 per cent of the votes for himself and his party CCM . By focusing on this period, the book will also contribute to throwing light on the processes and outcomes of the first phases multi-party democracy in Tanzania and how it is linked to other transitions in society.

The Post-Independence Model,
The Legacy of Nyerere and Beyond

In order to understand the role and influence of the colonial legacy, *Kjell Havnevik* in chapter two, first identifies and spells out some of the elements and compromises underpinning what he calls the post-independence development model. He subsequently addresses important areas of the legacy of the former Tanzanian president Julius Nyerere (1961-1985). Havnevik argues that Nyerere's ideas and strategies have had a profound and lasting influence on Tanzanian development. Evidence shows that Nyerere's ideas came to modify the post-independence model in important ways through the Arusha Declaration of February 1967.[12] But Nyerere's ideas and policies and the successes and failures of their implementation cannot be understood unless positioned in a societal context where domestic class forces and global interests are taken into account.

The post-independence model, Havnevik claims, comprises a number of trade-offs that relate to social, economic and regional imbalances of the colonial legacy and the social forces and processes that influenced and were influenced by the nationalist movement. The most important trade-offs of the post-independent model were those related to developmentalism vs political pluralism and consensus generation vs a conflict oriented political context. It was through the balancing of these contrasts that new Tanzanian leaders could carve out a path for nation building. The model thus rested on a social contract based on the Tanzanian people's unified anti-colonial struggle which reflected their aspirations and hopes regarding increased employment, higher wages and the satisfaction of basic needs.

In the first period of independence, the Tanzanian government saw the transformation of the economy coming through industrialization and modernization of agriculture. The frame for these changes was the nation state and that the benefits of the modernization were expected to "trickle down" to everyone. Resources for modernization were expected to come from the former colonial master, Great Britain. However, external resources

---

[12] See for instance M. Meredith, *The State of Africa – of history of fifty years of independence*. Simon and Schuster 2006, pp. 249-260.

received were limited and social differentiation took hold in Tanzanian society. Capitalist production relations expanded and exploitation and the divide between the state and people widened. Nyerere's vision of societal equality and justice was about to break, and a modification of the nation building model was required according to Nyerere. He translated his ideas and thoughts about such a modification into the Arusha Declaration. Here the emphasis of development is shifted from industry to agriculture and ujamaa villages, nucleated rural settlements or villages based on self-reliance and self-help that were to drive rural and national development.

Nucleated villages across rural Tanzania were seen to better enable the government to provide schooling, health facilities and water to rural people. Concentrated settlements and enhanced local cooperation were foreseen to lead to increased agricultural productivity and institutional development. Land was to be owned collectively by the villages. Rural cooperatives should be extended in order to increase the volume of production and increase export incomes. Industrialization was at this stage considered unrealistic - the conditions in Tanzania pointed rather to agriculture as the key to development. But did the agriculturally based ujamaa strategy have the ability to promote the desired transformational outcomes? Did the emphasis on agricultural production and exports not lead to stronger integration into global markets that could undermine self-reliance in the longer run? Was the ujamaa strategy with a strong emphasis on village driven rural development forward or backward looking?

Different interpretations emerged as to whether Nyerere's ideas and strategies could lead towards societal transformations. Three such interpretations are presented in the last section of the chapter, the ethical, the indigenous and the Marxist interpretations, in order to convey the different perspectives on the "ujamaa" strategy, its sources and potentials.

Development assistance to Tanzania increased dramatically after the proclamation of the Arusha Declaration. As an example of its character *Jarle Simensen* in chapter three analyses the Tanzanian-Norwegian development cooperation under Nyerere's presidency. Shortly after the launching of the Arusha Declaration, Nyerere visited the Nordic countries emphasising the social-democratic elements of the strategy. According to Simensen, highly placed development assistance officials in Norway stated that, "it sounded like music in our ears". Even when the Tanzanian government used force to move people into villages during 1973-76, The World Bank and international donors continued their support. But, in the 1970s, and in spite of the Arusha Declaration, the focus of development assistance shifted away from agriculture to boosting import substitution industrialization and large scale projects that could use the competence, know-how and products of the assistance providers, the donors.

The dramatic increase in development assistance and its non-agricultural emphasis ran counter to the spirit of the Arusha Declaration. In the mid-1970s development assistance accounted for nearly 30 per cent of the state budget, a doubling over the last decade. How could this happen? What was the character of this development assistance relationship? Did it lead to dependency that undermined desired transformational outcomes? Analyses of development cooperation during Nyerere's presidency and the emergence and modifications of the post-independence model will provide a historical perspective for the analysis of current transitions related to agriculture, governance and new forms of development cooperation and democracy.

The historical interpretations, according to Havnevik, provide alternative perspectives on the pre-conditions for the transitions in the 1980s and 1990s. The ethical interpretation claimed that Nyerere's ideas and thoughts and their translation into political strategies contributed significantly to nation building and peace. In addition this provided a basis, through rural change processes, for future transformational outcomes. The Marxist oriented interpretation, on the other hand, argued that Nyerere misread the pre-conditions for transformational change. Ujamaa and rural policies led to integration into the global economy without agricultural productivity increases. Lack of emphasis on industrial development in the Arusha Declaration instead undermined broad based economic development. The donor driven industrialization that occurred in the 1970s could not be supported by a weak agriculturally based economy. Let us now take a closer look at some of the findings of the current agrarian related transitions, presented in chapters four to seven.

Agrarian Related Transitions

In chapter four *Deborah Bryceson* uses case study material on Katoro-Buseresere, a rapidly expanding settlement 150 kms west of Mwanza town, as an illustration of Nyerere's blueprint for agricultural and rural development. Population growth in the settlement took off during the villagisation programme in the 1970s. But here, as in other areas of the country, tendencies towards de-agrarianisation and de-peasantisation emerged with economic reform in the 1980s. Thus rural dwellers moved away from agriculturally based modes of livelihood. The social, economic and political characteristics of peasantries throughout the ages started to erode. Commercialisation, changes in intergenerational relationships and rural-urban migration altered the terms of national development. Out of the Tanzanian population of about 37 million (2004), 63 per cent, reside in the rural areas, compared to 95 per cent at independence in 1961. According to Bryceson, the Katoro-Buseresere settlement for its part "blossomed into a thriving trading settlement during the economic liberalization policies and artisanal mining boom of the 1990s". Wealth accumulation and class differentiation are glaring features of the locality and local capitalist investors are taking a stronger grip on land and are expanding the use of wage labour.

Do these developments then not testify to the failure of Nyerere's vision of equality, reciprocity and development on the basis of agriculture? On the surface, it may be so, but according to Bryceson the deeper analysis shows that continuities and links to Nyerere's ideas and vision are still important. Agrarian forms of livelihood are still the foundation to the settlement's material and to some extent cultural security. The settlement's livelihood options have increased, now also encompassing urban type activities. The rapid population growth in Katoro-Buseresere, to a large extent from in-migration, reflects the area's ability to offer welfare improvements relative to the surrounding rural areas.

Katoro-Buseresere's features contradict the egalitarian productionist model espoused by Nyerere's ujamaa policy, but on the other hand they associate well with his modernization and forward oriented outlook, where settlements should be dynamic and ethnically diverse, not dispersed and backward looking. Bryceson argues that Nyerere stood as well for a cosmopolitan multi-ethnic and multi-religious identity. In the new development context he might have approved of the developments in Katoro-Buseresere, its embracing of the political dimensions of ujamaa and ethnic harmony, in the same way he realized that single-party politics could not carry the day in new global development narratives emerging in the early 1990s. The question remains, however, whether Katoro-Buseresere is representative of the rural dynamics of Tanzania and whether wealth accumulation and differentiation related to expansion of small-scale mining and gemstones can secure transformational outcomes.

In chapter five, *Rune Skarstein*'s contribution to the agrarian transition issue relates to a national context in terms of comparing production and productivity of food grains in two periods. The first time period is that of the pre-reform years 1976-1985, and the second of the reform and post-reform period 1986-1998. The study is a detailed analysis of available statistics across these time periods and concludes that production and productivity in the reform and post-reform period were lower than those of the pre-reform period. The implication is that the market liberalization strategy has not led to increased labour and land productivity that could assist in the growth of the agricultural surplus. This conclusion emerges from approaching the problematic from different angles in order to reduce the risk of various types of errors. It is argued that the reform model's

excessive focus on market forces as determinant of prices of outputs
and inputs cannot increase agricultural productivity and promote livelihoods in a sustainable manner. Rather, prices should be used as important policy instruments to reduce the uncertainty faced by rural smallholders. The market liberalization approach which has dominated since
the mid-1980s underscores the importance of the state in assisting smallholders to consolidate their holdings and in promoting livelihood based
poverty reduction strategies.

How can the contradiction that emerges between reports of the dynamics unfolding in Katoro-Buseresere and the conclusion related to the
negative nationwide outcome regarding production and productivity
in major grain production be explained? Is the end-point of Skarstein's
analysis, the year 1998, too early for capturing the positive agricultural
dynamics associated with transitions during the Mkapa regime? Or is
it so that the dynamics observed in Katoro-Buseresere are a survival
dynamics rather than transitional dynamics that can promote structural change?

In order to investigate whether the agrarian transition has deeper
roots, *Aida C. Isinika and Khamaldin Mutabazi* in chapter six, make
an inquiry into changes in attitudes and institutions related to land
administration and conflict resolution with a reference to gender
aspects. Changes in this area may provide important insights since they
constitute a critical foundation for rural life and production. Increases
in land conflicts are seen as a proxy for land pressure. The outcomes
of conflicts in relation to gender aspects say something about how and
whether institutions related to land administration and conflict resolution change in the context of broader societal reforms. The study
looks at these developments between 1990 and 2003, a period which
saw important legal and administrative developments related to land,
including the land policy of 1995 and the Land Acts of 1999. These
Acts, however, did not come into operation until May 2001 and have
later been amended.

The study investigates land conflicts with reference to gender in two districts
with somewhat different customary land ownership systems, Njombe
district in the Southern Highlands (within Iringa region) and Maswa
district in Shinyanga region, more to the north. There are a number of
pressures on land related institutions that derive from population increase,
the impact of villagisation of the 1970s, migration and intermarriages,
economic and political reforms and changes in policies and laws related to
land issues. In parallel there has been a process of decentralization which
has changed the location and character of administrative and legal institutions responsible for land issues.

The customary land ownership system prevails in both districts, and there is only a slow movement in the direction of land markets. According to Isinika and Mutabazi land conflicts increase when land becomes scarce. This can be measured through the level of development of the land market and the intensity of land disputes. Yet the attitudes in the areas, both among men and women (88 per cent of those interviewed), were that a rising land market would lead to landlessness with deepening of poverty and food insecurity. Although many men found that markets made it easier to convert land into other investments assets, very few had experienced possibilities to buy land on the market. Therefore, outright sale of family or clan land is not yet widespread, reflecting a dominant agrarian structure. As observed by Bryceson as regards to Katoro-Buseresere, agrarian forms of livelihood are still the foundation to material and cultural security even in emerging expanding settlements.

The study clearly shows that customary land tenure systems discriminate against women. However, women still retain important usufruct rights as well as rights of inheritance and transfer, although the latter varies between the systems. It is also generally perceived that land rights offered by indigenous institutions are quite robust. Knowledge about formal changes in laws and institutions is very limited at the local level, reflecting that indigenous institutions are still relied upon to allocate land and address land disputes. It was found that more than 60 per cent of the respondents were not aware of the ongoing land reforms. Less that 25 per cent of the men in both districts realized that land titling could enhance security of tenure. As a consequence, the emerging land markets are largely unregistered.

Notwithstanding these findings, it emerges clearly that there has been an upsurge in land conflicts in both districts after 1992, mostly between villagers who were not necessarily relatives belonging to the same clan. The findings also indicate some changes in attitudes and institutions as regards land with reference to gender. Women are more active in filing complaints and the customary land ownership institutions are providing more space for women to transfer and inherit land. Although women had increasingly taken on the role as plaintiff, their proportion amounted to only about 16 per cent of the total cases filed in each of the two districts.

Rulings in the formal system of land disputes also tend to respect women's rights more strongly than before. This reflects as well that the land related legislation has provided better formal representation for women in the land administration and conflict resolution machinery at all levels. However, these findings indicate only slow change in attitudes and perceptions as to the need for land markets, land registration and changing the male dominated customary land ownership systems. Although changes are faster in rural peri-urban like areas where developments are more dynamic, as in Katoro-Buseresere, transformational outcomes that can radically change the conditions for agricultural production and productivity cannot be seen to be emerging in the rural areas covered by this study.

In chapter seven *Gerald C. Monela and Jumanne M. Abdallah* show that transitions in the forestry sector are important both in terms of forestry practices on the ground and regarding policies and legal aspects. Formal forest management and conservation in Tanzania date back to the German colonial period, but with negative effects on the forests. The government in the 1990s realized that both central and local governments had failed to provide adequate protection and management of the forest estates, which led to an alarming rate of deforestation and degradation of state controlled forests. Declining government capacity to protect the forests related to finances, fewer human resources following retrenchment of staff during economic reforms and the general attitude of communities towards state properties, as not belonging to them. The advent of the global institutional reforms underlined the need for democratization, decentralization, participation and people's empowerment. The administration at all levels within the Forestry Sector in Tanzania responded quickly to these changes. This led to a process where villages and all the administrative layers of the government provided mutual support for each other towards greater involvement of local communities and beneficiaries in general.

This paradigm shift in Tanzania has resulted in the adoption of Participatory Forest Management (PFM), which includes Joint Forest Management (JFM) and Community Based Forest Management (CBFM). Under the CBFM approach, local communities are both owners and duty bearers, reaping all the benefits accrued from the resources. Although the importance of community forest management was felt in the 1980s, the CBFM started making news in Tanzania in the mid-1990s after the success stories from Duru-Haitemba and Mgori Forest reserves. The CBFM approach at Duru-Haitemba had a positive impact on the resource base and people's livelihoods. The forest is healthier than before and people are satisfied with the products they collect from the forests. To date both CBFM and Joint Forest Management are spreading in the country. Empirical evidence also indicates declining signs of human disturbance as well as increased stocking in forests under JFM.

Positive outcomes from community management led other villages to follow suit. In addition the Forest Policy of 1998, the Forest Act of 2002 and National Forestry Strategy 2001-2010 were informed by the practice on the ground. In 2001 the Ministry of Natural Resources and Tourism also issued guidelines for community forestry where the experience of Babati and Mgori were held up.

The Tanzanian experience with PFM shows possibilities for a conservation pattern which takes into account power relationships and control over forests while increasing citizen participation at the community level. However, there are also widespread indications that collaborative management is failing to meet all the required expectations in the country. The shortcomings of PFM include: (i) few villages have formalized their forest management plans as required by the policy and legislation; (ii) introduction of PFM is currently hampered by the cost and time it takes to transfer management rights to non – government stakeholders; (iii) revenues reported from areas under JFM – particularly in catchment forests-, remain particularly low; (iv) agriculture is the principal land use in Tanzania and remains the major livelihood of poor people, and the expansion of agricultural activities in semi-arid areas is through shifting cultivation, often using inappropriate farming practices; (v) accommodating diverse interests of local communities especially where some actors are not adequately represented in decision making organs; (vi) about 90% of total energy consumption is from fuelwood with no signs of alternative energy sources becoming available.

Even if all the forests in Tanzania are placed under either JFM or CBFM the challenge remains as to how to harvest fuelwood and timber sustainably. The question also remains whether community based forest management programmes/projects have sufficient value to stimulate community participation. The authors argue that future forest investments should address constraints emanating from the implementation of collaborative management and efforts to promote alternative energy and livelihood sources for poor communities.

Governance and Development Cooperation Transitions

One way to measure or to get an indication about governance problems is to look into trends in corruption. In chapter eight, *Brian Cooksey* examines the record of Mkapa's government in reducing corruption in Tanzania and attempts as well to come up with conclusions.

The study refers to the findings by the World Bank Institute (WBI) on Tanzania's corruption control during 1998-2004 which show little, if any, significant change, in terms of voice and accountability and governance effectiveness. As regards the rule of law there has been a slight deterioration and in terms of political stability and regulatory quality there has been marked erosion. The conclusion is that on average, governance in

Tanzania has not changed significantly during Mkapa's era. This stands in contrast to the impression given by the general praise of the Mkapa regime as mentioned earlier.[13]

In comparison with other countries, the WBI shows that two-thirds of the countries covered by its data bank have better scores than Tanzania. However, there seems to have been a substantial reduction in petty corruption relating to foreign business and investment but the degree of corruption linked with household service delivery does not seem to have declined. On balance, the public perceives such corruption to be increasing. Grand corruption trends are difficult to quantify but evidence does not indicate that corruption linked to construction, tendering, procurement and misuse of central government and foreign funds is under control. There was, however, at the end of Mkapa's reign a broad agreement that his presidential era was a marked improvement over the excesses of the previous Mwinyi era (1985-1995). This perception, however, is gradually changing in negative direction as to Mkapa's legacy since corruption at high government levels during his second presidential period, 2000-2005, were exposed in 2008 and 2009 during the presidency of Jakaya Kikwete.

On the other hand mainland Tanzania inherited from the Nyerere era a political culture and governance system which has managed to rise above ethnic, religious and cultural divisions. This can explain the relatively low levels of conflict and violence in Tanzania compared to other African countries. This has also hindered systematic political violence and social disruption in relation to exploitation of the country's rich and varied natural resources. Yet, unsustainable exploitation of natural resources is increasing in relation to forest, fisheries, wildlife and gold and gemstones outside the main gold mines.

Cooksey also shows that Mkapa's discourse on corruption changed markedly through his ten year reign from a crusading anti-corruption stance that showed impatience with due process to a turnaround stating that proof of corruption now lay with the public, not that the accused government officials should prove their innocence. Mkapa's record, including the more recent revelations, shows that there is no obvious solution to the corruption problem.

As to the impact of corruption on development outcomes, evidence shows that corruption does undermine governance, but it does not necessarily prevent growth or poverty reduction. This emerges clearly in the Asian

---

[13] Later, however, during 2008, major corruption incidences among government officials, including high level ministers, that dated back to Mkapa's second presidential period were revealed. Grand corruption continued to emerge during the reign of the current president, Jakaya Kikwete, that led to the president's dismissal in 2008 of the prime minister and as well the entire cabinet.

context where corruption is deepening without much affecting growth rates and poverty reduction. Maybe the benefits of political and institutional stability experienced by many East and South-East Asian countries make corruption more predictable than in Africa. Corruption in connection with political instability and a fluid institutional context, like in Tanzania and Africa, might undermine transformational outcomes or put them at risk.

In chapter nine, *Samuel Wangwe* focuses on the changes in development assistance modalities for development cooperation during the Mkapa era. He argues that there have been important changes since the 1980s, when aid dependence and conditionalities by donors dominated, to the current state where a partnership between the development partners and the Government of Tanzania (GoT) has emerged and continues to evolve. Tanzania experienced economic crisis from the late 1970s followed by structural adjustment in the 1980s and subsequent economic and institutional reforms into the 1990s. As donors pushed for more and speedier reforms during the 1990s, especially in terms of commitment and mobilization of local resources, the GoT felt that they were interfering strongly and eroding local ownership of the development agenda.

Subsequently, the terms for development cooperation were redefined as recommended by a group of experts in 1995. On this basis there has been regular dialogue between the GoT and development partners (DPs), emphasising consensus in order to ensure enhanced GoT leadership in development programming, increased transparency, accountability and efficiency in aid delivery. These aspects are contained in the framework for partnership to guide the management of external resources; the Tanzania Assistance Strategy (TAS), has been broadened further into the Joint Assistance Strategy (JAS), that incorporates all partners; domestic and external, aimed at operating at a higher level of commitment to the principle of best practices in development cooperation. These have been identified as basket funding, sector wide approaches (SWAPs) and general budget support. The GoT has also developed more comprehensive development strategies including the National Strategy for Growth and Poverty Reduction (NSGPR) commonly known by the Kiswahili acronym (MKUKUTA). Decentralization and devolution of power to local governments and lower levels is being pursued to ensure and enhance local ownership of development.

A review of the new arrangements for aid delivery has shown improved planning and coordination of development assistance. A framework for monitoring implementation and strengthened GoT leadership and ownership and macro-economic management has significantly improved this, along with domestic revenue mobilization. Participation in policy dialogue has been broadened and is becoming institutionalized through the public expenditure review (PER) and other processes. Consequently tensions have been reduced between the Tanzanian government and donors and trust has been enhanced. General budget support since 2002/2003 has improved the predictability of government resource flows as disbursement has ranged from 80% to 100% of commitment.

Wangwe points out however that these developments are not uniform across the range from the national level down to local communities. For example, while the level of ownership is high at the level of the Ministry of Finance, it is much lower at sectoral ministries. Leadership in dealing with local governments is not good and the role of the Parliament in the policy process is still limited to approving the budget and other legal instruments for policies where they are required. Participation of the mass media is also weak. Wange argues that unless Sector Wide Approaches (SWAPs) and basket funding are aligned to the district planning and budgeting processes, they are unlikely to work smoothly for decentralization by devolution.

While Wangwe acknowledges the continued requirement for development assistance over a long time to come, he cautions against aid dependence, and points to the need for an exit strategy that will eventually wean Tanzania and other developing countries from aid, a double edged sword. The emerging dangers of deepening aid dependency are not compatible with recent aid fatigue among DPs. Wangwe therefore suggests that an important component of the dialogue between GoT and DPs should be to develop a realistic exit strategy. This could be done by identifying common targets for phasing out aid to the public sector budgets. On technical assistance, which has been largely supply driven with little inbuilt capacity building, Wangwe proposes that it should be subject to more open, transparent and competitive procurement procedures and should be linked to facilitating institutional capacity building.

In chapter ten *Jonas Ewald* shows that the outcome of the political reform since the early 1990s is ambiguous. Although Tanzania has seen peaceful transitions through four presidents since independence in 1960, and gone through a peaceful transition from one party to a multi-party state, the new democratic system has as well shown up divisions and conflicts that the one party system managed to contain, albeit in an authoritarian way. Ewald focuses his analysis around the relationship between economic reforms, which picked up speed during the 1990s, and the democratic process on the political front.

Reviewing the political structure, Ewald highlights the characteristics of the ruling party (CCM), a well structured organization with developed and fairly democratic procedures, despite allegations of corruption in internal nomination processes during elections. CCM also derives its strength from its historic and contemporary close ties with government structures, administration and the media. Such ties inevitably weaken the eighteen opposition parties existing around 2005, of which only five were more fully developed political parties with representation in parliament. The opposition also remains weak because of internal conflicts, revolving around presidential candidates and corruption in managing party resources.

Both the media and the judiciary are relatively independent. But corruption in both institutions continues to be a concern. Lack of resources and short-age of educated staff with reasonable salaries further reduce the capacity of the legal system to enforce laws. The Legal Sector Reform Programme faces many challenges. The political and administrative reforms, along with globalization and economic liberalization have created more expectations and deepened the need for democratic governance. Consequently, there has been more public awareness and involvement in debates regarding corruption and participatory processes. However, the culture of dominance and patronage by the administration remains a major constraint.

Ewald attempts to assess whether the interface between economic, political and administrative reforms in Tanzania has established a pro-poor growth regime. He finds that the macroeconomic gains have not trickled down to the majority of Tanzanian citizens. A large amount of the population still lives below the basic needs poverty line. Despite some improvements in the education sector, net enrolment to tertiary education remains the lowest in East Africa, which reflects low capacity to build human capital.

While the reforms have created opportunities for entrepreneurs, it is argued that the reforms have undermined people's trust in the nation building process of the state. On the other hand, increased donor support has strengthened the administration's resource base, and hence the ruling party in monetary and prestige terms. The weak resource base of parliament, opposition parties and civil society organizations hinders them from developing their capacity to challenge the public administration.

Looking at the political reforms in relation to the electoral process in 2000 and 2005, Ewald first revisits previous elections when there was one political party. With economic liberalization and deepening globalization, the one party system had outlived its role (as argued by Cranford Pratt) in forging ethnic unity and thereby protecting the country from the divisive competition which multi-party politics may generate. Ewald shows, however, that the old one party legislation has not been replaced, rather that it has been amended to accommodate the multi-party system. On this basis, the opposition continues to demand a new constitution, as recommended by the Nyalali Commission in 1992. In Zanzibar, the transition to multiparty elections has been shrouded in problems, including killings linked to unresolved pre- and post-election issues.

The three multi-party elections demonstrate that CCM has consolidated its position, both in the presidential and parliamentary elections, as opposition parties have faced crushing defeats. This trend continued in the December 2005 elections when Jakaya Kikwete of CCM won the presidency with 80 per cent of the vote. Ewald attributes this development primarily to the electoral system of single member constituencies with winner takes all. He advocates instead a proportional system, which would have increased the opposition parties' representation in parliament.

Ewald concludes that economic reforms have a direct bearing on the democratization process. Hence, support to the economic and administrative reforms must be designed so that they do not undermine the room for manoeuvre of the opposition, the parliament, civil society, the media and other political institutions. This chapter therefore raises relevant questions regarding the transformational character of the ongoing economic, administrative and political reforms. Was the transition to democratic rule (via multi-party elections) profound in terms of allowing people fair representation and influence in the political process or did political reform merely help old structures to modify and survive?

CHAPTER TWO

A HISTORICAL FRAMEWORK FOR ANALYSING CURRENT TANZANIAN TRANSITIONS: THE POST-INDEPENDENCE MODEL, NYERERE'S IDEAS AND SOME INTERPRETATIONS

Kjell Havnevik

Introduction

This chapter will identify and analyse perspectives, ideas and processes that are important for understanding the historical framework for current Tanzanian transitions. This is done in terms of identifying a post-independence model and the important political and societal compromises that underpin it. The analysis of the historical framework has to go beyond economic issues and include political, social and cultural aspects. Tanzania and most African countries have emerged from a long period of colonisation. The constraints of the colonial legacy for the range of political options at hand for the post-independent state are important parameters for assessing and understanding the post-independence development path. Tanzania is special for its attempt to change the course of its development path. The ideas and perspectives around influencing and implementing such a change are in important ways related to Julius Nyerere, the former president (1961-1985), who subsequently became the official "father of the nation".[1] His perspectives became strong inputs for modifying the post-colonial model, partly because of the resonance of the ideas themselves, but partly because Nyerere at the time held executive power as president of the country. The chapter will also analyse how Nyerere's ideas and philosophy were translated into politics and policies. Different interpretations of Nyereres's contributions will be put forward in order to

---

[1] Julius Nyerere was one of the few high level politicians in Tanzania who was considered "clean", i.e. who had not appropriated wealth illegally. This had created an important moral example for at least part of the younger generation. However with Nyerere's death in 1999, his role as moral example weakened and corruption in high government circles seemed to increase from 2000 onwards, as revealed by the recent disclosures during 2008. Being "Father of the Nation" meant that Nyerere received an income that prevented him and his family from being exposed to poverty. It seems evident that lack of social and economic safety nets for government employees after retirement is an important driving force for rent seeking and corruption. This structural cause for African corruption tends to be overlooked in the moralistic analysis of the north of the state in Africa in general.

show the varying understandings of the ideas, their impact and potentials. In combination these will provide a historical framework that may help us understand better the pre-conditions for the current transition in Tanzania and how or whether they relate to transformational outcomes.

The Post-Independence Model

Background

The emergence of a post-independence model is intimately tied to the rise and struggle of the nationalist movement in the 1950s which emphasised independence, unity and equality. In this section I will identify, describe and analyse briefly the major elements and trade offs of the post-independence model during its first phase prior to the proclamation of the Arusha Declaration in February 1967. The major pre-occupations of the post-independent state during this period were modernisation of the economy and consolidation of the state. My argument is that the economic, social, ethnic and regional structures and imbalances that had developed in Tanganyika before independence must provide the backdrop against which to understand the social forces and processes that influenced and were influenced by the nationalist movement. In addition they provide a background for understanding the economic and political choices that the leaders of the post-independent state made as regards the nation's development path. The room for manoeuvre of the nationalist movement was constrained both by the colonial legacy, the character of the nationalist movement itself and its leadership and the challenges encountered in creating nationhood.

It is, in my assessment, possible to distinguish a single basic post-independence development model, resting on a number of central trade-offs or compromises, that undergo modifications over time in response to economic, political and social pressures. A model, however, is always a simplification of reality. Its relevance will depend upon how it is able to capture central issues, processes and relationships based on knowledge and insights of a wider societal context. Joan Robinson in her treatise on economic heresies, states that, "It is easy enough to make models on stated assumptions. The difficulty is to find the assumptions that are relevant to reality".[2] The understanding of this post-independence model in turn rests on the conceptualisations of a set of basic trade-offs that underlies the model and the shifts in emphasis within and between its different trade-offs over time. These trade offs provide an understanding of a framework within

---

[2]   Robinson, Joan 1971, *Economic Heresies. Some old-fashioned questions in economic theory.* MacMillan, London and Basingstoke, p. 141.

which the political choices and prioritisations of the post-independence state were structured.

Before specifying the content of the various trade-offs with reference to the elements of the colonial legacy, let me outline the three major "sectors" of the post-independence development model. The dominant development agent that emerged on the eve of independence was the post-colonial state. No social group was strong enough to impose its interest on the state formation, which provided a basic underpinning of the nationalist ideology, that the state was a "state for all". Thus the state took upon itself to be the main actor and agent in the promotion of the modernisation process. This process was to unfold within the framework of the nation state with an aim to promote economic growth and increase fulfilment of basic needs for all. The state, within this framework, had a critical regulative role in counteracting the economic, social, political and regional imbalances associated with the colonial legacy. This included as well the need for the state to create a broad consensus around major nation building policies. Thus there was a strong linkage between the regulatory functions of the state and creation of the space for consensus around nation building policies and strategies.

The capital sector was the second major driving force of the modernisation process. It consisted of local, mainly Asian, and European, including British, stakeholders. The external capital sector was strongly linked to the latter through the historical colonial relationship. The major tasks of the capital sector, in co-operation with the state, were to promote industrial development and to modernise agriculture. These were key challenges of the modernisation process that the new government of Tanganyika had taken upon itself to implement.

The third sector, agriculture, comprised both smallholders and the plantation sector. In the perspective of modernisation, the deficient technologies of the smallholders had to be upgraded. This was an important task which was connected with the striving towards industrialisation. In its interaction with smallholders, the state also entered into complex relationships with formal and informal local institutions.

Within this frame of major actors or sectors of post-independence development, a number of trade-offs had to be addressed by the state, including (i) consensus generation versus a more conflict oriented policy context, (ii) developmentalism versus a pluralistic political system, (iii) state versus non-state provision of basic needs and (iv) continued external dependency versus an internally oriented development strategy. In the following some of the basic contents of the four trade-offs will be presented with emphasis on the most dominant ones, i.e. (i) and (ii).

Consensus generation versus a more conflict oriented policy framework

Tanganyika was approaching the end of colonial rule with a structure of limited social differentiation, but growing regional and social divisions in some areas. As TANU (Tanganyika National Union) membership grew, its social basis became increasingly diverse, and according to Iliffe, "no one social group dominated, but certain patterns of support recurred".[3] This implied that no African social group was sufficiently strong or economically dominant to aspire to the leadership of the nationalist movement. It was instead a small group of educated Tanzanians with the teacher Julius Nyerere at the forefront who created TANU and stayed on as its leaders. A small, but well organised labour force and a large mass of poor farmers, "constituted the social base of the nationalist movement".[4] This social reality was reflected in the first motto of TANU, "Freedom and Development".

As TANU moved to the rural areas it did not, however, explicitly exploit the hostility that had developed over the Native Authorities' role in implementing the rules and orders associated with colonial agricultural policy. The leadership of TANU neither endorsed nor encouraged resistance to this policy and its development schemes. Nyerere and his colleagues were disturbed by vigorous and possibly violent local protest which TANU had neither initiated nor could control. In the quest for modernisation and wishing to present a responsible image to the colonial state, they tended to uncritically accept the judgement of professionally qualified officers on such technical issues as the need for cattle-culling, tie-ridging and terracing.[5]

The national issue that provided overwhelming support for TANU throughout Tanganyika was the attempt by the colonial state to give disproportionate political power to the European and Asian minorities within the political institutions of post-colonial Tanganyika. This led to deep-rooted fears on the part of the African population that, "Tanganyika might yet be dominated by Asian and European minorities".[6]

As chairman of TANU, Nyerere had done his best to create ethnic and tribal unity in the struggle for independence. In the negotiations over constitutional issues with the colonial government, Nyerere had argued that, "the interracial co-operation and the intertribal unity which TANU had generated and was sustaining were political and social assets of enormous value.

---

[3]   Iliffe, J. 1979, *A Modern History of Tanganyika*. Cambridge University Press, Cambridge, p. 523.
[4]   Kiondo, A. 1989, *The politics of economic reform in Tanzania 1977-1988*. Phd Thesis, University of Toronto, p. 11.
[5]   Pratt, C. 1976, *The Critical Phase in Tanzania 1945-1968: Nyerere and the emergence of a socialist strategy*. Cambridge University Press, p. 34.
[6]   Ibid., p. 28.

They would be threatened if Africans came to feel that they would have to fight for their independence".[7]

TANU's consensus generating role, although important, had clear limitations. Firstly, the consensus centred around modernisation and nationalism. By placing the nation as the framework for modernisation, the nationalist movement and later the post-colonial state, came to repress and undermine cultural, ethnic, social and religious diversity as well as certain ways to make a livelihood. For instance, many of the major pastoralist groups, including the Maasai, had their land alienated by both encroaching agriculturalists and by the post-independence state that appropriated pastoral land for the enlargement and creation of conservation areas, wildlife parks and state farms. The forced movement of pastoralists into nucleated villages in the 1970s and 1980s further undermined the pastoral way of living.

Not much is known about the relationship between indigenous religions and nationalism. Many religious practitioners did not participate in politics, while others seemingly considered TANU a threat to the indigenous order. Traditionalists, however, usually lacked the skills of the modern politicians and "TANU leaders were modernists who, like Nyerere, habitually spoke of indigenous leaders with an embarassed smile".[8]

Christian attitudes to nationalism varied. Christian churches and missions were extensively intertwined with the colonial state. The colonial state paid nine-tenths of mission teachers' salaries. The Christian churches were also linked to the critics of the colonial society. For instance, many TANU leaders had been trained in mission and church schools, including Julius Nyerere and Oscar Kambona, the secretary of TANU. These leaders transferred an ideology of Christian altruism to TANU which differed from indigenous ethics.[9] But to place all Christian religious movements in the nationalist camp, is according to Ranger a serious error, ".we can begin to construct a much more complex pattern of religious politics. This was sometimes anti-colonial, and sometimes allied to movements of nationalism, but so far from taking these connections for granted we need to treat them as problematic, as needing explanation, just as all other kinds of social and political implications of religious movements need explanation".[10]

Discussing the Muslim response to nationalism, Iliffe contends that "Muslim reactions to TANU were probably more completely positive than those

---

[7]   Ibid., p. 52.
[8]   Iliffe op. cit.1979, p. 550.
[9]   Ibid., p. 547.
[10] Ranger, T., 1986, "Religious Movements and Politics in Sub-Saharan Africa". In *The African Studies Review*, Vol. 29, June, p. 51.

of Christians".[11] Muslim activists helped to establish TANU and Muslim brotherhoods provided strong support for the nationalist movement due to their predominantly African membership and regional extension. Nearly all lines of Muslim opinion supported TANU, although there were also some exceptions. The National Union of Tanganyika, with its main base in Dar es Salaam, suggested in 1959 that independence should wait until Muslims had attained the same level of education as Christians. But TANU used its influence and mobilised local sheikhs to counter this idea.[12]

By linking the modernisation approach with traditional values and cultures such as redistribution and reciprocity, TANU was able to pre-empt a growing opposition from traditional cultural and religious bodies and thereby, at least in its early phase, provide some political and cultural cohesion to the post-colonial model. The launching of the Arusha Declaration in 1967 signalled some form of African socialism where the policies of ujamaa, were the major element. Nyerere wished to tie the values of ujamaa with the values and norms that had prevailed in pre-colonial Tanzania and use this as a model for the future. When first introducing the ujamaa concept in the early 1960s, it was more strongly linked with the modernisation idea, without the strong emphasis on culture and tradition.[13] Arguments for the technical benefits of villagisation were first promoted by the World Bank in 1961.[14]

Developmentalism versus a pluralistic political system

One of the early decisions, in 1963, of the post-independence state was to abolish the power and role of the chiefs and indigenous institutions and replace them by formal institutions. By so doing, the relationship between the central state and the rural population changed. Yet the unpopular chiefs that had lost legitimacy due to their close collaboration with the colonial state did not disappear fully. However, this radical break with the local institution of the colonial and pre-colonial systems, offered a new scope for state-peasant relationships that came to be further formalised through villagisation.

The first national development plan of the then Tanganyika covered the period 1961 to 1964 and was prepared by British civil servants. It largely amounted to a compilation of individual projects promoted by government

---

[11] Iliffe op. cit. 1979, p. 551.
[12] Ibid., p. 552.
[13] Nyerere, J. 1962, "Ujamaa – The Basis for African Socialism". TANU Pamphlet. Dar es Salaam and Nyerere 1966, "President's Inaugural Address", In Nyerere: *Freedom and Unity*. A selection of writings and speeches 1952-65. Oxford University Press, pp. 176-187.
[14] World Bank 1961, *The Economic Development of Tanganyika*. John Hopkins Press, Washington D.C.

ministries. The overall modernisation emphasis clearly emerged in the plan through promotion of import substituting industries. This meant that instead of importing finished goods, Tanganyika aimed to build her own industries to provide domestically produced goods. This policy was further underlined in the second development plan, 1964-1969, which was more Tanzania's own plan still, however, basically prepared by an expatriate team. Here it also emerged that modernisation had to rely on continued support of progressive and innovative farmers and mechanisation of agriculture through creation of highly capitalised nucleated villages. The government expected investments for modernisation to come from the British state and from foreign and local private sources.[15] Basically small farmers were left to fend for themselves. Of greatest importance to them was the growth and spread of the co-operative movement.

The co-operative movement had been strongly behind the nationalist policies and immediately after independence the government invested great efforts in spreading it beyond non-cash crop producing areas. This approach aimed to increase the marketed agricultural output and to weaken the role of the Asian ethnic minority as intermediaries in trade and crop purchasing. Government involvement in agricultural marketing gradually increased and by the end of 1966 twelve national agricultural boards had been created with regulatory or advisory or monopoly functions.[16]

A three-tier, agricultural marketing system, i.e. the primary societies, the regional co-operative unions and the marketing boards, was made the single legal channel for marketing of agricultural produce. A major thrust of post-colonial policies was to enlarge and control the agricultural surplus. The agricultural surplus is that portion of production which is beyond what farmers consume themselves, reuse as seeds or feed to animals. The role of the agricultural surplus is maybe best understood through its functions or use as food for the non-agricultural population, as raw materials for the industrial sector and as "export crops" to generate external revenue. There is a strong link between the size of the agricultural surplus and the potential for an economy to grow in a diversified way. The total marketed agricultural output in an economy may be used as an indicator of the agricultural surplus. However, since it also includes marketed transfers within the agricultural sector itself, this indicator tends to exaggerate the size of the surplus.

The government expanded its regulation and control of the agricultural sector. As early as 1966, the government appointed a Special Committee

---

[15] Pratt op. cit., 1976, p. 97.
[16] Wagao, J. 1982, *State Control of Agricultural Marketing in Tanzania 1961-1976*. Economic Research Bureau Paper 82.7, University of Dar es Salaam, p. 5.

of Enquiry in the co-operative movement which concluded that the move-ment was suffering from basic defects and problems. These were stated to be an uninformed membership, shortage of qualified manpower, absence of democracy at union level and political interference.[17] A later report of inquiry, Kriesel et al 1970, confirmed these findings and recommended more autonomy for societies that were doing well. The Special Committee of 1966, however, argued for the need for "a greater degree of central responsi-bility and central accountability".[18] This latter recommendation opened the way for increased government interference in the co-operative movement.

The post-independence state gradually undermined the unity of the nationalist movement. In 1962, however, the state had already taken initia-tives to control civil society organisations that had helped promote the nationalist movement into power. Early attacks were aimed to destabilise the labour movement. The government also banned senior civil servants from participating in trade unions. Legislation was pushed through that disarmed individual labour unions and in June 1962 the right to strike was drastically limited. A few months later the Preventive Detention Act, i.e. the right of the government to seize and jail people without proper juridi-cal procedure, was passed and this Act was used against leaders of trade unions and traditional chiefs who challenged nationalist policies.[19]

Subsequently, in February 1964, the National Union of Tanganyika (NUTA) was established as a single national labour union affiliated to TANU. The union had thus lost the autonomous position in society that it had opted for in the anti-colonial struggle. The creation of NUTA had followed the January 1964 army mutiny, which was related to the trade unions' and the military's demands for Africanisation and higher wages. The consolidation of the post-independent state required external force as Nyerere called in British troops to quell the mutiny. Sixty British marines were landed by helicopter at military barracks on the outskirts of Dar es Salaam and half an hour later the mutiny was over.[20]

Only six weeks before the army mutiny Zanzibar and Pemba had been given their independence from Britain and a month later the revolution on Zanzibar took place. Details of the revolution are obscure until this day since none of those strongly involved in it has written about it, except John Okello, a Ugandan, who himself claimed to be its leader. In the

[17] URT 1966, *Report of the Presidential Special Committee into Co-operative Movement and Marketing.* Dar es Salaam, pp. 9-10.
[18] Havnevik, K. J. 1988, *State Intervention and Peasant Response in Tanzania.* Phd thesis. University of Bradford, England, p. 44.
[19] Pratt op. cit.,1976, p. 187.
[20] Listowel 1965, "The making of Tanganyika". Chatto and Windus, pp. 430-40, Edgett Smith, 1971, *We Must Run While Others Must Walk*, Random House and Coulson, A.1982, *Tanzania: A Political Economy.* Spokesman, Nottingham, p. 140.

pre-revolutionary period, most of the 1950s and into the 1960s, the clove harvests were poor, the main crop on the island. This led to unemployment and economic depression. Violence increased and was directed towards the government and against the Arabs, in particular those who kept small shops all over the island.[21]

Analysts argue that it is likely that not only Okello prepared for plotting against the government, but also the Afro Shirazi Party leadership under Abeid Karume with the support of Nyerere. The Umma party led by Abdulraman Babu was also likely to have been prepared for plotting against the government.[22] Karume became the new president of Zanzibar and only a few weeks later a union agreement had been negotiated with Tanganyika. "The United Republic of Tanzania" was proclaimed on April 23 1964.[23] The union with Tanganyika, how it was done, and the terms under which it was pursued, have until today represented a major problem for political stability in Tanzania.

TANU and state control of the politics of Tanzania continued to deepen. In July 1965 a new one-party Constitution was introduced with the underlying assumption that, "the nation is harmonious and united and that the elections involved the choice of trusted individuals who will then legislate on the nation's behalf".[24] This "state for the people" ideology envisaged the state as a unifying factor and a provider of "each and every thing to all people equally, while protecting them from external exploitation, manipulation and /or domination".[25] Coulson claims that Nyerere's modernisation theory, in rejecting the past as traditional and inherited patterns of production as destructive and backward, is "authoritarian and implies social engineering (or management by the state apparatus) rather than democracy, although Nyerere himself does not take the logic that far, at least not in his writings".[26]

Kiondo (1989) has argued that the increasing predominance of authoritarianism over democracy led to a specific form of 'statism' in Tanzania. This is understood in terms of a simultaneous expansion and centralisation of state economic activities and reduction of possibilities or channels for popular participation. According to Kiondo, statism can be traced to the early post-independence struggles between the newly

---

[21] Coulson, A., ibid., 1982, p. 132.
[22] Lofchie, M. 1967, "Was Okello's Revolution a Conspiracy?" Transition (Kampala) 33, pp. 39-42; reprinted in Cliffe, L. and J. Saul (eds), 1972, Socialism in Tanzania: An Interdisciplinary Reader, Vol. I, East African Publishing House and Heineman Educational Books, pp. 31-38 and Coulson op. cit., 1982, p. 133.
[23] Coulson op. cit., 1982, 132-133 and Edgett Smith 1973, pp. 122-136.
[24] Pratt op. cit., 1976, p. 207.
[25] Kiondo op. cit., 1989, p. 12.
[26] Coulson op. cit., 1982, p. 329.

created post-colonial state and labour unions. Pratt was unwilling to draw any conclusions about the longer term consequences of what he calls the, "Tanzanian democratic one-party system". He argued that "in its early manifestations as well as in its original purposes it was intended to provide and did provide an effective popular check upon authoritarian tendencies within the TANU leadership" (!).[27] Nevertheless, Pratt conceded as well that "the electoral system could easily be adapted to a more authoritarian style of leadership".

State versus non-state provision in increasing satisfaction of basic needs

In its quest for meeting popular demands in the early post-colonial period, the government raised minimum wages in 1961 and 1963 that led to a significant improvement in the position of poor wage earners. The post-colonial state's policies intended to modify the ethnic and regional imbalance of commercial agriculture by promoting progressive farmers and mechanisation. At the same time this led to increased social differentiation in the rural areas. This development was compounded by increasing state control of some of the co-operative movements of larger farmers. This undermined the expectations of smallholders and marginal farmers who had supported the nationalist movement in the belief they would see substantial improvements in their material livelihoods. Like-wise workers, civil servants and others who had supported the nationalist movement did so with the hope of seeing the spread of social services, and getting access to better education and employment opportunities. Failure to meet these demands and aspirations after independence was bound to strengthen the divisive forces in society. According to Amir Jamal, the long time Minister of Finance in Nyerere's various governments, and one of the staunchest nationalists with an Asian background, "The critical test is one of being able to reconcile the short-term priorities with the long-term objectives".[28] Not only Tanzanian leaders, but also those in other Sub-Saharan African countries, were faced with a similar challenge to balance the demands of the nascent petit bourgeoisie

---

[27] Pratt op. cit., 1976, p. 208.

[28] A. Jamal quoted in Pratt op. cit., 1976, p. 1 and Lonsdale, J., 1981, "States and Social Processes in Africa: A Historiographical Survey", in *The African Studies Review*, Vol. XXIV, Numbers 2/3, June/September, p. 196. Nyerere's efforts to undermine ethnic tension also made him include non-black members in his cabinet, among them Amir Jamal, Derek Bryceson, of British origin, as Minister of Agriculture in the first post-independence government and in later cabinets, and Al Noor Kassum, of Asian background. Al Noor Kassum has written a biography of his life and his experiences as a Tanzanian and UN civil servant, see Kassum 2008, *An International Tanzanian*.

with the reproduction of the supply of basic needs to meet the demands of the broad masses.[29]

Continued external dependency versus an internally oriented development strategy

One way of accessing resources to meet development needs and demands for social services etc, was through external sources. Contrary to popular belief, the policy emphasis in the early post-colonial period was continued dependence on the former colonial power, Great Britain. This related both to civil service manpower and investments. These policy emphases emerged from limited financial resources and that Tanganyika did not have any, or only a small, middle or bourgeois class, generally a low level of education of the population and weak and externally dependent economic structures.

The decision by the leadership of TANU and the post-colonial state to continue its dependence upon the former colonial power, set clear limitations for the speed of Africanisation in the national institutions that emerged. The major share of the senior government positions, the police and the military were in the hands of the former colonial masters. Trade and business in the early independence period were mainly conducted by non-Africans. In addition British economic assistance fell way below expectations. When pressures mounted for further Africanisation of the state and national institutions, the state leadership had to retreat somewhat from its external dependency policy.

The trade-offs of the post-independence model – some concluding comments

Despite its increasingly authoritarian character, it is still possible to regard the early post-colonial state as being in pursuit of modernisation through a variety of channels and initiatives. From 1964 onwards when important democratic institutions were undermined and channels for popular expression closed, autonomous institutions still remained. In spite of increasing government interference in the co-operative movement, the movement remained autonomous. In the industrial sector, the state actively promoted the private sphere. To regard the first phase of post-colonial rule as a trade-off between developmentalism and political pluralism captures one of the critical arenas where the state had to balance contending forces and interests. Nyerere himself on several occasions mentioned the, "analogy

---

[29] Bangura, Y. 1989, "The political and social context of structural adjustment in Sub-Saharan Africa", in *Nytt från Nordiska Afrikainstitutet*, no. 24, pp. 22-24.

between a wartime coalition government in a constitutional democracy and the need for a united effort in Tanganyika to achieve stable government and rapid development. The war 'against poverty, ignorance and disease' required a national effort similar to the effort needed to win a war against an enemy power".[30] A one-party system was seen as both a proper and genuinely democratic response to national crisis. Yet, it also carried the seeds of authoritarian rule.

The modernisation strategy, however, led to growing economic and social differentiation. The politicisation of government institutions further weakened the division between the state/party and civil society. Political power was the basis for economic control and the regulatory mechanisms in the hands of government bureaucrats could easily be used for rent seeking and personal enrichment. In the early independence years, Nyerere was already concerned about the unity and commitment to the common good, a hallmark of TANU. This, in his opinion, was being destroyed by the scramble for status, income and personal power by party members. A growing divide between TANU leaders and the state bureaucracy on the one hand and peasants, workers and ordinary people on the other had to be addressed.

Although the expansion of regulatory mechanisms of the state provided opportunities for rent seeking, many of the early government initiatives aimed at addressing ethnic and regional imbalances. One approach used by Nyerere to counter the narrowing space for consensus was to incorporate different political factions into the decision making process.[31] Such imbalances were, by the leaders of the nationalist movement, seen to undermine a common ground for development and political stability.

The decision of the post-colonial state to depend on Britain went against the aspirations of the anti-colonial struggle for genuine national sovereignty. This strategy choice was modified due to the limited British support and it was fully overturned with the Arusha Declaration in 1967. The relationship between the leadership of the nationalist movement and its social base had developed from the common anti-colonial struggle and can be seen to represent some kind of social contract that rested on the expectations from the successful outcome of the struggle. The developmental path, however, could only partly satisfy these demands and expectations. The developmental emphasis had tilted the basic trade-off away from a pluralistic political system. The political legitimacy of the post-colonial state would be increasingly questioned as developmental benefits did not emerge.

---

[30] Pratt, op. cit., 1976, p. 68.
[31] Omari, C. K., 1995, "The management of tribal and religious diversity". In Legum, C. and C.K. Mmari (eds), *Mwalimu – the Influence of Nyerere*, British-Tanzania Society, London, p. 29. See also note 28 above.

Rather than moving in direction of a society emphasising equality for all, Tanzania was moving towards deepening economic and social differentiation and capitalist oriented ways of production. Nyerere's design for societal development was about to break. It was not an economic crisis that was the underlying cause, but the undermining of elements of the post-independence model. The various trade-offs and compromises were no longer able to hold sway. A bridging of the gap between rich and poor, between the urban and rural and between TANU and its social base, required re-emphasis on the social profile of the development model and introduction of policies and initiatives that could halt the spread of capitalist production relations. This important modification or shift of political course came with the Arusha Declaration of February 1967.

There is, however, a more fundamental question relating to the post-independence nation state in Africa that goes beyond this discussion and that has been raised by historians. This focuses on whether there exists a possibility of establishing an imported notion of the nation state on the African post-colonial legacy. The historians return to the pre-colonial period when African societies were "governed through a set of norms that were ethnic, interethnic and supraethnic, thus 'national' in scope."[32] Historical evidence shows numerous examples from the pre-colonial period of black African socio-political formations that grew from the merging of different socio-political and cultural systems, under the guidance of customary or written law. The interpretation of historians claims that the historical process of endogeneous, or internal, African development processes, focussed on national development was sacrificed and undermined through the imposition of the colonial reign. Evidence from Tanganyika supports this argument. Among the Sambaa in Pare Mountain, Feierman, found that a fundamental transformation took place in local social structures in connection with the colonial conquest, "The forms of local mutual assistance in the colonial period, which are commonly referred to in the literature as pre-capitalist, were not at all the same as the pre-colonial ones".[33]

But was Nyerere not aware of this problematic when he designed the post-colonial state and its structures in Tanzania? The next section will inquire into Nyerere's ideas and philosophy and their implications for the Tanzanian post-independence model.

---

[32] Ki-Zerbo 1995, 'Which way Africa?' Reflections on Basil Davidson's The Black Man's Burden, in *Development Dialogue* 1995:2, The Dag Hammarskjöld Foundation, Uppsala, pp. 107-108.

[33] Feierman, S., 1990, *Peasant Intellectuals-Anthropology and History in Tanzania*. The University of Wisconsin Press, p. 63.

Nyerere's ideas and perspectives, the Arusha Declaration and Ujamaa – and the modification of the post-independence model

Introduction

In July 1968 Nyerere, in the introduction to the book, "Ujamaa – Essays on Socialism" wrote that since 1962 TANU had been committed to building a socialist society. But the meaning and implications of the socialist philosophy were "left vague". The pamphlet that Nyerere had written, "Ujamaa – The Basis of African Socialism," had been published in English and was not easily available to Tanzanians. And thus according to Nyerere:

> Many active party workers, and also many of our teachers and civil servants, therefore remained unclear about even the most important principles of the socialism they were responsible for promoting or serving.[34]

It had gradually become clear to Nyerere that the absence of a "generally accepted and easily understood statement of philosophy and policy was allowing some Government and Party actions which were not consistent with the building of socialism, and which encouraged the growth of non-socialist values and attitudes".[35] It was the role of the Arusha Declaration, adopted by TANU in February 1967, to supply the definition of socialism in Tanzanian terms and give the direction that society had to take in order to achieve its goals.

This section will investigate the early ideas of Nyerere, as presented in 1962, and other documentation that may help us understand his commitment to the ideas and perspectives and how they were translated into politics. Particular reference will be made to give to the notion of *ujamaa*, its philosophical background and the way it was carved out as a major policy of transformation for agricultural and rural development. The subsequent sections will present different interpretations of his ideas and their foundations that may be useful for assessing the Arusha Declaration and subsequent Tanzanian development.

Nyerere's philosophy and ideas regarding development in a socialist context

In Nyerere's early thinking he spoke of a socialist society requiring a socialist attitude of mind and that such an attitude was needed to ensure that

---

[34] Nyerere, J., 1968, "Ujamaa – Essays on Socialism". Oxford University Press, p. vii.
[35] Ibid., p. viii.

people cared for each other's welfare. He argued that the appearance of millionaires in any society is no proof of that society being affluent, "For it is not efficiency of production, nor the amount of wealth in a country, which make millionaires; it is the uneven distribution of what is produced. The basic difference between a socialist and a capitalist society does not lie in their methods of producing wealth, but in the way that wealth is distributed".[36] His next question would be why African societies do not produce any millionaires since there exist sufficient wealth and resources to produce a few. His answer was, "because of the organisation of traditional African society - its distribution of the wealth it produced - was such that there was hardly any room for parasitism".[37]

In traditional African society according to Nyerere, everybody was a worker as there was no other way of earning a living for the community. The elders, who appeared to be enjoying themselves and for whom everybody else was working, had in fact worked hard all through their younger days. The wealth he or she now possessed was bestowed on them not personally, but it belonged to them as members of the group of elders that had produced it. The wealth itself gave the elders neither prestige nor power. The respect paid to them by the younger generation was theirs because they were older than the youth and had served the community longer. The poor elder enjoyed as much respect as the rich one. When Nyerere stated that everybody in traditional African society was a worker, it was not 'worker' as a term opposed to 'employer', but also as opposed to 'loiterer' or 'idler'. The capitalist exploiters were unknown to traditional African society. There was no other form of modern parasite such as loiterer or idler who accepted the hospitality of society but provided nothing in return. In traditional African society capitalist exploitation was impossible – loitering was an unthinkable disgrace.[38] "Thus, working was part and parcel, was indeed the very basis and justification of this socialist achievement of which we are so proud."

The other use of the word worker, in its specialised sense as 'employee' as opposed to 'employer', "reflects a capitalist attitude of mind which was introduced into Africa with the coming of colonialism and is totally foreign to our own way of thinking."[39]

---

[36] Nyerere 1962, *Ujamaa – The Basis of African Socialism*. Published as a TANU pamphlet in April 1962. *In Nyerere, Ujamaa – Essays on Socialism*. Oxford University Press 1968, p. 2. This quote clearly shows at this stage, at least, that Nyerere was not leaning on Marxist theory which emphasises the critical role of production relations rather than wealth distribution, as a basis for understanding societal dynamics. With the launching of the policies of ujamaa and self-reliance in 1967 there is a shift, however, in Nyerere's thinking towards controlling the means of production in order to attain the objectives of the Arusha Declaration (see also below).

[37] Ibid.

[38] Ibid., pp. 4-5.

[39] Ibid., p. 6.

In traditional African societies, according to Nyerere, people had never aspired to the possession of wealth in order to dominate any of their followers. The coming of the foreign capitalists made the Africans want to be wealthy too. So, some of us, according to Nyerere, would not hesitate to exploit our brother for gaining personal wealth. This is foreign and incompatible with the socialist society that Nyerere wished to build. Thus the first step required was one of re-education to turn back to the attitude of mind of traditional African societies. And in rejecting capitalism and the capitalist methods that go with it, there is also, according to Nyerere, the need to reject individual ownership of land. "To us in Africa land was always recognised as belonging to the community." An African's right to land was a right to use it, not any other right, "nor did it occur to him to try to claim one".[40] To obstruct the growth of parasites in the post-colonial societies, Nyerere argued that the government "must go back to the traditional African custom of land-holding".[41]

When reflecting on tribal society, Nyerere claimed that the individuals of families within them were either rich or poor depending on whether the tribe itself was rich or poor. Mechanisms of redistribution would see to it that everyone attained the same level of welfare, be it high or low. So if everyone in Tanganyika worked hard prosperity would come and be shared by everyone. But also in the view of Nyerere, according to true socialist principles, prosperity must be shared.

The foundation and the objective of African socialism is according to Nyerere the extended family. The true African socialist sees all men as his brothers – "as members of his ever extending family". According to the first article of TANU's creed this is emphasised, "I believe in Human Brotherhood and the Unity of Africa". According to Nyerere, 'Ujamaa', then, or 'Familyhood', is the right way to describe Tanganyikan socialism. It is opposed to capitalism which is exploitative, and also to doctrinaire socialism which builds its society on a philosophy of inevitable conflict between man and man. Nyerere further states that the peoples of Africa have no need to be converted to socialism or to be taught democracy, since both are rooted in the traditional past of African societies.

As to the urge for unity, Nyerere states that the struggle to break out of colonialism had made Africans learn the need for unity in nation building, Nyerere, emphasised this strongly in the early 1960s:

> New nations like Tanganyika are emerging into independence as a result of a struggle for freedom from colonialism. It is a patriotic struggle that leaves no room for differences and unites all elements of

---

[40] Ibid., p. 7.
[41] Ibid., p. 8.

the country; the nationalists who led them to freedom must inevitably form the first government of the new States. Once the first free government is formed its supreme task lies in building up the country's economy so as to raise the living standards of the people, eradicate disease, banish ignorance and superstition. This, no less than the struggle against colonialism, calls for the maximum united effort by the whole country if is to succeed. There can be no room for difference or division. ... This is our time of emergency, and until our war against poverty, ignorance and disease has been won, we should not let our unity be destroyed.[42]

According to C. K. Omari, Nyerere saw the achievement of independence as attained through the unity of the people fighting as one unified force against a common enemy – colonialism. With independence the common enemy shifted from colonialism to the challenges posed by development.[43]

But Nyerere emphasised as well that the unity of and the recognition of the family to which all the people of Tanganyika belonged had to be extended further, beyond the tribe, the community and the nation or even the continent, "to embrace the whole society of mankind. This is the only logical conclusion for true socialism".[44]

Nyerere like Ki-Zerbo returned to the analysis of the pre-colonial period for assessing the possibilities for post-colonial development in the framework of the nation state. Both saw virtues, values and processes of endogenous development that were promising for Africa's future. However, this potential development was undermined by the coming of colonialism which led to changes in values, imposition of alien institutions, exploitation of resources for external interests and a structuring of the economy away from internal integration. Whereas Nyerere saw a possibility to reconnect with the values and attitudes of the pre-colonial period through the nation state, ujamaa and modernisation, Ki-Zerbo and others hardly recognised any possibility to reconnect with the pre-colonial features and processes. And what is more, most African leaders, according to Ki-Zerbo, did not take note of or stand up for African values and attitudes, but tried to copy the European way.

However, Nyerere wanted to pursue his vision of a development that reconnected with African traditional values. When the first years of post-colonial development in Tanganyika did not meet with expectations of equal-

---

[42] Sigmund, P. (ed), 1963, *The ideologies of developing nations*. Praeger, New York. Quoted in C.K. Omari, "The management of tribal and religious diversity", in Legum, C. and C. K. Mmari (eds), *Mwalimu – the influence of Nyerere*, British-Tanzania Society, London, 1995, pp. 24-25.

[43] Ibid., p. 25.

[44] Nyerere, op. cit., 1968, p. 12.

ity and the promotion of a socialist attitude of mind, Nyerere attempted to redirect Tanzanian development according to his vision. This was reflected in the Arusha Declaration that was announced in February 1967.

The transfer of ideas into politics – the Arusha Declaration

The Arusha Declaration first spells out that the policy of TANU is to build a socialist state and that the principles of socialism are presented in the TANU creed which includes individual human rights, including freedom of expression, and an interventionist role for the state. It is declared that the state needs effective control of the means of production in order to ensure economic justice and prevent accumulation of wealth in private hands which is inconsistent with a classless society. The creed encompasses Nyerere's early ideas and perspectives but goes further in terms of arguing for state intervention in the economy. It is likely that that the document was fully formulated by Nyerere himself.[45] The second part of the Arusha Declaration addresses the policy of socialism and emphasis is given to the absence of exploitation, that the major means of production and exchange are under the control of peasants and workers, that the government must be run according to the principles of democracy and that socialism is a belief. The most important part of the Arusha Declaration addresses the policy of self-reliance. The emphasis is again on the war against poverty and oppression, but what emerges most strongly is the conceptualisation of a self-reliant development. This indicates a shift, in comparison to the thinking and policy at independence, away from external dependence for development assistance and loans in the direction of the country's own resources and capacities.

But the change announced went deeper than that. It is also stated that it would be unwise to rely on money for development when the nation is in a state of poverty. To rely on external financial assistance would be stupid for two reasons. Firstly the money would not come, as experienced by Tanzania in the early independence period. But even if the money had been available, "is this what we really want?" And Nyerere's answer went, "Independence means self-reliance. Independence cannot be real if a nation depends upon gifts and loans from another for its development".[46] But external gifts and loans are acceptable and valuable, according to the Arusha Declaration, if they help increase, or act as a catalyst, to the country's own efforts. And loans are better than gifts because of the acceptance

---

45 Green, R. 1995, in Legum, C. and C. K. Mmari (eds), p. 82. We learn, however, that there is a shift in Nyerere's thinking that control over the means of production is key to attain social justice, whereas he in his writings in 1962 had emphasised that it was in distribution, not in production conditions that the seeds to inequality and exploitation were situated (see note 36 above).

46 The Arusha Declaration 1967. In Nyerere, J. 1968, *Ujamaa – Essays on Socialism*, Oxford, pp. 22-23.

that they have to be repaid, "show that you intend to use the loan profitably and will therefore be able to repay it".[47] The Arusha Declaration further claims that the excessive emphasis on money had caused Tanzania to commit the big mistake of putting too much emphasis on industries. It was a mistake because Tanzania did not have the means to develop many modern industries, neither did the financial resources and the technical know-how exist. To borrow money to establish industries would lead to dependence and interference with the policy of socialism. Another possibility mentioned in the Arusha Declaration, to invite foreign capitalists to Tanzania to establish industries, which might have succeeded, "would also succeed in preventing the establishment of socialism unless we believe that without first building capitalism, we cannot build socialism".[48]

So the main message of the Arusha Declaration, presented towards the end of the part on self reliance, is to base future development on agriculture and the people of Tanzania. Development is brought about by people, not money, and the four prerequisites for development, according to the Arusha Declaration, are, (i) people, (ii) land, (iii) good policies and, (iv) good leadership. The emphasis on food production and agriculture stands out:

> And because the main aim of development is to get more food, and more money for our other needs, our purpose must be to increase production of these agricultural crops. This is in fact the only road through which we can develop our country – in other words, only by increasing our production of these things can we get more food and more money for every Tanzanian.[49]

As to attaining self-reliance based on agriculture and people, the Arusha Declaration states that, "the people have to be taught the meaning of self-reliance and its practice".[50] This attitude of Nyerere, that rural people themselves do not know or have the capacity to promote self reliance in practice, runs through his thoughts and initiatives. It indicates a hierarchical structure and top down development approach. Can this approach be reconciled with his simultaneous emphasis on equality?

---

[47] Ibid., p. 24. Here Nyerere directly addresses the importance of accountability in relation to external loans and development assistance. Loans and development assistance can work as catalysts when the premises of development have been outlined by the country itself. However, the Tanzanian government and Nyerere himself soon came to overlook these perspectives when the grabbing of development assistance and loans started in the 1970s in the face of global economic stagnation. On the other hand the donors were more than willing to provide loans and development assistance to compensate for declining demand for their export products from markets in the rich countries. Development assistance thus became a market channel for industrial commodities of the north, including Norway. See also Havnevik, K. et al. 1988, "Tanzanian Country Study and Aid Review", The Center for Development Studies, the University of Bergen, Norway.

[48] Ibid., p. 26.

[49] Ibid., p. 29.

[50] Ibid., p. 33.

The concretisation of ideas on ujamaa and rural development

Shortly after the announcement of the Arusha Declaration two presidential papers were issued, "Education for Self-Reliance"[51] and "Socialism and Rural Development".[52] It was the latter that promoted the concept and policy of ujamaa.

In its first sentence it is stated that the traditional African family lived according to the basic principles of ujamaa. This implied that people lived and worked together "because that was how they understood life, and how they reinforced each other against the difficulties they had to contend with – the uncertainties of weather and sickness, the depredations of wild animals (and sometimes human enemies), and the cycle of life and death".[53] The emphasis was on unity and reciprocity which were manifested in the notion that the basic goods of life were 'our food', 'our land' and 'our cattle'. This pattern of living was based on three assumptions of traditional life, (i) respect that reflected a genuine recognition of mutual involvement with one another, (ii) that basic goods were held in common and shared among all members of the unit and, (iii) that everybody had an obligation to work.

But Nyerere admitted as well that there were flaws in the traditional system. One was the acceptance of human inequality and a second was that, "the women in traditional society were regarded as having a place in the community which was not only different, but was also to some extent inferior. It is impossible to deny that women did, and still do, more than their fair share of the work in the field and in the homes".[54] This fact was against the socialist conception and according to Nyerere: "If we want our country to make full and quick progress now, it is essential that our women live on terms of full equality with their fellow citizens who are men."[55]

Another aspect of traditional life that had to be broken out of, according to Nyerere, was poverty. Poverty was the result of two things, ignorance and the scale of operations. These could, in Nyerere's thoughts, be corrected without affecting the validity of the principles of mutual respect, sharing of joint production and work by all. These principles can also be the basis for economic development if modern knowledge and modern production

---

[51] Nyerere, J. 1968, "Education for Self-Reliance". Policy booklet published in March 1967. In Nyerere 1968, *Ujamaa – Essays on Socialism*, Oxford, chapter 4.

[52] Nyerere, J. 1968, "Socialism and Rural Development". Policy booklet published in September 1967. In Ibid., chapter 7.

[53] Nyerere 1968, "Socialism and Rural Development", p. 106.

[54] Ibid., p. 109.

[55] Ibid.

techniques are employed. These latter elements could be added to allow for increased output per worker which makes the efforts of producers provide them with more satisfaction. This then was the basis from which Nyerere attempted to lay out the principles of ujamaa in the rural areas of Tanzania.

To allow for wage labour in agriculture would lead to development of a class system which would be inconsistent with the principles of socialist Tanzania and the values of the traditional system. Therefore, according to Nyerere, "the principles upon which the traditional extended family was based must be reactivated".[56] The first thing that is required for development is that people must work harder, by using their own hands and brains. Each person has to produce more by harder, longer and better work. The co-operative movement must in addition be made more efficient both in terms of management and democracy and an efficient and democratic system of local government has to be established as well. Tanzanian rural development must be based on the equality of all citizens and their common obligations and rights. The goals of Tanzanian society can only be achieved, "if the basis of Tanzanian life consists of rural *economic and social communities where people live together and work together for the good of all*".[57]

In the end, Nyerere's prescription for Tanzanian rural development is to link the egalitarian principles of traditional and pre-colonial Tanzania with the utilisation of modern methods that can satisfy the human needs in the organisational unit of the village: "This means that most of our farming would be done by groups of people who live as a community and work as a community. They would live together in a village; they would farm together; market together, and undertake the provision of local services and small local requirements as a community. Their community would be that traditional family group, or any other group of people living according to ujamaa principles, large enough to take account of modern methods and the twentieth century needs of man."[58] Private activities may be allowed in villages and they may vary between villages, but always on the basis that no member is allowed to exploit another.

In discussing how to move from the current situation to the new position, Nyerere argues that, "viable socialist communities can only be established with willing members; the task of leadership and of the role of Government is not to try and force this kind of development, but to explain, encourage, and participate". And further, "it is vital that whatever encouragement

---

[56] Ibid., 120.
[57] Ibid.
[58] Ibid., p. 124.

Government and TANU give to this type of scheme, they must not try to run it; they must help the people to run it themselves".[59]

This statement signals a bottom up approach which contradicts Nyerere's emphasis in other texts that peasants need to be educated in order to promote self reliance.

Ujamaa villages should be developed without reliance on great external capital injections because of the great dangers of an increasing debt burden and its consequences for smallholders. Ujamaa villages should be established by the people themselves based on self-reliant activities and government support in terms of proper agricultural extension. No one model should be pushed or imposed on any village. However, according to Nyerere, experience that has been collected from existing ujamaa villages, "such as those now operating within the Ruvuma Development Association, could be helpful, and the Ministry of Local Government and Rural Development should try to make this experience available to people from different parts".[60]

In conclusion, Nyerere's vision for rural development in Tanzania is to move from "being a nation of individual peasant producers who are gradually adopting the incentives and the ethics of the capitalist system. Instead we should gradually become a nation of ujamaa villages where the people co-operate directly in small groups and where these small groups co-operate together for joint enterprises".[61]

Interpretations of Nyerere's ideas and policy recommendations

Introduction

Interpretations of Nyerere's ideas are many and varied. Some claim that Nyerere's writings and speeches are difficult to analyse because they lend themselves to "easy misreading as hopelessly self-contradictory". Tensions

---

[59] Ibid., p. 131. Nyerere was a great admirer of the activities and organisation of the Ruvuma Development Association (RDA). According to the then chairperson of the RDA, Millinga, Nyerere in the 1960s used to ask the leader of RDA whether he could send people who came to Tanzania to learn more about ujamaa to see for themselves at the RDA in Ruvuma (personal communication with Millinga in November 1979). In 1969 RDA was banned and all the assets were expropriated by the state, the expatriates that assisted RDA was sent out of the country. The Executive Committee of TANU had voted in 1969 that all ujamaa activities had to be in control of the Party. It is speculated that Nyerere voted against the decision to ban the RDA, see Coulson, A. 1982, *Tanzania – A Political Economy* and K. Havnevik 1993, *Tanzania – The limits to development from above*. The Nordic Africa Institute, Uppsala.

[60] Ibid., p. 143.

[61] Ibid.

and secondary contradictions in Nyerere's thinking emerge, but, "it is a misreading to suppose they are basic". The occurrences of such inconsistencies are due to the dynamic development of Nyerere's thinking. There is an evolutionary aspect in his central vision as to development, at times more revolutionary, "or at least discontinuous, so far as economic instruments are concerned".[62] Other aspects pointed at in helping to explain contradictions in his thoughts and speeches relate to the fact that Nyerere's thoughts are not simple and in addition he has fulfilled many roles at the same time. Thus his messages, ideas and speeches have been put forward in different capacities, for different audiences and at different levels.

The ethical interpretation

This interpretation is shared by many both inside Tanzania, in Africa and outside. It was particularly strong in the 1960s and into the 1970s when Tanzania and Nyerere tried to chart out an alternative development path through the Arusha Declaration. The immediate response was huge domestic support and sympathy and support from churches, solidarity movements, international institutions, including the World Bank, and donors. Nyerere's and Tanzania's policies with their strong emphasis on basic needs satisfaction struck a chord in particular with social democratic governments in particular the Nordic ones, who themselves were consolidating their welfare societies.[63] As a result, Tanzania's new development path was given ample financial and development assistance support from the very beginning and for a policy that emphasised self reliance.

Support from church societies in the north was widespread and strong and the Right Reverend Trevor Huddleston, a long time friend of Nyerere, at a later stage underlined "the strength of Nyerere's commitment to equality as the basis for African socialism, ujamaa". He was sure that Nyerere would describe himself as a Christian socialist and emphasised as well the global and human aspects of his ideas. According to Huddleston, for Nyerere the word Catholic would always mean universal and in the international setting Nyerere, sees all institutions as necessary "not for their own preservation and power but for the purpose of sustaining and promoting global co-operation and interdependence".[64]

But maybe the strongest proponent of the ethical interpretation is the late professor of political science, Cranford Pratt, who for many years

---

[62] Green 1995, in Legum and Mmari (eds), op. cit., p. 81.
[63] See also the contribution by Jarle Simensen in chapter 3. Nyerere, during the 1960s and into the 1970s, received warm welcomes in all the Nordic countries, in particular, and much beyond the social democratic parties. For instance the Prime Minister of Norway, in the early 1970s, John Lyng, from the conservative party gave much praise to Nyerere in his biography.
[64] Huddleston, T., 1995, in Legum and Mmari (eds), op. cit., p. 7.

worked at the University of Dar es Salaam and became a personal friend of Nyerere. When summing up his interpretations from decades of analyses of Tanzanian development, Pratt concluded that Nyerere during his presidency had four major preoccupations, (i) developing the Tanzanian economy, which was seen as a basis for attainment of all other objectives, (ii) securing national control of Tanzania's economic development, (iii) creating participatory political institutions that would sustain the unity and common purpose that were reflected in the anti-colonial struggle, and (iv) building Tanzania as a just society where everybody would share the benefits of development.[65]

This interpretation considers the ujamaa policy and villagisation of the early 1970s as basically a transformation that would help rural people to, "be much more accessible to the agricultural extension worker, the rural dispensary, the primary school and other agents of development".[66] Its analysis of the Tanzanian policy shift towards national control of economic development away from dependence on international capitalism and major industrialised countries, is that it followed from a number of foreign policy crises in the first five years of independence. This led to radicalisation of the nationalist ideas which resulted in a more inward oriented economic strategy and a more clearly non-aligned foreign policy. This implied a clear shift of the trade-off on the external versus internal dimension since, "Tanzania had begun its independence with a foreign policy that was unquestioningly oriented towards Britain and the West".[67] Nyerere and Tanzania's new found critical stance towards Britain, the United States and Germany was based on disappointments as to their negative stand on sanctions against the Apartheid government in South Africa, on Tanzania's desire to retain relations with East Germany, on Tanzania's wish to accept development assistance from China and other communist countries, and in addition to Britain's lukewarm response to the illegal Smith regime in Zimbabwe.

By the mid-1960s Nyerere had become more realistic in his assessment of international politics, seeing that the desire of other countries to assist Tanzania in its economic struggle, was only secondary to these countries' interests in aligning with the major political blocs in the West and East. The Cold War had put countries up against each other and according to Nyerere, "the world is divided into various conflicting groups and each one of these groups is anxious for allies in Africa and even more anxious that its

[65] Pratt, Cranford, 1999, "Julius Nyerere: Reflections on the Legacy of Socialism". In *Canadian Journal of African Studies*, Vol. 33.
[66] Ibid.
[67] Ibid.

opponent shall not find friends".[68] Such nationalist sentiments spilled over into other areas and the nationalisation to enhance national control of the economy was also founded on a nationalist purpose. And further, the only way in which nationalist control of the economy could be achieved was through the economic institutions of socialism.[69]

The ethical interpretation shows genuine support for Nyerere's stand that poor countries would have few, if any, advantages of integrating into the international economic system and that the IMF's and the World Bank's drive to open up Tanzania to the global economy in the 1980s was flawed. It is likewise supportive of Nyerere's attempts to develop participatory democratic institutions based on the one party system. The thinking is that Tanganyika in 1961 was left with alien institutions, e.g. the Westminster parliamentarian model, transplanted by the British colonial regime. This system led only to limited involvement of Tanzanians in elections and that the political elite focussed their personal ambitions on the Government and the National Assembly. TANU, the party, that represented the movement around which Tanganyikans had mobilised thus lost it role. In 1965 the constitution was changed to allow for the "democratic one-party state". The ethical interpretation goes a long way towards defending the move to a one-party state and in Pratt's words in the late 1990s, "It was a highly original effort to provide meaningful popular elections, greater answerability of the political leadership and genuine political participation by ordinary Tanzanians, while protecting Tanzania from the divisive ethnic, regional, and religious factionalism which could easily destroy its fragile unity and which a fully open competition between rival parties might generate".[70] Although the interpretation also sees flaws in the one-party state system, it takes a lenient attitude towards recurrent detentions and human rights abuses. Although such abuses should never have been tolerated, it is claimed that "they were painfully defended by Nyerere as necessary for the stability of the nation".[71] It is further acknowledged that the strong oligarchic tendencies within the party, "were never fully contained and indeed grew more apparent and threatening".[72]

The merit of the one-party constitution of 1965, according to this position, is that for two decades it provided a political framework, which was largely unchallenged, and which contributed to stable civilian rule and allowed discussions of policies and development strategies more openly than compared to any other African country. And further that the system

---

68 Nyerere 1966, *Freedom and Unity: Uhuru na Umoja*, Oxford University Press, pp. 314-315.
69 Nyerere 1973, *Freedom and Socialism*, Oxford University Press, p. 197.
70 Pratt, op. cit., 1999.
71 Ibid. and Nyerere 1966, pp. 305-315.
72 Pratt, op. cit., 1999.

allowed for a peaceful transition to a new president in 1985 and a complete turnaround of economic policies at the same time.

The interpretation of the central importance that Nyerere attached to equality is said to separate him from Western liberalism which primarily focussed on individual liberty and with weaker attention to equality. His Christian faith may explain part of it, but Nyerere's, "central emphasis on equality, we may safely hypothesize, was in part shaped by his wide and eclectic reading in his years at university in Edinburgh and in the years immediately after, readings in which classical liberalism, British socialism, and pan-African anti-colonialism were more prominent than Marxism".[73] But there was maybe a stronger strand of reflections in Nyerere's early writings that focussed on human dignity and equality that was related to the indignity and humiliation of being ruled by foreign powers.

Nyerere's socialism was an expression of the ethical core of Tanzanian and African traditional life. The equality enjoyed here was that of, "closely integrated and caring societies such as Nyerere assumed most Tanzanian tribal societies had been and indeed still were".[74] But as well Nyerere recognised that this equality and way of life were being undermined by an African bourgeoisie that was powerful and difficult to hold back. He was thus increasingly preoccupied with combating the tendencies towards class differences and many of his political initiatives, including the Arusha Declaration and the policies for rural development, can be explained on this basis.

The indigenous interpretation

This interpretation grows out of an interest in investigating whether indigenous forms of accountability can be scaled up to the level of the modern state. In such a focus the background and experiences of Nyerere's ideas and policies in Tanzania present an interesting case. Nyerere himself has on many occasions claimed that his, "social and political thought is very substantially related to 'traditional' African values".[75]

Stöger-Eising in her analysis attempts to explore to what extent Nyerere's visions of African socialism and democracy can be linked with his own 'tribal' background and what elements that might be linked to European influences.

Nyerere was born in a small and remote Zanaki village named Butiama, located 50 km from Musoma in northern Tanganyika. The Zanaki lived

---

[73] Ibid.
[74] Ibid.
[75] Stöger-Eising 2000, "Ujamaa revisited: Indigenous and European Influences in Nyerere's Social and Political Thought", in *Africa* 70 (1), p. 118.

scattered in the countryside and the number of houses in a homestead cluster depended on the number of the husband's wives and of married dependent sons. The Zanaki still practise polygny, i.e. men having more than one wife, but to a lesser extent than in the past. The writings of anthropologists and early European travellers to Africa indicate that the lowest political unit in Zanaki society is the lineage. A lineage is a lineal descent group whose members trace their descent from an ancestor/ancestress through known genealogical links. In a clan, which resembles a lineage, the descent group does not know its genealogical links. In Zanaki society the lineal descent group is called *hamati*. At a more structural level in Zanaki society exists what is termed *erisaga*, a form of 'social security' association where several neighbouring homesteads constitute a distinct community. The members of the *erisaga* work co-operatively in e.g. harvesting and house building. The *erisaga* functions as a voluntary association for mutual co-operation and self-help in order to address the uncertainties associated with rural life.[76] Such institutionalisation of reciprocal support or exchanges may at times spell the difference between survival or not. For the 'traditional' Zanaki, "reciprocal generosity is a core value".[77]

The *hamati* is not always locally based like the *erisaga*, but may include different members in different homesteads and different provinces. Abiding by the authority of the *hamati*, which is the primary loyalty group among the Zanaki, is, according to Stöger-Eising, "a critical requisite of 'traditional' Zanaki life".[78] In the past the rights and duties associated with the *hamati* were well known and conflicts and crimes were resolved and sanctioned accordingly. The leaders of the *hamati* were usually wise and charismatic male elders. Several *hamatis* or lineages constitute a clan which is the next level of socio-political integration of the Zanaki. The most famous Zanaki clan was that of a rainmaker who claimed that his forefathers had been in the Zanaki area for twenty-two generations. But clan leaders, such as the rainmaker, were not secular political authorities, but they were given their position because of their being 'seers' or specialists on ritual matters. Linked to this is the principle that individual status in the Zanaki social order is 'social' rather than 'political', "the highest form of social prestige and nyangi can be attained only through generosity".[79] Nyerere's own description of his youth in Butiama, a Zanaki village, was, "I grew up in a perfectly democratic and egalitarian society".[80]

[76] Bischofberger 1972, "The Generation Classes of the Zanaki (Tanzania)". *Fribourg, Studio Ethnographica Friburgensia*, p. 14, Mkirya 1991, "Historia, Mila na Destrui za Wazanaki". Ndanda and Peramiho, Tanzania, Benedictine Publications, p. 85 and Stöger-Eising op. cit., 2000, p. 120.

[77] Ibid., p. 123.

[78] Ibid., p. 121.

[79] Bischofberger op. cit., 1972, p. 22.

[80] Stöger-Eising, op. cit., p. 119.

When the German colonisers entered the Zanaki area east of Lake Victoria in 1898, they had the idea, like most Europeans at that time, that African tribes had a chief at the head of their social structure. When this was not the case, they invented tradition to make it fit their own perceptions. In this way flexible and dynamic socio/cultural/political realities were merged into one, "bounded by all the rigidities of an invented tradition".[81] When not finding a chief as expected, the head of the Germans in the area appointed eight chiefs, one for each of the Zanaki provinces. One of them was Nyerere's father, Nyerere Burito who was know to be a 'seer'. Julius Nyerere's middle name, Kambarage, came from one of the local 'rain spirits'. The year he was born, rainfall was especially plentiful, hence the name.[82] According to Nyerere, he grew up like other boys in the area and in surroundings of rural equality. No privilege was bestowed upon him because his father had become a chief.[83]

The appointment of chiefs by the German colonisers posed a challenge to the rainmaker and the principle of authority based on social aspects. The rainmaker, after all, had not been appointed a chief by the Germans. The new chiefs discarded the function of resolving social disputes, but, "these colonially created traditions – at that time – affected only small changes in Zanaki social norms since they nevertheless retained their cultural coherence".[84] This argument is based on the finding that the intrusion of colonial political structures only marginally influenced the genera-tion class system in Zanaki society. This system comprised the loyalty to the descent lines or *hamati* which encouraged vertical integration and to the *erisaga*, which was critical for personal identify formation within the community. The generation class system thus encouraged a horizontal integration cutting across lineage and clan lines which generated social links and reciprocity far beyond the boundaries of descent (lineage and clan) and locality (*erisaga*). The relationships affiliated with the genera-tion groups may go "beyond the borders of one's own ethnic group".[85] These age and generation systems, so important for forming a person's social and political status, most often emerge in non-centralised political

---

[81] Ranger, Terence, 1993, "The invention of tradition revisited: the case of colonial Africa", in Rang-er and Vaughan (eds), *Legitimacy and the State in Twentieth Century Africa*: Essays in honour of A.H.M. Kirk-Greene. Basingstoke, MacMillan, pp. 62-111 and Berry, Sara, 1993, *No condition is permanent, the social dynamics of agrarian change in sub-Saharan Africa. University of Wisconsin Press, Madison.*

[82] Hatch 1976, *Two African Statesmen: Kaunda of Zambia and Nyerere of Tanzania.* Secker and War-burg, London. Mentioned in Stöger-Eising, p. 127.

[83] Stöger-Eising, op. cit., pp. 123-124.

[84] Ibid, p. 124. Reporting personal communication with District Councillor Mwigura M. Kanyonyi. This interpretation runs counter to that observed by Ki-Zerbo op. cit. and Feierman op. cit. re-ferred to above.

[85] Ibid.

systems and take on important political functions. According to Stöger-Eising they constitute non-centralised forms of political power, which are alternatives to Western centralised ones. Although the importance of this system had declined during the twentieth century, it was still, "the most important 'traditional' political, social and cultural institution of the Zanaki when the colonisation of Tanganyika began.[86]

Outstanding features in Zanaki society and traditional culture were thus a complex socio-political structure without a centralised political structure. The generation class system promoted egalitarianism, the diffusion of power and as well the dialogue as a means to resolve conflicts. The pursuit of individual advantage at the expense of the community "was frowned upon".

Whereas the supportive and ethical position argues that Nyerere's emphasis on equality and justice was generated by his studies in Edinburgh, Stöger-Eising, claims that this reading "did not so much create Nyerere's political world view *de novo*; rather I shall argue that it reinforced and enriched the moral and political sensibilities he had imbibed in his native Zanaki culture".[87] She argues that Nyerere's underlying commitment to equality as the guidance to his thoughts resulted in his emphasis on issues such as democracy, human rights, egalitarianism, education for self-reliance and women's liberation. These aspects were more like arteries supporting the heart of Ujamaa, not the heart itself.[88] Nyerere's essays on 'Socialism and rural development' and 'Education for self reliance' have, according to Stöger-Eising, to be seen as the philosophical underpinning for the Arusha Declaration, which is more programmatic. Hence, the three documents must be seen as a whole.[89]

There are two important themes, according to Stöger-Eising, that are clearly Western in origin, poverty and the discrimination of women. His early writings on the need for liberation of women, which were clearly influenced by John Stuart Mill, were extended to embrace the struggle for 'human rights', which was also a concept that had emerged from Western thought. Whereas Nyerere argued for the need to protect individual human rights, he was careful to underline that this should not compromise the 'common good', human dignity for all, which had to come first. Nyerere's pre-occupation with finding a balance between the individual and the community is not a new political idea, but was addressed by Jean-Jacques Rousseau much earlier. In particular the Rousseaun conceptualisation of a 'social contract' has by some been seen to be reflected in the construction

---

[86] Ibid.
[87] Stöger-Eising, p. 129.
[88] Ibid, p. 130.
[89] Ibid., p. 32 and Coulson op. cit., 1979, p. 2.

of a one-party state with authoritarian leadership. Rousseau considered that a 'social contract' was required for governments to function for the benefit of all. The one-party state could, in Nyerere's view, be seen as a way of extending the non-centralised or acephalous ideas to a modern nation state. According to Nyerere's early thoughts, the nationalist movement and its vanguard political party had to be the driving force of development, since party division at such a critical stage would be irresponsible. The Westminster political system was simply inappropriate for Tanzania and was scrapped.

The creation of a Tanzanian identity resembles, according to this position, the horizontal integration that so strongly featured in Zanaki culture. Nyerere strongly opposed the exploitation of ethnic loyalties to build power. In contrast he used ethnic loyalties to promote an integrated Tanzanian national unity. Nyerere utilised the mechanisms that had been at play in the Zanaki generation class system both for strengthening the cohesion of TANU and for promotion of national identity and unity. Nyerere went on at a later stage to employ the same ideas for African unity.

The indigenous position argues that Nyerere's emphasis on the values and virtues of traditional society is not merely a rhetorical device employed by an African politician or a romantic notion of a Westernised African university graduate. Neither does it serve as an 'invention' of African tradition. On the contrary, Nyerere had lived many of the experiences that he later came to formulate as philosophical and political ideas. Some of them came to serve as important vehicles for attempting to set Tanzania on an alternative development path. Nyerere must have been aware that Zanaki society was only one example of how Tanzanian and African societies were structured. But in constructing a socialist and democratic society he nevertheless seems to have built on the ideas of the non-hierarchical Zanaki cultural patterns alongside philosophical ideas from the West. Many claim that Nyerere glorified the African past and underestimated the extent to which it was affected and undermined by colonial rule. The reconnections he tried to make with the traditional life in his political ideas and programmes, thus became oversimplified and unrealistic.[90] Others, more extreme, dismiss Nyerere as being ignorant of African society.[91] According to the indigenous position, as argued by Stöger-Eising, such a notion is to miss the point completely. Her overall assessment is that Nyerere's reference to "the democratic and egalitarian African traditions are, in fact, accurate in regard to the cultural and political surroundings in which he was socialised. He selectively chose

---

[90] Refer to Ki-Zerbo op. cit., 1995 and Feierman op. cit., 1990.
[91] Watzal 1982, "Ujamaa. Das Ende einer Utopie? Die politicshe Bedeutung einer philosophisch-anthropologischen Konzeption". Hochshule der Bundeswehr. Munchen.

those African ideas he felt were worth honouring, those values upon which a healthy Tanzania should be based".[92]

The class interpretation

The ethical interpretation of Nyerere's ideas indicates an acknowledgement of the existence of economic classes in Tanzania and that Nyerere was struggling to contain the bourgeoisie in its attempt to expand capitalism in Tanzania. But the position never attempted to define or analyse the Tanzanian post-independence model in terms of classes. The indigenous interpretation for its part focussed mainly on linking Nyerere's ideas and perspectives to the realities of the socio-cultural context of his youth or to external ideas and influences.

The first attempt at analysing the post-colonial developments in Tanzania in terms of class struggles was done by Issa Shivji in a special issue of Cheche, a University of Dar es Salaam publication, in 1968. The early publication had the title, "The Silent Class Struggles in Tanzania". In 1972 a mimeo appeared where 'silent' had been dropped from the title, which was now, "Class Struggles in Tanzania" which in 1976 was published internationally by Monthly Review Press in London and New York. In this edition Shivji took the opportunity as well to respond to the critiques of his earlier publications on the thematic. With the Monthly Review publication the ideas and reflections on the class character of the Tanzanian state were thrown open to a wider public, many of whom disliked the notion of class analysis but also to those who were unable to fit the categories of class into analysis of African social formations.

Shivji placed his analysis within a Marxist framework in a wider sense, arguing that Marxism was not simply a body of conclusions where one could pick one aspect or conclusion or the other, but that Marxism as a whole constituted a world outlook with its own philosophical base.

Shivji argued against the standard notion that Marxism, which was essentially developed for highly developed capitalist societies, implied that the non-capitalist character of African societies would make Marxism irrelevant as a tool of analysis. Basically Shivji argued that the underdevelopment in Africa had to be seen in the context of global developments where "the colonial state was largely responsible for establishing certain economic structures and integrating the colonial economy with the metropolitan economy. In the process it certainly helped or hindered the development of various classes or strata".[93] Thus the historically determined system of

---

[92] Stöger-Eising op. cit., 2000, p. 139.
[93] Shivji, Issa, 1976, "Class Struggles in Tanzania". Monthly Review Press, London and New York, pp. 32-33.

social production in Africa has emerged as an integral part of the world capitalist system. Class divisions in Tanzania are therefore integrated with the 'colonial' economic structures.

But classes in the African and Tanzanian context cannot be transferred from the European context where the dominant class, the bourgeoisie, had developed and matured within the "womb of the feudal system". The accumulation of capital from commercial activities that this class managed to bring about was gradually transferred into industrial capital thereby bringing about the industrial revolution and the expansion of the capitalist system. The bourgeoisie class was the agent of the capitalist and industrial mode of production and it struggled for its expansion with the landed aristocracy, the agents of the feudal mode of production. This struggle led to the defeat of the landed aristocracy in France which culminated in the bourgeoisie's democratic revolution in 1789. In England it ended up with a compromise where the aristocracy to some degree transformed itself into a bourgeoisie. This was reflected as well in the repeal of the corn law in England in 1840. This led to free importation of grain that helped reduce the wages of labour in industries but also to marginalise or under-mine grain production on marginal lands in England, thus weakening the landed aristocracy. Nationalism in this context was the struggle to over-throw the parochialism of the feudal mode of production and develop first national and later international markets for manufactured goods emerging from the factories of the industrial bourgeoisie.

Shivji argued that the national bourgeoisie in the African context is neither national or bourgeois. The leading class in the African socio-economic context is rather the petty bourgeoisie which refers to those social strata that belong neither to the bourgeoisie nor to the proletariat, those without land or assets and with only their labour power to sell.[94] In capitalist societies the petty bourgeoisie was not a ruling class, neither was it part of it. Whereas in Africa the petty bourgeoisie, including teach-ers, lower level state functionaries, traders etc, "led the independence struggle and came to control the state apparatus, thus becoming a ruling class, albeit in a subordinate place to the international bourgeoisie".[95] Thus Shivji, to the dislike of many, including the 'members' of the class itself, placed Nyerere and his colleagues in the post-colonial govern-ment as members of the new Tanzanian ruling class. This class, due to its intermediate character, was rather weak because it had weak economic roots. This opened up the opportunity for the 'ruling group' of the petty

---

[94] See also Kalecki, Michael. 1976, "Observations on social and economic aspects of 'Intermediate regimes'". In Kalecki, *Essays on Developing Economies*. Harvester Press, pp. 30-37. First published in *Co-existence*, Vol. 4, No. 1, 1967, pp. 1-5.

[95] Ibid., p. 22.

bourgeoisie to wield a much freer hand and take control of the state. It is this 'ruling group' that Shivji calls the 'bureaucratic bourgeoisie'. Prior to the Arusha Declaration when the state had not yet acquired an economic base through nationalisations, Shivji argues that the bureaucratic bourgeoisie could be seen as a stratum of the petty bourgeoisie. And further, because the anti-capitalism of the petty bourgeoisie is that of a small property owner, this class on the eve of independence had hardly "any conception of structural change and struggle against the international capitalist system". This implies that "the economic measures taken immediately after independence objectively resulted in further integration of the economy in the world capitalist system".[96]

So the class struggle that unfolded in Tanzania in the early post-colonial period was that between the petty bourgeoisie with a weak economic basis of its own and the commercial bourgeoisie which grew stronger with expansion of capitalist relations of production and increasing integration of the economy into the global economic system. Thus, according to Shivji, the class struggle on the part of the petty bourgeoisie could not be waged without state power. This was due to the inability of the petty bourgeoisie to establish a strong economic base for itself. Before the Arusha Declaration in 1967, the African petty bourgeoisie had not been able to make substantial inroads into the commercial sector, rather the state first concentrated on bolstering its peasant base through expansion of the co-operative movement and villagisation schemes to expand its territorial economy with support from foreign capital, i.e. the international bourgeoisie. Thus the major pre-occupations of the state in the pre-Arusha Declaration period were to facilitate "the further integration of peasants in the cash economy, raising their production for export, raising of the productivity of workers, encouraging and attracting foreign capital (private, state and from international agencies)". By so doing the early post-colonial state base was constituted "in the territorial neo-colonial economy".[97]

According to Shivji the Arusha Declaration provided for the bureaucratic bourgeoisie an economic base through state nationalisations that made it "really become a bourgeoisie". The Arusha Declaration made the state and state institutions, including the parastatal companies, the dominant factor of the economy. But by carving out for itself its own internal economic base, the bureaucratic bourgeoisie also came into conflict with its former ally, the international metropolitan bourgeoisie. This resulted in the tensions that were observed between Tanzania and Great Britain in the aftermath of the Arusha Declaration. But according to Shivji, "since the

---

[96] Shivji op. cit., 1976, pp. 64-65.
[97] Ibid., p. 71.

'bureaucratic bourgeoisie' is incapable of restructuring the internal society and thereby disengaging from the world capitalist system, their objective class interests in the long run converge".[98]

As to Ujamaa Vijijini, (Swahili for Ujamaa in the villages), the policy that was adopted alongside the Arusha Declaration, Shivji claims that it is not based on a proper analysis of Tanzania's economy and its integration in the global capitalist system. What Nyerere calls 'embryonic' agricultural capitalism that can be arrested through implementation of ujamaa policies, Shivji sees as an underdeveloped capitalism which is not properly grasped in Nyerere's "Socialism and Rural Development". Thus, according to Shivji, the Ujamaa policy therefore, "is not conceived as part of an overall strategy to transform the *colonial, vertically integrated economy* to a *nationally integrated economy* ".[99] And even though the volume of production of primary crops can be increased, "this in the long run does not help for, *inter alia*, the terms of trade have been deteriorating drastically" (italics in original text).

The low level of agricultural productivity in Tanzanian agriculture cannot be remedied by the Ujamaa policy alone, because productivity, whether in agriculture or industry, is related to the level of industrial development. A weak industrial sector, unable to provide the relevant inputs to enhance production in agriculture, will also hinder the development of agricultural productivity.[100] Shivji's conclusion is thus that the ujamaa policy like its predecessor, the villagisation programme, "is to integrate the non-monetarised (or the so-called 'subsistence sector') within the cash economy. Given the overall neo-colonial structures of the territorial economy this means integration within the world capitalist system".[101] A further proof for this is said to be supported by Lionel Cliffe who had noted that almost all the ujamaa villages established were formed in so-called 'marginal subsistence areas', and not in high-productive areas.

Ujamaa then, from the point of view of Shivji's class analysis, is a policy aimed at accelerating the overall process of monetarisation and the associated peasant differentiation and is thus a continuation of the rural policy that had historically been pursued in Tanzania. A real transformation would, according to Shivji, require a disengagement from the world capitalist system and the establishment of a "nationally integrated economy". Such a transformation is not seen as a simple technical question of changing economic structures, but is rather related to political struggles against internal and external classes with "vested interest in maintaining and

---

[98] Ibid., p. 85.
[99] Ibid., p. 104
[100] Ibid.
[101] Ibid., pp. 106-107.

perpetuating the existing relations of production". Since the ujamaa policy, in Shivji's assessment, does not emerge from a political analysis involving class struggles, it will not be able to address the question of transformation of the rural economy. This Shivji claims is well illustrated in the way ujamaa is implemented.

From the point of view of the class analysis raised by Shivji, the Arusha Declaration should be understood as a political programme for the leadership of the petty bourgeoisie class to gain for itself an economic foundation and turn itself into a bureaucratic bourgeoisie. By controlling the state power in the early post-colonial period, the petty bourgeoisie could use that power to undermine the commercial bourgeoisie which was contending for access to state power. Shivji accepts that the bureaucratic bourgoisie to some extent also played a progressive role in adopting a non-racial ideology, in its vigorous anti-imperialist stance and in bringing about the historical necessity of expanding the public sector as well.[102]

But the basic and underlying ideology of the bureaucratic bourgeoisie was petty bourgeoisie "given that its very material base is a dependent one". The approach and method of work of the bureaucratic bourgeoisie are therefore much "characterised by bureaucratic decision-making and technocratic implementation", implying that this is a basic feature of the ideology of the class. Bureaucratic decision making and technocratic approaches to implementation, are seen by Shivji to be two sides of the same coin. "The dependent and underdeveloped nature of the class is reflected in the fact that, in practice, despite its 'ideology', there is neither bureaucratic efficiency nor sound technocratic expertise".[103]

Some concluding comments

The interpretations of Nyerere's ideas and perspectives, as shown above, differ widely. The core of the interpretations are, nevertheless, that they are related to different driving forces for development based on frameworks that diverge in terms of the understanding of history and the course of development. The ethical interpretation underlines Nyerere's emphasis on equality and consolidation of the state as a state for all in order to protect these values. This separated Nyerere from Western liberalism that primarily promoted individual liberty and individualism. The ethical position also interprets the emerging repressive state governance system as necessary for protecting the core of the development model.

---

[102] Ibid., p. 98.
[103] Shivji, op. cit., 1976, p. 97.

A hierarchical structure where power is concentrated at the top is seen as a way, at least in a transitory phase, to protect the notion of equality for all from penetration by capitalism and market based development with emphasis on individualism.

The indigenous interpretation concludes that Nyerere's ideas of equality and self reliance as framed in the ujamaa policies, were based on his own personal experiences from being raised in Zanaki society, and not from influences from studying or reading. Two themes are, however, seen as being of Western origin, the need for liberation of women and the struggle for individual human rights. However, these themes were secondary to the overarching priorities of promoting and protecting the common good and dignity for all. It is in such a perspective possible to discern societal priorities being located at different levels, where the higher level priorities shall not be compromised by those at lower levels. The one-party state, it is claimed by the interpretation, was not in Nyerere's view seen as a structure for centralisation of power and repression, but as a way of extending non-centralised ideas to a modern nation state.

The class interpretation strongly argues that Nyerere's ideas and policies, in particular those promoted through ujamaa, were based on a faulty analysis of Tanzania's integration in the global capitalist system. Ujamaa was a way to cement this integration and through state intervention in the economy Nyerere and his associates created what can be termed the bureaucratic bourgeoisie class. The Tanzanian leaders at independence needed state power to obstruct capitalist expansion promoted by the commercial bourgeoisie, in particular the Asian traders and international companies. But the class interpretation claims that this did not represent a break with international capitalist interest, rather it conserved Tanzania as a primary producing country with no ability to restructure the economy. The class interpretation accordingly defines a hierarchical bureaucratic structure where power is centralised and used to maintain the position of the bureaucratic bourgeoisie class. Nyerere's notion of equality linking it to traditional African societal values is, according to the Marxist position, a misreading of history. And it is anyway, when it came to practical politics, subordinated to the quest for the petty bourgeoisie to transform into the bureaucratic class in order to hang on to power.

We are faced with at least three different interpretations of Nyerere's ideas and politics. The ethical and Marxist interpretations have the same broad focus, while the indigenous one is oriented towards historical and micro-level understanding.

The interpretations emphasise as well different aspects of the post-inde-pendence development model and put different weight on the compromises underpinning it. But in addition they take the analysis beyond the first decades of the post-independence period and make predictions for the future. In this way the historical framework, Nyereres' ideas and perspectives and the different interpretations provide a setting for analysing the pre-conditions for and the processes related to the current transitions in Tanzania which are the major focus of this book. The historical framework and the interpretations will also be of help in analysing the character of the transitions and whether they are of transformational character or not.

CHAPTER THREE

THE NORWEGIAN-TANZANIAN AID
RELATIONSHIP – A HISTORICAL PERSPECTIVE

Jarle Simensen

The history of the Norwegian-Tanzanian aid relationship can be divided into two periods. The turning point was in 1985, when the Scandinavian countries went along with the International Monetary Fund and the World Bank to demand economic reform as a condition for continued aid. We may talk of a shift from sovereignty to conditionality as a guiding principle in the aid relationship. The following is concerned with the period up to 1985. Three phases can be distinguished: technical assistance in the 1960s, financial aid – mainly in the form of project aid – from the 1970s, and the first phase of more direct budget aid from the late 1980s onwards. We shall look at the institutionalization of the aid relationship, the cultural encounter involved and the extraordinary story of the image of Tanzania in Norwegian and Nordic aid opinion.[1]

The Nordic Alternative

The Norwegian aid relationship with Tanzania started as part of a joint Nordic effort. It is difficult today to imagine how strong the idea of Nordic cooperation was in this field around 1960, when all the Nordic countries established their agencies for international aid. Here was, at last, a field where the Nordic Council, "Nordisk Råd", could move beyond words and take joint action. Previous experience had been gained through the Nordic Field Hospital in Korea, through a close coordination in recruiting to the United Nations Technical Assistance Programme after 1949 and through the continuous Nordic consultation in international agencies, from student to state level. The ties between the social democratic parties were particularly strong, crystallized in the personal friendship between Tage Erlander and Einar Gerhardsen. Development was particularly close to the heart of social democrats, and Gunnar Myrdal gave eloquent expression to the idea

---

[1] Where no other reference is given, the factual basis of the following analysis can be found in Jarle Simensen: *Norge møter den tredje verden, (Norway Meets the Third World).* In *Norsk utviklingshjelps histore (The history of Norwegian Development Assistance), 1952-1975,* Vol. I Bergen 2002.

that development aid represented an extension to the international field of the ideas of the Nordic welfare state.[2]

A Ministerial Committee under the Nordic Council took charge of coordination and in 1960 appointed a committee that started the search for so-called "countries of cooperation".[3] How did they land in East Africa? A process of elimination took place: there was a need to avoid favouring one Nordic country over the others in the choice of target area, and a particular sort of "purist" mentality also seems to have been at work: development aid was seen as a new start in foreign policy and international affairs, clean of national self-interest.

Nigeria and Ethiopia were considered because of existing commercial and missionary ties – Sweden and Norway had even helped build the imperial Navy and Air Force in Ethiopia in the 1950s – but were discarded for those very reasons. The main Norwegian missionary field, Madagascar, with French as the official language, was out of the question. Personalities played a part in the final choice: Olof Palme knew Julius Nyerere from international student politics, and a charismatic Swedish missionary in Tanganayika, Barbro Johanson, made a strong impression both in Stockholm and Oslo – she later went on to become a member of Nyerere's first cabinet. Language and climate also spoke in favour of East Africa.

The purist pretension, as we know, was to remain an element in Nordic aid throughout, particularly in Sweden and Norway. In reality the self-interest component became strong, here as elsewhere, about 50% of bilateral aid has come back to the donors in the form of payments for goods and services, in spite of the principle of non-tied aid. In some areas this has been of importance for employment opportunities. A Socialist Democratic Party member on the Board of NORAD later asked why this fact could not be more effectively exploited in opinion campaigns, and he was joined in this by NORAD's Director of information, Leif Vetlesen.[4] The question remains unanswered.

The practical materialization of the joint Nordic effort was the so-called Nordic Tanganyika Project in Kibaha south-west of Dar-es-Salaam.[5] It was a large-scale educational centre, dominant in the landscape, with 50

[2] Myrdal is quoted in David H. Lumsdaine: *Moral Vision in International Politics. The Foreign Aid Regime 1949-1989*, Princeton 1993: 186.
[3] The ministers responsible for development aid in the three Scandinavian countries during this formative period all happened to be women: Aase Bjerkholt, Lise Groos and Ulla Lindstrøm. A useful collection of documents is *Aase Bjerkholt's papers*, three boxes, in Simensen's archive.
[4] Kjell Magne Fredheim and Leif Vetlesen, NORADs styremøte, 9.-10.1. og 11.10. 1974.
[5] Nils Røed: *Utdanning for utvikling: The Nordic Tanganyika Centre 1961-1970*, MA-thesis, Department of History, University of Oslo, 2004.

Nordic and 300 Tanzanian staff and about 560 students in 1969. It was taken over by Tanzania in 1969, and remains an example of a successful aid project to this day. It was based on a vision: a high school, an agricultural centre and a school for health personnel within the same institution. There was a certain Nordic flavour to its activities, an emphasis on applied oriented curriculae, practical service and grass root contacts. The changing strategies at the agricultural centre – from two weeks demonstration courses for local farmers, to out-reach efforts in the region and back to an ordinary agronomist school – is a fascinating piece of agricultural history.[6] This was a sparsely populated and agriculturally backward region, the location of the centre having been decided by political considerations. Kibaha was dear to president Nyerere, and was intended as a national model, he wanted more of the same kind, but this was not to be. Why?

The immediate reason was that each national aid agency in the Nordic countries by the end of the 1960s had enough money to build up their own portfolios which would satisfy bureaucratic ambition, promote a national profile and serve commercial and humanitarian interest at home more effectively than Nordic cooperation. In this sense development aid was nationalized. But Kibaha also illustrates the problems of creating joint administrative operations at the Nordic level, once separate national agencies exist in the same field. On the spot there were frictions, structurally determined, between leaders of the three different professional centres and the leadership at headquarters, complicated by the need to balance national representation. More important, and probably decisive, was that it proved impossible to create an independent and effective joint organization at home. Only the secretariat leader was defined as a Nordic civil servant. Conflicting national bureaucratic interests and differences in tradition and regulations governing personnel, accounting etc. created constant problems and absorbed time and energy. The secretariat was placed within the framework of Sida, with predictable friction as a result. A Swedish proposal to create one joint Nordic aid agency was not seriously considered at the time, but was not dropped altogether.

---

[6] An OECD expert group recommended a combination of solidly educated so-called "prototype farmers" and new settlements where agricultural techniques could be combined with health and education efforts in an integrated strategy. It might sound like an early version of *ujamaa* but it also sounded like an echo of colonial settlement schemes. The whole idea was discarded by a Canadian expert engaged by NORAD, who maintained he had seen "the roads around Africa paved with failed settlement schemes" (NORAD archives: Evaluation of the Nordic Tanganyika project at Kibaha in Tanzania. Report prepared at the request of the Board of Nordic Development Projects by an evaluation mission arranged by the OECD Secretariat, Paris 1969).

The Nordic Tanganyika Project remains an interesting organizational case in Nordic aid history. By coincidence it took place at the same time that a prominent Danish economist, Kjeld Phillip, in 1966 became head of a commission appointed by the East African presidents to find a solution to *their* project of regional integration.[7] The only significant coordinated Nordic effort in Tanzania after this was the Institute of Development Management in Morogoro, but here each donor country was responsible for its own staff contribution. The model of joint administration was left behind, but twice-yearly consultations between top-level personnel from the aid agencies in the Nordic countries were established as a routine. And Tanzania soon became the largest recipient of Norwegian and Nordic aid.

Technical assistance and cultural encounter

The precise nature of the institutional link-up in the aid relationship is an interesting area of study, and much under-researched. In the first phase during the 1960s, apart from Kibaha, aid was mainly restricted to technical assistance. The development plans on which the relationship was based had a double function: on the one hand they expressed the aims and ambitions of the newly independent states, on the other hand they mapped out the economy in the terms of prevailing international categories of planning and accounting, which represented one aspect of the closer integration of the new African countries into the world market. In the case of Tanzania the new five year plan of 1969 was worked out by an international team of economists, funded by the Ford Foundation, and recruited from Norway, Great Britain, the US, India, Germany, Israel and Czechoslovakia! In the course of their work the planners generated a lot of ideas about useful aid projects including deliveries from their own countries. Thus Eskild Jensen, the Norwegian economist, who had started as the first chief of staff in the newly created Norwegian Development Agency, identified local needs and Norwegian aid opportunities within fisheries education, coastal transport and tourism, and large scale aid projects were later established in these areas. On returning to Oslo, Eskild Jensen went on to become head of division in NORAD. Another NORAD economist, Steinar Skjæveland, served as advisor in the division for External Finance in the Financial Ministry and helped produce a manual for formulating plans and projects in such a manner as to attract foreign donors. One case in point was a five year health plan to be financed by aid. As aid increased there can be little doubt that the structure of the Tanzanian state apparatus

---

[7] Kjeld Phillip: "Den østafrikanska gemenskapen". In *Afrikainstitutets skriftserie*, nr.16, 1969.

was partly shaped to fit into the international aid system, and aid was a precondition for its expansion.

A few glimpses can be given of the cultural encounter during this early period of the aid relationship. Coming from a country with no colonial experience and little international business, except for shipping, there was a fascination with Africa: "My heart was here, this opened the world to me".[8] An anthropological survey of about 50 Peace Corps members took for its title a quote from one of the interviews: "*Africa remains in our bodies and minds*". [9] Personal letters might reflect the naive and partly confused attitudes of newcomers to Africa: They are so poor, and all this we have done to them! Our servant will not sit with us at the table, but eats in the kitchen or on the staircase like a dog. We have been to the mission station and slavery museum in Bagamoyo, and you cannot believe how much slave trading the missionaries have been doing![10] – At the other end of the scale is a 300 page diary from the years 1967-69 by Katrine Frøland, a Trondheim professor who with her husband took part in establishing the chemistry departments both in Nairobi and Dar-es-Salaam. The diary is a valuable historical source coloured by a one hundred percent dedication to Tanzania.[11]

The most voluminous source group on the cultural encounter are the regular, half-yearly reports from NORAD personnel in the field. Although to some degree standardized and bound by the inhibitions of the NORAD context, they are concrete, written in everyday language and frequently reflective. They could have been systematically utilized as a basis for institutional learning, and should be exploited for research. A particularly articulate group was the about ninety high school teachers ("lektorer"), who served in Tanzania between 1967 and 1975, scattered in many parts of the country at the time when Nyerere's educational policy was put into practice.[12] Interestingly, most of them are sympathetic to the reforms, which bore a resemblance to educational ideas about comprehensive schools and new pedagogical methods in the Nordic countries at the time. The Norwegian teachers took responsibility for compulsory classes in practical work – harvesting in the field or doing repairs in the schools – with a

---

8   Interview with Eskild Jensen, 10.9.1998.
9   Ada Engebrigtsen: *"Afrika sitter i kropp og sinn ..." : fredskorpsengasjement: opplevelse og formidling : Rapport fra en undersøkelse om hva fredskorpsarbeid har betydd for tidligere Fredskorpsdeltakere og for brobygging i det norske samfunnet*, Oslo 1992.
10   Personal letters, nr.1, 1999, Simensen's archive.
11   Katrine Førland: *Dagboksblader*, manuscript, 369 pp., Kenya and Tanzania, 11.2.1967 to 25.8.1969, in Simensen's archive.
12   Katrine Wilson: *Åtti norske lektorer i Tanzania mellom 1968 og 1980. Et eksempel på norsk ekspert bistand, MA-thesis*, Department of History, University of Oslo, 2005. A rich and honest personal account is Tutte Whist Klouman: *Møte med Afrika*, Oslo 2002, manuscript, 224 p., Universitets-biblioteket, UHS, Oslo and in Simensen's archive.

non-snobbish attitude and seemingly with more sympathy than the students and their parents.

 Some of the teachers comment on the ambivalence of recipient attitudes, reflecting general patterns of frustration in a gift relationship – it is desired but also resented. In one case from Tabora student essays on "The role of the expatriate teacher" released a flood of negative comments on the "neo-colonialists". This might be a reflection of general TANU Youth League agitation at the time, which in the opinion of one senior Norwegian teacher contained "mob language reminiscent of the Nazis, with dema-gogic clichés and hateful attacks on foreigners who poisoned the folk soul of Tanzania".[13] Foreign teachers had been specifically mentioned. The degree of party control and surveillance was disturbing. When a Danish teacher in Tabora, who was mingling in local society, kept two students in his house beyond the prescribed hours, it was not treated as a disciplinary matter, but referred to the Regional Commissioner as a security case. The teacher was expelled, and so were the two students involved. The head-master advised the foreign teachers to be careful in establishing friendly relations, not to meet Africans "at awkward hours" and to keep a certain distance to the students.[14]

The most spontaneous reports and reactions we find among the Peace Corps personnel. Radical spokesmen of the Peace Corps Association in Norway, influenced by the atmosphere of 1968, were all for Tanzania as a progressive country, it was even proposed that the Peace Corps should form part of Tanzania's National Service, a suggestion that would scarcely have been attractive to Nyerere.[15] The Peace Corps had a difficult and late start in Tanzania from about 1973, and at the start many were frustrated by the backwardness, the political regulations and the lack of security. "It is not a happy people, but things will scarcely improve if I make off for home."[16] But the general tendency was that the Peace Corps members identified with *their* country. Backwardness in itself might inspire an effort. One report formulates this in terms illustrative of James Buchanan's

---

[13] NORAD: Personal file, Sverre Klouman, 6.1.1969, with enclosed cutting from the *Sunday News* of December 15, 1968 reporting a speech by the chairman of the TANU Youth League and cabinet member Mr. Sijaona: "Mr. Sijanona told about 6000 people at Arusha Stadium after a procession through the town streets, that after failing politically, the capitalists were now trying to poison the minds of the people against their own culture....When Tanzania needed teachers, foreigners came to help – but to the detriment of youth. They did not comb their hair or wash their clothes, Mr. Sijaona said, and he was thankful that the Ministry of Education had taken steps "to curb such tendencies in teachers."

[14] NORAD: Personal file, Sverre Klouman, 2.10. 1969

[15] Dag Seierstad: *Hva skjer i Afrika? Makt og avmakt i afrikanske samfunn,* Oslo 1969, sitert i Simen-sen 2003:192.

[16] Peace Corps worker report 1984, quoted in Leif Vetlesen: *Det norske fredskorps. Fra Trollvasshytta til Afrika,* Oslo 1986:147.

theory about the "Samaritan's dilemma": "It is probably the case that we Norwegians almost *demand* that a developing country shall be dirt poor. If they start showing signs of something different, we often react negatively by instinct, perhaps because we feel our position and role threatened."[17]

Financial aid and project orientation: Stiegler's Gorge

From about 1970 the aid relationship changed character. Having been restricted mainly to the provision of experts, the emphasis now shifted to financial aid. This shift had been foreseen during the previous period of technical assistance, the increased aid budget necessitated new financial outlets and we have seen that the Norwegian experts on the ground were on the look-out. In the period that followed, the Norwegian aid contribution came mainly in the form of large-scale projects combining financial and technical aid – Tacoshili in coastal transport, Mbegani in fisheries education, the Sao Hill timber mill – which came to occupy much of NORAD's attention and aid debate through the 1980s. Seen from Oslo such large scale projects were attractive. They absorbed large amounts of money which might otherwise have been stuck in the pipeline, they provided interesting opportunities for Norwegian consulting firms and also prospective deliveries of machinery. And there was now a belief on both sides that industrialization must be given priority, in spite of the Arusha Declaration to the contrary.

This shift in the aid strategy went together with a further institutionalization of the aid relationship. Each project was regulated by a separate agreement which defined the extent of aid and the responsibility for the execution of the project. One precondition for this was the introduction of a long-term aid planning machinery in the form of four year rotating "framework programmes" for the whole bilateral aid budget and a corresponding four

---

[17] Peace Corps worker report 1984, quoted in Vetlesen, *op.cit.*:148. For James Buchanan's theory, see his article "The Samaritan's dilemma", in Edmund S. Phelpes (ed): *Altruism, Morality and Economic Theory,* New York 1975: 71-81. The concept is successfully put to use in Hilde Selbervik's path-breaking study, *Power of the Purse? Norway as a Donor in the Conditionality Epoch 1980-2000,* Dr.art. dissertation, Department of History, University of Bergen 2003. The largest Norwegian missionary aid project, Haydom Hospital and Health Centre, reveals something of the same problematic. It was created by the Norwegian Lutheran Missionary Association in the sparsely populated Mbulu district in Tanzania under the direction of two generations of the Evjen Olsen family, and with partial support from NORAD. By 1988 there lived about 20, 000 people around the hospital, more or less connected to its activities. In spite of its success, the paternalist tradition of the project began to be questioned when "local capacity building", "sustainability" and "out-phasing" became catchwords in international aid discourse in the 1990s. But the exceptional nature of this aid relationship was illustrated when Prime Minister Sumaye came to Norway, unheeded by the media, to attend the funeral of Evjen Olsen in 2004. See Arild Engelsen Ruud and Kirsten Alsaker Kjerland: *Vekst, velvilje og utfordringer.* Vol.II of *Norsk utviklingshjelps historie,* Oslo 2003:216-217.

year "land programme" for the main recipient countries. Regular routines were now developed in the contact with the Tanzania authorities.[18] On the surface it was a partnership. Before the yearly budget under the "land programme" was drafted in Oslo, a list of priorities had been sent up from Tanzania through the local NORAD representative, who, together with Norwegian advisors in the Tanzanian ministries, might have given hints as to what would go down well in Oslo. Next, a yearly Norwegian delegation would go to Dar-es-Salaam, to large scale initial meetings and to specific consultations in the agencies concerned to collect facts and opinions before returning to Oslo. During negotiations the Norwegians might give further signals as to what to them seemed desirable and non-desirable projects, an example given was that both parties knew that support of an airport was out of the question. No conflict seems ever to have arisen – but how can a conflict arise within a gift relationship? Back in Oslo the country budget was finalized, detailed project planning started, consulting firms were engaged and personnel recruited. In the large-scale projects NORAD took direct employer and operational responsibility. No Tanzanian advisor was in place in NORAD when the plans for Tanzania were formulated.

The flaws of the project strategy are now common knowledge and need only be listed here: over-dimension, technology excess, lack of proper integration into the national development strategy, weak market orientation, the subsidy problem (with exhaustion when aid was withdrawn), premature hand-over and a lack of long-term commitment. In historical perspective, including the perspective of mission history, the time horizon of aid projects has been absurdly short. Where the NORAD commitment has lasted longer, as in the case of forestry education at Morogoro and mechanical engineering in Dar-es-Salaam, it has seen considerable success. And there was the basic dilemma that as the Tanzanian state weakened, NORAD tended to take more direct operative responsibility, thus further weakening the state and neglecting the training of local counterparts. In the case of Tacoshili the director of the Tanzanian Transport Company in later interviews was strikingly critical of Norwegian attitudes: "We were never really taken on board.... We were not given any choice, it was take it or leave it...... We could not tell the truth, we feared it would cost us the support". He had experience with other donors who he maintained were more open.[19] How representative this example is we do not know. The reactions of local recipients in the field have never been systematically studied, it must be a task primarily for local researchers.

---

[18] Paal Bog, "Planlegging og prioritering av norsk utviklingshjelp". In *Forum for utviklingsstudier*, 9, NUPI, Oslo, 1974.

[19] Interview by Kirsten Alsaker Kjerland with M. E. Sanare, director of National Transport Company, Tanzania 2000, quoted in Engelsen Ruud and Alsaker Kjerland 2003: 92.

One project may serve to illustrate the aid relationship in this period, the planning of a gigantic dam and power plant at Stiegler´s Gorge.[20] Its potential had been noted from colonial times, and the dam was Nyerere's dream. Norad took over responsibility for planning in 1971 with great enthusiasm: "The director finds this project of particular interest. It may play an important part in Tanzania's development, and it concerns an area where Norway has particularly good qualifications."[21] For the consulting firms, who were given open-ended contracts, it provided unprecedented opportunities for profit and competence building. Africa expertise at the Norwegian University for Science and Technology in Trondheim was fascinated. What NORAD was *not* told at the start was that the World Bank had already carried out a pilot study and concluded that the investment needed was too high for Tanzania´s limited energy market. So, Norwegian planning ran its course, with a grand prospecting and research camp on the spot, and the costs by 1980 reaching 14 times the original budget. Engineers on NORAD's staff had been sceptical from the start, and in 1979 demanded a stop in planning and a review of the financial realism of the project. In Oslo the case went to the Cabinet, who in 1978 made it clear that responsibility for finance must rest with Tanzania alone. A delegation went to Tanzania to negotiate a termination of the project, but was confronted with the obligations of a signed contract and persuaded by new calculations and financial plans. Environmental concerns increased and a report from the Christian Michelsen Institute in Bergen analysed the ecological consequences.[22] Paradoxically the forced villagization removed the scattered farm settlements with traditional agriculture that could have benefited from flood control. One researcher complained about the "ideological taboo which today surrounds *ujamaa*".[23]

This case illustrates as well interesting institutional aspects of the aid relationship. There were conflicting opinions on both sides. In Dar-es-Salaam the Finance Ministry thought the plans unrealistic, but the sceptics were not allowed to come into contact with the Norwegian delegation. The Tanzanian Electricity and Water Agency, TANESCO, was against Stiegler's Gorge, and had an alternative regional plan for the Rufiji river basin. A negative Canadian report was not published. For president Nyerere, Stiegler's Gorge was a matter of faith, and profitability calculations were not his strongest side. But the core of the case finally became clear: without a market for the electrical power

---

[20] Simensen 2002: 162-167.
[21] *Ibid.*, 164.
[22] Kjell Havnevik: *The Stiegler's Gorge multi-purpose project: 1961-1987.* DERAP working papers: A 131. Bergen 1978.
[23] Helge Kjekshus: Økologiske aspekter ved Stiegler's Gorge-prosjektet, in Forum for utviklingsstudier, nr 10, 1977.

there could be no international finance, and without finance there could be no dam. After another period of procrastination NORAD's director in 1981 went to Tanzania in person to tell his friend, the President, that the plans must be shelved. By then about Nkr150 million had been spent, equalling in today's money about Nkr 500 million or 80 million dollars.[24]

The one-party state and the Tanzania syndrome

The reception of Tanzania in Norwegian and Nordic opinion provides an interesting area of research. A prominent Scandinavian Africanist, Göran Hydén, in 1967 named Tanzania "the shining star" of Africa[25], and in NORAD the Arusha Declaration had the status of an icon. Nyerere received a positive press, across party lines, right into the 1980s, and his visits to Scandinavia were celebrated events. How can this be explained? This was after all a one-party state with preventive detention and a suppressive security apparatus, hostile to private ownership and an independent middle class. It was described as a "*socialist*" state, a "peasant and workers' state", following communist terminology. It stood in stark contrast to the Scandinavian model of development, built on personal liberties, self-owning farmers, independent trade unions and an entrepreneurial middle class. It came at a time when Norwegian opinion was much taken up with the Cold War, with the party states in Eastern Europe and the consequences of Mao's "Great Leap Forward" in 1958-62. We can only indicate a few elements of explanation.

Modernization theory, which guided aid thinking in the 1950s and 1960s, was not primarily concerned with democracy, there was a tolerance for the so-called "developmental state", and Weber's concept of charismatic rule as a transitional stage on the way from traditional to modern society was common. Immanuel Wallerstein in his *Africa: The Politics of Independence* from 1961 provided an apology for the party state as holding the floor during the time of nation-building. Thus authoritarianism in Africa was explained and to some degree taken for granted, less so in its military form, and there was a widespread concept of a trade-off between democracy and development. It was only towards the end of the 1970s that the double standards this involved were pointed out by African critics and human rights appeared on the international aid agenda. The concept of "social development" which gained ground in international aid discourse from the late 1960s and

---

[24] This calculation presupposes that the money was equally spent over the project years and that an average of the consumer price index for the period can be used.

[25] Göran Hydén: *Tanzania : vision och verklighet*, Afrikainstitutets skriftserie nr.11, Uppsala, 1969.

the radical turn in Norwegian and Nordic development opinion about 1970 also worked to the advantage of Tanzania. The Norwegian White Paper on aid policy in 1972 introduced what have since been the guiding formulations: preference should be given to recipient countries who conducted a "development oriented and socially just policy". Underdevelopment theory achieved something of a hegemonic status in Norwegian interpretations of Third World development which can be registered in aid information material and not least significantly in school textbooks.

But the Arusha Declaration also struck deeper cords in Nordic mentality: egalitarianism, respect for practical work and physical labour, the importance of peasant culture in national life, and the use of family and village images in the creation of modern social ideology. The "New Norwegian" language movement, dating back to the period of nation building from the 1860s, contained social and cultural ideas of this kind, and it is significant that the two Norwegian volumes of Nyerere's speeches came out in New Norwegian.[26] We have already mentioned the special appeal of Nyerere's educational philosophy. To all of this must be added the personal charisma and charm of Nyerere, who on visits to the Nordic countries played up the social-democratic elements of his programme, according to the NORAD director "it sounded like music in our ears".[27]

It is rather more difficult to explain the continued enthusiasm for Tanzania after "Operation Planned Villages" started in 1974-75. Even seen alongside other utopian efforts at agricultural social engineering in modern history, the removal of 13 million people from their homes by 1976 – about seventy percent of the total population – was an extraordinary figure.[28] In this process Nyerere revealed other features of his personality: his contempt of traditional rural mentality, his admiration for the discipline of industrial organization, his characteristics as *haambiriki,* he who will never change his mind, and *Mse Mose,* he who leads his people to the promised land. The welfare and productivity argument for *ujamaa* could, at least initially, make an impression, as it did on McNamara in the World Bank and also on the visiting chairman of NORAD's board

---

[26] *Sosialisme i Tanzania. Artiklar og talar,* Oslo, 1970; *Fattigdom og frigjering. Artiklar og talar,* Oslo, 1976, both in the series Orion Utsyn. A Swedish edition is *Socialism i Tanzania,* Nordiska Afrika-institutet, Uppsala 1968.

[27] Interview, Arne Arnesen, 23.9.1998.

[28] James C. Scott, *Seeing Like a State: How Certain Schemes to Improve the Human Condition Have Failed.* New Haven, 1998; Kjell Havnevik, *Tanzania. The Limits to Development from Above.* The Nordic Africa Institute, Uppsala, 1993.

in 1973, Jacob Modalsli.[29] But how could the methods and disastrous results *for so long* be disregarded by the Scandinavian donors? Peasant collectivization had normally been perceived as the great communist scare in Norwegian opinion.

To account for this lack of reaction the concept of a "Tanzania syndrome" can be applied, in the sense of a system of perceptions and policies captured by prevailing ideology and interest. The aid momentum in itself is probably an element in this, so much was invested in Tanzania and prestige was at stake. Ideological identification blinded the eye. And large bureaucratic machines will always have a problem forming a true picture of reality; concerns about the status of the institution and the advancement of personal careers will tend to prevent honest reporting and filter reports as they go upwards in the hierarchy. Internal debate is dampened for the same reasons. In the case of the Norwegian Foreign Ministry the frustrations bred by such an institutional culture came into the open, mainly anonymously, in the house-cleaning that followed the handling of the Tsunami crisis in January 2005. In international aid, particularly in the case of Tanzania, there was in addition the "tyranny of the good cause", the fear of playing into the hands of the enemies of aid on the populist right.

It can of course be maintained that few Norwegian aid workers were actually in the countryside as first-hand witnesses. But when a Norwegian teacher in Moshi, close to brutal operations, questioned Norwegian aid to Tanzania under such circumstances, he was firmly put in place by the local NORAD representative, who maintained that the extent of removals was exaggerated and that criticism was based on political antipathy against collectivization, a policy he claimed was well known when Tanzania had been chosen as a "main cooperating country".[30] When a new NORAD representative in the years that followed returned to Oslo with critical views, and when it became clear that his concerns were shared by many in the administration, it was made clear from the top that no change of policy would take place. The ideological commitment remained, and the sovereignty principle was maintained. Personal relationships also played a part, as in the case of NORAD's director, Arne Arnesen and President Nyerere.

---

[29] NORAD, Ø.A.0008.08, Ta 29.6 PP, Jakob Modalsli: Rapport fra reise I Øst-Afrika I tiden 10.-30. mars 1973. When Modalsli visited Kibaha, 16 *ujamaa* villages had been put under the centre, where the students could help with physical work during their compulsory practical classes and in Modalsli's words "get soil on their hands to counteract the general tendency to become intellectuals and look down on physical work". Modalsli was taken on a visit to one *ujamaa* village and was impressed: "Political speeches, slogan shouting and responses from the assembly revealed that a spark had been lighted. Here they are building on something of the best in village solidarity, adding a new dimension which points towards more modern forms of production and above all a more intensive work effort by the village members." Modalsli's report on this point could have been taken from a speech by Nyerere.

[30] Simensen 2002:159.

It took a Norwegian TV journalist, Einar Lunde, to bring Tanzanian realities to public attention in Norway. Against warnings both from the Norwegian Embassy and the acting Tanzanian Foreign Minister he took up the case of Christina Lugangira, who was arrested as a hostage for her brother, a suspected member of a coup planning group in 1983, who had escaped from the country. The case provides an illustration of the power of the *recipient* in a gift relationship; there was reason to ask who was actually giving 300 million kroner per year to whom.[31] The prisoner was released without charge after two and a half years. Independently of this case Lunde, in 1985, obtained the TV-interview where Nyerere admitted that some of his policies had been seriously wrong, an interview which became an international sensation.

The concept of a closed system can be widened, at a stretch, to include the whole of the Norwegian aid establishment.[32] A crucial point is that the non-governmental organizations, about 200 of them by the year 2000, have been so closely integrated into the aid system that many of them can scarcely be called "non-governmental" any longer. Consultancy firms also vegetate on the aid budget, journalists are paid travel grants – at a time when the media are scaling down on their own correspondents outside the West – and most of development research has been funded through the Foreign Ministry. Recent anthropological theory has been taken up with the problem of "discourse anemia", the lack of an alternative language to the official "aid-speak" which can report things as they are, and not as they are expected to be, a mechanism which has also been at work in the history of Norwegian Christian missions to Africa.[33] The everyday language of aid workers in the field might be entirely different, cynical to a degree, compared to official discourse. When NORAD moved part of its training programme for the Peace Corps to Tanzania, the recruits were deliberately isolated from the old-timers on the spot, partly with reference to the language they used.

Budget aid and the missing link in the aid relationship: Macro-economics

In 1974 the Tanzanian finance minister stated that foreign aid now equalled 28% of the state budget, a doubling in ten years. Considering that the main aim of the Arusha Declaration had been *self-reliance*, specifically

---

[31]   Einar Lunde, *Safari blant folk og røvere i Afrika*. Oslo, 1998.
[32]   Terje Tvedt, *Utviklingshjelp, utenrikspolitikk og makt*. Oslo, 2003.
[33]   Karina Hestad Skeie, *Building God's kingdom in highland Madagascar. Norwegian Lutheran missionaries in Vakinankaratra and Betsileo 1866-1903*, Dr.art. thesis, History of Religion, University of Oslo, 2005.

mentioning independence from foreign aid, it called for a comment. The finance minister thought this was an "insignificant portion", and that is was "absolutely necessary". Nyerere at the same time went on the offensive and justified the demand for aid as "compensation for long-time exploitation, for the great price variations in the commodity market and for the lack of social insurance arrangements at the international level".[34] During the subsequent decade of economic downhill in Tanzania the aid percentage rose steadily in the direction of half the state budget, the Norwegian share being about nine percent and the Nordic share about twenty-five percent of total foreign aid to Tanzania in the period 1982-85.[35]

A significant change in the aid relationship was the shift to more programme aid and direct budget aid in the form of import subsidies and balance of payment support. Large sums were also channelled through the state development banks. None of this could be subject to regular audit by Norwegian standards. Most critical was the deficit in the foreign currency account, mainly caused by the fall in agricultural production and export and the consequent need for food imports. The financial crisis of 1983-85 made it clear that a state had been created which could not be supported by the economy.

In hindsight it is extraordinary that macro-economics do not seem to have been on the agenda of the aid relationship. The "country programme" negotiations seemingly did not take up the total economic and financial situation within which the specific projects and programmes took place. What we may call the "sovereignty fallacy" probably blinded both parties to the fact that Tanzania, like many other African states, had become a client state of a very special historical nature. Not many aid administrators on the Norwegian side had the information and the theoretical grasp to pull aside the veil of diplomatic aid discourse and present to Norwegian public a comprehensive picture of what was actually going on at the macro-economic level. This did not happen until the Norwegian Ministry of Development Cooperation commissioned a so-called country study of Tanzania in 1988.[36] But by then the aid relationship had been fundamentally changed by the crisis of 1984-85, when the IMF and World Bank, with the Nordic countries aboard after a period of hesitation, demanded economic reform as a condition for continued aid and loans. Conditionality replaced sovereignty as a leading principle in aid history.

---

[34] Simensen, 2002:168.
[35] *Ibid.*, 167-68.
[36] Kjell J. Havnevik, Finn Kjærby, Ruth Meena, Rune Skarstein and Ulla Vuorela, *Tanzania. Country Study and Norwegian Aid Review.* University of Bergen, Center for Development Studies. 1988.

CHAPTER FOUR

AGRARIAN FUNDAMENTALISM OR FORESIGHT? REVISITING NYERERE'S VISION FOR RURAL TANZANIA

Deborah Fahy Bryceson

In looking back over the past half-century, it is abundantly evident that Julius Nyerere, more than any other, shaped Tanzania's developmental path. From the 1950s, when he first led the struggle for independence, to 1985, when he finally stepped down from the national presidency, he was the country's agenda-setter. He continued to exert political influence until his death in 1999. His legacy as *mwalimu*, the teacher, lives on in people's minds – foundational to national identity, political unity and a sense of moral idealism - despite a general repudiation of Nyerere's economic policies over the last two decades.

This chapter attempts to go beyond the controversy surrounding Nyerere's charisma as a 'successful' political nation-builder who nonetheless is deemed to have 'failed' to achieve his national economic welfare objectives. While many commentators have remarked about Nyerere's thwarted agrarian socialist plans, would Nyerere himself have seen it in this way? What elements of the Nyerere vision continue? What elements have sunk to oblivion? As the founding father of the nation, was Nyerere an idealistic agrarian fundamentalist or a pragmatist who saw agriculture as the starting point and foundation for future national development?

Following a review of the Nyerere agrarian-based blueprint for national development and the obstacles encountered in its implementation, this chapter considers what has evolved in place of Nyerere's vision - the unforeseen reality of 21st century Tanzania. Illustration of the contradictory nature of today's rural Tanzania will be provided by an examination of the development trajectory of Katoro-Buseresere, an agrarian-cum-sprawling-multi-purpose urbanizing settlement in northwestern Tanzania, which reflects the Nyerere legacy and recent unpredicted economic and political trends in the country.

Nyerere's Blueprint: *Kilimo na Ujamaa*

During the first decade of independence, the question of whether agricultural or industrial investment would take the leading role in

Tanzanian development was not at issue (Rweyemamu 1973, Seidman 1973, Bryceson 2000). Nyerere saw no need for debate.

> This truth is said so often that people forget it....Yet it remains true. Agricultural progress is indeed the basis of Tanzanian development-and thus of a better standard of living for the people of Tanzania. (Nyerere's speech at the Morogoro Agricultural College, 18 November 1965, in Nyerere 1968a: 104)

In choosing agriculture, specifically peasant smallholder agriculture, other developmental options were circumvented. At independence, Tanzania's major peasant-produced crops coffee, cotton and cashew exports, valued at UK£ 18.4 million, were not overly dominant as foreign exchange earners relative to the plantation crop, sisal (UK£15.4 million) and diamond and gold exports (UK£ 5.8 million), but the economic potential of the latter two were politically tainted (Tanganyika 1961). The 1950s had been a period of considerable mine prospecting. South Africa's Anglo American mining giant had emerged as an attentive investor. However, relations between apartheid South Africa and Tanzania were not surprisingly strained[1] and in the aftermath of the Arusha Declaration, the government's nationalisation policy deterred foreign investors. Very little mining survey work was undertaken during the Nyerere years. Tanzania's mining wealth remained buried securely for the future.

Meanwhile, the future of Tanzania's large-scale plantation agricultural sector was increasingly less certain. During the independence struggle, TANU had been committed to raising plantation remuneration beyond the abysmal level of bachelor wages and finally delivered on their promise in 1963 with the establishment of a territorial minimum wage. Employers retaliated by reducing the size of their labour force. The collapse of sisal prices in the world market in reaction to the growing importance of rival synthetic materials compounded shrinking rural wage labour opportunities (Bryceson 1990). These circumstances reinforced Nyerere's conviction that:

> For the foreseeable future the vast majority of our people will continue to spend their lives in the rural areas and continue to work on the land. The land is the only basis for Tanzania's development; we have no other. (Nyerere 1967: 118)

Unambiguously Nyerere prioritized *kilimo*. During the independence struggle, the peasantry had served as the springboard for nationalists' successful seizure of political power. Peasant grievances against the colo-

---

[1] At independence Nyerere refused Tanganyika's entry into the British Commonwealth unless South Africa was expelled from membership in light of its apartheid policies (Kaunda 1985).

nial state's insistence on labour-intensive conservation practices and Asian merchants' domination in agricultural produce marketing were key issues that TANU championed, winning the hearts and minds of the rural masses. True to his election promises, Nyerere fashioned a government that was sensitive to the basic needs and aspirations of the rural peasantry.

Food security was a key peasant concern. The colonial government had introduced famine relief as a fallback for farming households if they suffered food crop failure (Bryceson 1990). The Nyerere government, mindful of the dangers of trying to raise export crop production on the basis of subsistence-oriented peasant farming as well as taking account of rising food production pressures associated with urbanization, introduced a raft of subsidy supports to encourage the expansion of smallholder staple food output and boost agricultural productivity (Bryceson 1993). The objective was to earn foreign exchange for national development and the supply of food to feed the expanding urban population.

Ujamaa, the Kiswahili word that Nyerere (1962, 1967) imbued with portent meaning during the 1960s and his epitaph in the eyes of the world at large, has often been conflated with western notions of socialism and collectivization of production. The concept can be likened to the word 'democracy' invoked in the United States or Britain to symbolize the national collective, unity of purpose, and cherished way of life. The analogy can be extended further. Just as the western nation-state forged its 'democracy' out of sentiments opposed to autocratic ecclesiastical, feudal and monarchic political traditions, under Nyerere, *ujamaa* congealed from a reaction to the anomalous blend of tribal and colonial traditions of divide and rule. Both democracy and *ujamaa* necessarily incorporated aspects of governance from their respective political legacies in the construction of the nation-state, nonetheless the underlying premise of the new state was radically different (refer also to chapter 2).

In the case of Tanzania, the particularism of tribal loyalties and the authoritarianism of the colonial order were roundly rejected. Nyerere's Tanzania was built on the base of an African nationalist identity, one that valued welfare concerns akin to the ethics of the peasant moral economy (Scott 1976). Peasant welfare was premised on access to land to enable rural households to provision their subsistence needs and food security as a human right. In this context *ujamaa* was intended to serve as the means towards national development and welfare improvement for the Tanzanian peasantry as well as being a goal in and of itself.

Unlike so many of the early African nationalist leaders in the neighbouring countries of East and Southern Africa, Nyerere rejected the perpetuation of chiefly rule as a form of local government even though this was the default option at independence and Nyerere was himself the son of a chief. Governor Twining, Tanganyika's last colonial governor, took it for granted that a rural tribal order would prevail after independence:

> ...the tribe is the most important group in the territory and that the chiefs are an essential part of this system and are indeed, the bulwark of the territory... it is the duty of every servant of government to uphold the respect and honour due to the chiefs so that the people may clearly see that the government recognizes the importance and the dignity of the position which they hold. (E. Twining, First Convention of Representative Chiefs, Dar es Salaam, 1957 recorded by C.M. Meek, quoted in Pratt, 1978:38)

Nyerere was a modernist who viewed local government as a catalyst for political and economic change rather than primarily a means of keeping law and order in a tribal cultural setting. Before independence in 1960 TANU had resolved that chiefly rule was not desirable (Iliffe 1979: 569). Chiefs were encouraged to become active in the party, which many did, enabling the government to quietly abandon the Native Authority system and establish District Councils in 1962 (Pratt 1978: 194). This move was to give Tanzania an enormous advantage in rural development. Native Authorities during the colonial period had embodied a spectrum of old and new influences. Literate clerks and rainmakers assisted hereditary chiefs. The clerks had interfaced with the central colonial government, keeping records and assisting in tax collection. Rainmakers and others claiming magico-religious powers communicated with the ancestors and natural forces. By replacing Native Authorities with District Councils, rural areas gained secular bureaucratic rule by people legitimized on the basis of their education and work experience rather than their chiefly connections and traditional sacred beliefs. This was vital to separating matters of state from religion and fostering a welfare development outlook in the countryside.

Nyerere stood for the secular state as an instrument for change. It is unlikely that the villagization programme and other development campaigns in the fields of health, education and agriculture would have been feasible if there had not been a cadre of people at district, ward and village levels who were literate and numerate and owed their employment and future career prospects to regional and national networks rather than local tribal affiliations. In this way, Nyerere built a mass political base with the combined themes of *kilimo* and *ujamaa*, serving as both the nation's ends and means for mass mobilization. He presided over a developmental state intent on raising the standards of living and life chances of rural producers throughout the country by heavily investing in the provisioning of social and productive services. Villagization was first and foremost aimed at accelerating the government's service provisioning capacity in the countryside. The rallying call for mass involvement in this undertaking was *ujamaa*, defined as a traditional collective spirit put to work for modern developmental objectives. In Nyerere's words:

> ...our people in the rural areas are prepared to work together for their common good; in many places they have never stopped this traditional custom, and would take quite easily to an extension of it. The problem is not the principle; the problem is that of getting people to adopt practices which retain the central idea at the same time as they allow for development and growth. For we are not just trying to go backwards into the traditional past; we are trying to retain the traditional values of human equality and dignity while taking advantage of modern knowledge and the advantages of scale and improved tools...in the past we worked together because that was the custom; now we have to do it deliberately and to do it in such a manner that modern knowledge can be utilized for the common good. (Nyerere 1968: 180-1, Speech to the University College branch of TANU Youth League)

Nation-Building Hiatus: Design Faults, Bad Materials or Environmental Subsidence?

The story of the Tanzanian rural socialist experiment from the Arusha Declaration through villagization has been told many times and is referred to at some length in other chapters of this volume (Shivji 1975, Bryceson 1988, Komba 1995). Here, it is pertinent to note that villagization was not about socialist collectivity as much as nuclearizing scattered rural household settlement into villages where health dispensaries, schools and agricultural marketing services and productive infrastructure could be more efficiently provided. This goal was premised on the delivery capability of a cadre of government and parastatal agents from the central and local governments who would competently and honestly make the goods and services available to the villagized peasantry.[2]

After having supported Tanzanian state expansion in the 1960s and 1970s, many western donors, led by the World Bank and IMF, criticized the role of the state as the central delivery agent. Government and parastatal agents were viewed at best as incompetent and at worst corrupt. Charges of corruption were aligned with a theory of urban-bias in vogue at the time. In his influential book *Why Poor People Stay Poor: A Study of Urban Bias in*

---

2 Pratt (1985) observes that Tanzania faced a scarcity of trained and experienced people in its civil service which imposed restrictions on its development goal attainment.

World Development, Michael Lipton (1977) had argued that terms of trade were heavily weighted against rural dwellers in India. Robert Bates (1981) transferred Lipton's thesis to Africa with dramatic effect by proposing that Nyerere's government, contrary to championing rural farmers, was perpetrating urban-biased policies directed at privileging urban dwellers with favourable urban wage levels and food subsidies relative to rural peasants' agricultural commodity prices. Over-centralization of government and parastatals in Dar es Salaam and the unaccountability of bureaucratic agency were seen to be at the root of the problem. At the same time the World Bank (1981) published its version of the urban bias theory and critique of bureaucratic under-performance of the African modernizing state. But in the early 1980s, urban bias, a historical feature of all rapidly urbanizing societies, as argued by W. A. Lewis (1978), was vaporizing. Tanzania's urban residents experienced a drastic deterioration in their real earnings and living standards that contrasted with the more long-range gradual decline in peasant remuneration (Bryceson 1990 and 1992, Jamal 1993 and 2001).

An awareness of the precise timing of interactive processes and events is essential for understanding what went wrong. As luck would have it, Tanzania's villagization could not have been more poorly timed. Nyerere inauspiciously launched his nationwide villagization programme in 1973, the same year as the first international oil shock. Oil prices increased by 350 per cent causing Tanzania's fuel import bill to balloon (Bryceson, 1990). The higher oil prices rapidly initiated a chain reaction. International shipping costs rose spurring domestic transport costs upwards for export crops and peasant incentive goods. Inadequate rainfall in 1973/74 and especially 1974/75 combined with the upheaval of villagization and transport constraints, led to food shortages in rural and urban areas.

Despite these blows, the country recovered in 1976 and 1977. Food imports and the trade deficit declined, but in October 1978 the country was invaded by Amin's Uganda sparking a war that drained the country of its financial reserves and transport capacity. Just as the war ended, the second oil crisis hit in 1979, precluding the possibility of economic recovery. The value of the oil import bill went up while the import volume declined. The transport system contracted, causing the effects of poor rainfall to be magnified. A downward economic spiral reflected in all economic indicators characterized the following years. Tanzania limped into what was to later be called the lost decade of the 1980s. Nyerere's final presidential term from 1980 to 1985 lurched from one financial crisis to the next.

Beyond *Ujamaa*: Tanzania's Post-Peasant Economy and Society

Tanzania's *ujamaa* socialist experiment ended in the early 1980s as the Nyerere government conceded indirectly and then increasingly directly to IMF demands. Villages that had 'over-villagized' during the campaigns, resulting in too many people moving into one settlement, were allowed to disaggregate into satellite villages during the first half of the 1980s. Their population concentrations had proved to be too demanding on local resources, notably water and firewood, and had encouraged the spread of infectious disease. In 1981-82, the Tanzanian economy experienced its lowest point since independence. In addition to crippling oil prices and donor hostility, drought conditions endangered Tanzania's food security. Internal and external pressures were entwined, undermining Nyerere's *ujamaa* policy. Village farms that often had been established only reluctantly by villagers were disbanded and village services, health dispensaries, schools and marketing, all unravelled as government cutbacks deepened under the IMF-enforced structural adjustment programme.

Peasant agriculture experienced severe setbacks in the 1980s. Production of coffee, cotton and cashew, the major peasant export crops, dipped well below average as indicated in Figure 1 showing export performance in relation to the overall trend. Juxtaposed to the rural population growth rate of 2.0% per annum (Figure 2), coffee, cotton and cashew exports growing at 2.0%, 1.1% and 0% respectively suggests stagnation if not decline in peasant agricultural export capacity over the post-colonial period. Remarkably, the late 1960s and most of the 1970s, so heavily criticized by the international financial institutions as Nyerere's era of misguided statist policies, registered good export performance particularly for cashew production relative to the SAP era of the 1980s.

Economic liberalization policies of the 1990s had a positive impact on the peasant commodity sector. The abysmal decline of cashew production was checked and cotton and especially coffee responded with above average export performance. Nonetheless, over the long-term the volume of Tanzanian exports per rural capita in the 21st century is only about 90 percent of the early 1960s level for coffee whereas it has been halved for cotton and cashewnut.

Despite Nyerere's efforts to build an economy on the foundations of peasant agriculture, by the early 1980s, processes of deagrarianization and depeasantization were set in motion. 'Deagrarianization' is defined as long-term occupational adjustment, income-earning reorientation, social identification and spatial relocation of rural dwellers away from strictly

Figure 1: Major exports 1950-2003

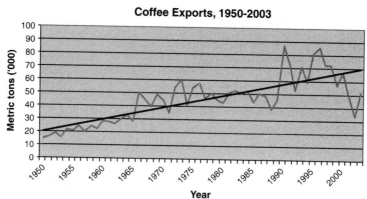

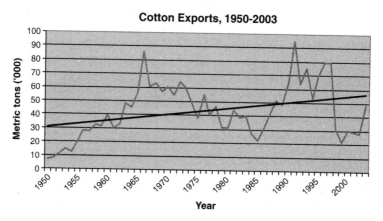

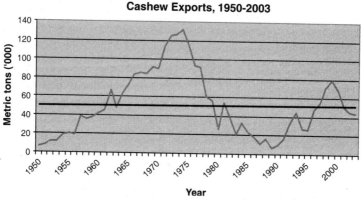

Sources:

1950-76 – East African Trade Reports

1977-84 – Tanzanian Trade Reports

1985-93 – Economics Research Bureau 1991 & 1994, Tanzania Economic Trends 3(4) and 6(1)

1994-2003 – Bank of Tanzania 2004, Annual Report 2003-04, p.118

agriculturally based modes of livelihood (Bryceson 1996). 'Depeasantization', the unravelling of peasant households and communities, as a cultural way of life and basis of economic livelihood, is more specific in terms of affecting small-scale rural peasant producers (Bryceson 2000). The social, economic and political characteristics of peasantries through the ages stats to erode. Classically peasants are denoted as rural producers who:

- farm to produce their subsistence as well as commodities for sale,

- produce in family household units,

- form a class subordinate to state authorities and national and international markets, and

- live in rural settlements that are relatively remote and traditionalist in outlook.

It is useful to consider Tanzanian agrarian change in light of these four characteristics.

There has been striking change in the balance between rural and urban settlement since the 1960s. In 1960 Tanzania's rural population numbered 10 million whereas in 2004 it was estimated to be 23.2 million growing at 2.0 percent per annum over the preceding four decades. Meanwhile the urban population has grown much faster (7.9 %) (Figure 2). In 2004, 63 % of Tanzania's estimated population of 36.5 million people resided in the rural areas as opposed to 95 % in 1961.

In the wake of the 1970s oil crises, Tanzania's peasant export crops lost their competitiveness as commodity transport costs from widely dispersed village sites throughout the country to ports rose. The large agricultural parastatals handling marketing had to borrow more and more heavily to finance their operations (Figure 3). The National Milling Corporation, in particular, shouldered an enormous overdraft. Declining parastatal marketing services as well as the continuing long-term decline in international prices for peasant export crops had a massive disincentive effect on peasant farmers. Their response was to diversify away from export crops. In areas with market accessibility this could take the form of staple food crops for urban demand or crops with a quick turnover, such as tomatoes and horticultural products, which constituted diversification into non-traditional exports (Ponte 2002). However, non-agricultural income diversification was the more generalized response throughout the country (Jambiya, 1998, Madulu, 1998, Mung'ong'o, 1998, Mwamfupe, 1998, Seppälä, 1998, Havnevik and Hårsmar, 1999 and Ellis and Mdoe 2003).

In the name of addressing 'urban bias' and 'getting the prices right' for peasant farmers, structural adjustment was implemented as a cost-cutting

Figure 2: Rural & Urban Population, 1960-2004

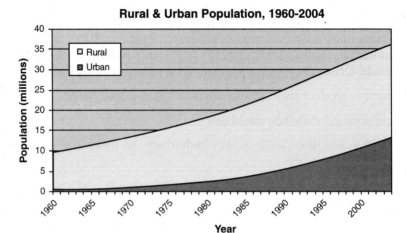

Source: World Bank 2004, World Development Indicators (vertical axis show millions)

exercise which gradually eliminated the social services and productive subsidies initiated under Nyerere's pro-peasant policy regime. User fees were introduced in health facilities and school fees were re-introduced reversing the government's universal primary education policy established in 1976. Subsidy removal and user fees imposed pressing cash needs on peasants (Bryceson, 2002a).

Depeasantization was triggered by structural adjustment. Rural households scrambled to earn cash through experimentation leading to upheaval in age-old ways of organizing rural household labour (Bryceson, 2002b). Some successfully innovated while others faced impoverishment. Several different tendencies emerged including rising:

- *cash-based activities* - More work activities became cash as opposed to subsistence based.

- *multiple activities and expansion of local economic divisions of labour* - Households and individuals within households sought to engage in one or more income-earning activities often on an experimental basis.

- *non-agricultural activities* – Involvement in trade, services and mining increased.

- *activities performed by household members of both sexes and a wide spectrum of ages* - Household members male and female, young, middle-aged and old were becoming involved in cash-based work whereas before most cash-earning had been the preserve of the male head of household selling agricultural export crops.

Figure 3: Commercial Bank Lending 1967-2003

Commercial Bank Lending, 1967-2003

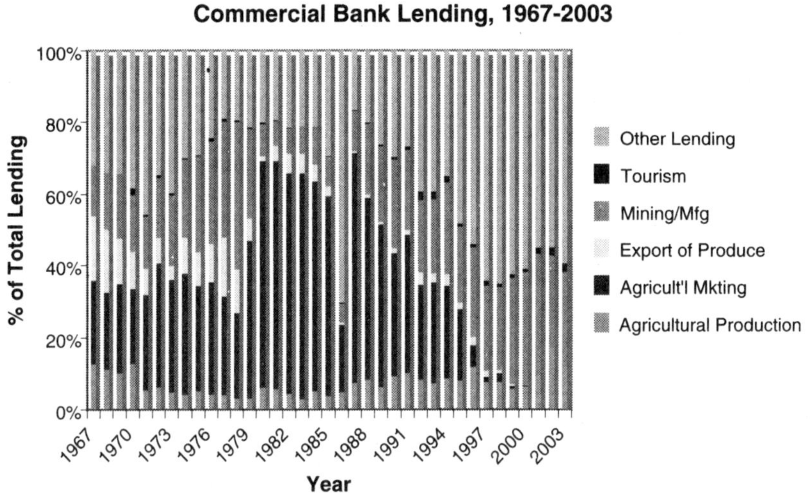

Source: Bank of Tanzania Annual Reports, 1967-2004 compiled by Goslinga 2005
* The anomaly in the agricultural marketing data for 1986 relates to the fact that during that year the regional cooperatives took over responsibility for staple food produce marketing from the National Milling Corporation causing a temporary hiatus in bank loaning for agricultural marketing.

- *Activities differentiated by income strata* – Certain activities such as beer brewing required low amounts of capital and were therefore 'easy-entry' activities as opposed to others, such as mine pit owners, transporters and guesthouse operators, which were reserved for the well-off with ready access to capital. In areas where income differentiation was rapid, there was a tendency for income-earning of the poor to veer more towards casual wage labour rather than self-employment which required capital outlays.

At household level, social implications of these economic tendencies were profound. Since the colonial period, male heads as export crop producers had been their households' chief income earners. As peasant export crop output declined during the 1980s, women and youth, as well as male heads of households, became involved in alternative income earning. Household members who formerly were not expected to earn an income were asserting a moral right to determine how their income was spent. Male patriarchal power within the peasant household was increasingly challenged.

Meanwhile, wealth differentiation between households became more pronounced, particularly in the bigger settlements where the division of labour proliferated the most. Concurrent processes of economic accumulation and impoverishment were generating rural land and labour markets. Case studies from the Institute of Resource Assessment's beyond the Shamba research project documented the outcome (Madulu, 1998, Mwamfupe, 1998). In rural Njombe, youth resorted to labour migration out of their home area to stave declining household income from maize cashcropping (Mung'ong'o, 1998). In some of the more densely populated parts of the country where out-migration was not enough redress, a rural proletariat was beginning to emerge which fuelled the incidence of local crime. In Lukozi, a village in West Usambaras, Tanga region, the village chairman observed in the mid-1990s:

> I would say that at least one in four households has a father, mother, son or daughter away from the village seeking an income, usually in the larger towns in the region...some do return eventually, but now we have a serious problem of crime, and our local court is very busy...agriculture alone does not pay nowadays. Everyone must *bangaiza* [struggle to scratch an income from whatever possible sources]. There is also so much begging now. All these are bad signs. Yes, of course part of this is due to the food shortage, but this did not begin today. My colleagues here who have been around longer will verify that it is nearly ten years since this phenomenon became evident (Jambiya 1998:8).

Figure 1 indicates that peasant agricultural exports temporarily improved during the mid-1990s following economic liberalization. This was remarkable in the face of farmers' lack of fertilizer usage connected with the removal of the fertilizer subsidy and the drying up of smallholder agricultural marketing credit resulting from the privatization of the National Bank of Commerce in 1997 and the reintroduction of foreign banks (Figure 3).[3] Meanwhile, world market prices were continuing to slide in real terms for Tanzania's major exports. What provided the impetus for agricultural export production despite all these impediments?

Fluctuating weather conditions do have an important bearing on annual output levels, but to understand long-term trends, we must turn to a consideration of what rural dwellers were doing in addition to agriculture. Tanzania's rural households emerged from a prolonged process of 'sink or swim' and those, who managed to stay buoyant, became adept swimmers. Structural adjustment had increased the need for cash and liberalization provided the opportunity. During the Nyerere period, strictures on many types of commercial transactions in the economy had prevailed with the hope of containing the extremes of wealth accumulation and impoverishment

---

[3] Goslinga (2005 citing Treichel 2005) reveals that liberalized bank lending ironically became restricted to a very small clientele of roughly 200 borrowers based on ethnic, religious and communal networks of trust in which Asians with large-scale businesses and 'net worth prestige' figured prominently.

in line with *ujamaa* objectives. Under liberalization, rural people were afforded the means of seeking their fortune both in an income and occupational sense. In my 1988 survey of grain traders, 60 percent of all traders interviewed started trading during implementation of the government's liberalization policy (Bryceson, 1993).[4] Earnings from trading and other non-agricultural activities could provide an impetus for intra-household capital transfers into smallholder agriculture.

The growth of artisanal mining activities took a similar course to trade. During liberalization, mining was no longer off-limits and local residents and migrants from neighbouring as well as more far-flung areas flocked to parts of the country endowed with gold, diamonds and precious stones to try their luck as small-scale miners. In 1995, the number of small-scale miners was estimated to be over half a million people, mostly men and many who would have been engaging in subsistence farming as well. More recent estimates have been scaled down to between 450,000 to 600,000 (Tan Discovery, 1996 and Mwaipopo *et al.*, 2004:27). Estimates are very subjective, especially as mining labour is highly volatile in its distribution over time and space.

There is a tension between formal and informal mining operations in Tanzania, with most artisanal pit owners and diggers experiencing marginalization. Their operations are feasible mainly for the surface deposits. Once digging is required beyond a few metres they are unable to make the capital investments in equipment and pumps required to make the mining technically viable and safe.

Outside of estimates of the mining labour force, Tanzanian national statistics are woefully neglectful of the documentation of mining activity in the national economy. Gold and diamonds are mostly sold informally by small-scale miners and physically transported by pit owners and wholesale traders to neighbouring countries and South Africa. Thus, exports from artisanal mining are severely under-reported.

Figure 4 shows the gradual rise in reported gold production in the late 1980s and 1990s followed by a dramatic increase when Afrika Mashariki and Buhemba mines started production in the 21st century. Tulawaka gold mine followed in 2005.

The recent surge in gold production has pushed the value of recorded mineral exports over the value of Tanzania's main peasant cashcrops for the first time. It appears that Tanzania is now on its way to having an economy driven by mineral as opposed to agricultural production.

---

[4] Women were more likely than men to have started at that time, possibly because they had found the former trade controls more intimidating than men had (Bryceson, 1993).

Is mining antithetical to Nyerere's *ujamaa* philosophy? Large-scale mining is notorious for its exploitative labour practices in the absence of regulation, a feature already noted in the Tanzanian context (Chachage 1995). Furthermore, countries with economies dominated by mining often display highly unequal wealth distribution patterns which have to be addressed with progressive taxation.

Given the meteoric rise of mining in the Tanzanian economy, it is pertinent to consider the role of mining in Tanzania's local rural economies. The following case study of a settlement near to the gold-mining activities of Geita and Biharmulo districts in Tanzania's Lake zone explores the influence of artisanal mining and trade in what hitherto was a typical cotton-growing village.

Katoro-Buserere: Nyerere's Model or Deviant Settlement?

Has Nyerere's effort to develop peasant agriculture and the spirit of *ujamaa* completely crumbled or does it remain embedded in the new economy? In this section, we probe the question by focussing on the history of Katoro-Buseresere, a rapidly expanding settlement straddling the border of Mwanza and Kagera regions roughly 150 kilometres from Mwanza town on the road to Bukoba and Uganda. Forming one contiguous spatial unit and unified local economy, Katoro is physically located within Geita district, Mwanza region while Buseresere is in Biharmulo district, Kagera region. Agronomically, the settlement is situated deep in Lake Victoria's cotton zone, where peasant farmers have grown cotton since the 1950s (McCall, 1980).

In 2002, the population was 30,472 having registered accelerating intercensal growth rates of 4.3 per cent between 1978 and 1988 and a very high 9.6 per cent between 1988 and 2002. Its location right on the Geita-Biharmulo district border and Mwanza-Kagera regional border has given it a strong edge as a trading centre. Contrasting tax regimes in the two districts have engendered competitive rivalry within the town. Many of the market stalls in the weekly Saturday market have recently relocated themselves from the Geita to the Biharmulo side of the settlement in response to market fees being raised in Geita district compared with Biharmulo district.

Most of the major guesthouses and shops, however, are located in Geita. Many are rumoured to be the property of mine owners who have recently made fortunes at the nearby Matabe gold mine approximately 30 km away. Whereas Geita is famous for its gold wealth with several mines dotted around the district, the gold discovery at Matabe is relatively new and very

Figure 4: Reported Tanzanian Gold Production, 1930-2003

Reported Tanzanian Gold Production, 1930-2003

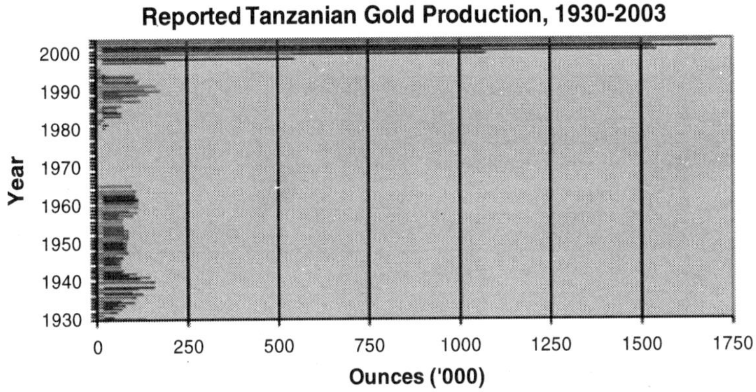

Source: Ministry of Energy and Minerals (various reports) compiled by Mwaipopo 2004 et al., 150-51.

welcome in a district known for its poverty. Matabe is physically situated in a game reserve which prevents people from building houses nearby. In this context, Katoro-Buseresere has benefited from its proximity to the mines. Katoro, in particular, has been favoured with investment in residential housing, shops and commercial guesthouses by successful mine owners trying to avoid tax demands from Biharmulo officials.

The local division of labour has proliferated with a profusion of small grocery-selling *dukas*, businesses, shops, bars and guesthouses in its centre. There are milling and peanut shelling facilities and several skilled tradesmen: carpenters, brickmakers, builders as well as water porters and bicycle repairers earning viable cash incomes. In addition to many bicycle taxis, there is one car taxi that operates in the settlement. Agricultural activities encompass the cultivation of rice, cassava, maize and cotton and the keeping of livestock.

Interviews with village elders and officials during a field trip to Katoro-Buseresere in April 2005 provide vivid accounts of unfolding settlement and livelihood change during and after the Nyerere years. A group of six elders, including Mzee Salvatore Kalema, a spritely 80-year-old with a razor-sharp memory, related the history of the settlement. He recalls the scattered farming households distinguished only by the presence of an Arab trader in the vicinity when he first came to the Katoro area in 1949. Mzee Kalema took the lead in attempting to attract infrastructural services to the area during the 1950s.

I met Father Lukraksi, a Roman Catholic priest on *safari* in Mwanza, in 1952 and asked him to build a church in Katoro. He agreed but there were

Figure 5: Value of Exports of Minerals and Peasant Cashcrops

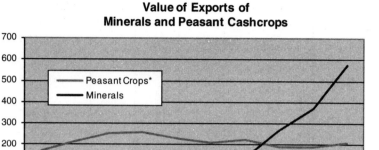

Source: Bank of Tanzania 2004, p. 118
* Peasant cashcrops include coffee, cotton, tea, cashew and tobacco

a lot of problems because the people here didn't like *maendeleo* [development]. I asked also for a school, but he was working in a parish in Kahama and he didn't think he could do it, but he asked permission at the Mwanza regional headquarters and they agreed. There was a school at Katoro and two others sprung up along the Geita road. Chief Edward Ludomila was the traditional leader, although now the area has been divided...in 1954, we asked for a hospital. It was agreed and built for the three settlements along the border of Biharmulo and Geita districts. At this time there were about 80 households here. In the same year the school was registered.

> During the 1950s we had to plant cotton. We were all required to plant 0.5 to 1.0 ha, both men and women. The government insisted and I didn't understand why. Life changed with cotton. In 1956 we formed a cooperative society, *Chama cha Ushirika Katoro Wakulima* (VCFU) which was part of the Victoria Federation Union under the leadership of Hon. Paul Bomani. We all knew Paul Bomani who visited us here and we also went to Mwanza to see him. In 1958 we built a cotton store here. By 1959, many people started moving here including Wasukuma because of cotton. The road was surveyed and built making it possible for vehicles to come and go.

The elders used national campaigns and events during the Nyerere era as benchmarks to recount their settlement's post-colonial history. All the interviewed *wazee* agreed that the 'village' began in 1974 when households located throughout the area were obliged to nucleate. There were more than the 250 households, which was considered the maximum for village formation.

> We were required to live together in villages. Villagization caused several villages to be formed whereas previously houses were scattered. People were brought together to be close to schools, health facilities, churches and mosques. Because a lot of these facilities were already in place in Katoro many people were moved here. It started to be like a town from that time because so many people were moved from the *porini* [bush]. Thereafter, our children experienced a serious attack of *surua* [measles] in 1975. Many children died. Too many people had come to Katoro. The officials had underestimated how many people were living in the surrounding bush. Thus in 1975 there was a policy to establish sub-villages.

> In 1976 we started village projects to deal with *pamba* [cotton]. We established a 150-acre village farm and every year the acreage and output grew. Our village was getting better and better. In 1977 we were getting TSh 30 per *laki* and in 1978 we were chosen as the best village in the district [*kijiji bora*] and awarded TSh 130,000 and a shield. We put the proceeds in a village account at the bank and used the accumulating money to build a school, a clinic for women to have their babies and other buildings. We continued to improve our school.

> In 1978 the village cooperative was very strong (operating as the primary buying agency). We sold all our cotton to the *Mamlaka wa Pamba* [Cotton Marketing Board]. Cotton marketing started falling apart because people were paid with promissory notes. They had to switch to other crops. Over time, the fertilizer and input subsidies were removed. Between 1980 and 1982 the village farm was dismantled in accordance with national policies, but the tradition of village projects continued.

Village elders reminisced with pride about the bumper cotton harvests they had in the past, regretting that currently they could not get loans for input purchase. The large conspicuous corrugated iron green warehouses for cotton storage dotted around the Lake zone, built with World Bank funding during the 1970s, are now largely empty.

The 1979 Uganda war in which Tanzania was invaded and then repelled Amin's troops driving them back into Uganda was economically destabilizing. Many of the troops passed through Katoro-Buseresere on their way to and from Uganda. In 1984 Operation *Nguvu Kazi* and *sungusungu* began, the former being an official government campaign to send the urban unemployed back to their homes area. *Sungusungu*, on the other hand, was primarily a local initiative aimed at addressing the lawlessness of the area. Burundese refugees, some of whom formed gangs hiding in the nearby forest, were believed to be ambushing unsuspecting parties travelling to and from Katoro. Mzee Kalema recalls:

> We were having a lot of trouble with *majambazi* [rabble rousers]. We had years of insecurity after the Ugandan war, the economic crisis of the 1980s, livestock rustling, theft from the fields and stored cotton, and Burundi refugees running amok. So we started *sungusungu*, which deterred the troublemakers from coming to Katoro.

Katoro-Buseresere evolved on a different trajectory from the rural egalitarian model of Nyerere's *ujamaa* with its commercial exuberance promoting consumer spending, a mining ethos of getting rich through luck and cunning, wealth accumulation on the basis of tax avoidance, numerous bars for recreational drinking and prostitution and state-of-the-art television entertainment using electricity generators and satellite dishes. Yet, this settlement owes its origin to Nyerere's villagization campaign. It retains an agrarian foundation with a large proportion of its residents engaged in farming for household food provisioning in the nearby fields surrounding the settlement.

Despite the presence of large numbers of immigrants, years of instability and incursions by lawless gangs of refugees, Katoro-Buseresere enjoys multi-ethnic harmony. Mzee Kalema joked about how the original ethnic groups, the Wazinza, Warongo, Wasumbwa and Wasubi, were engulfed by the very big and powerful neighbouring tribe, the Sukuma. When asked about the Sukuma influx Mzee Kalema cheekily recalls:

> The Wasukuma were *kaburi* [deadly]. We didn't want them. They first came as farmers, then civil servants and teachers. They came to support TANU and to produce cotton. They farmed like crazy... We have many tribes here and very good neighbourly relations. Ethnicity is not a problem. The majority now are: 1) Sukuma, 2) Ha, 3) Kuria and 4) the indigenous tribes who are now the minority: Longo, Subi, and Sumbwa. The Walongo were traditionally ironsmiths who made tools like hand hoes, machetes and axes and traditional weapons like spears and knives. Since the situation has now changed and industrial commodities are available, the Walongo have lost their identity as ironsmiths. Most of them have been integrated into the Sukuma culture.

Sukuma dominance had an ironic twist when *sungusungu* vigilante groups formed which co-opted adult male participation. The *sungusungu* groups were based on Sukuma tradition and involved Sukuma rituals and songs.

Mzee Kalema described how the men enthusiastically participated but many people did not have a clue about the lyrics of the songs they were singing because they did not understand the Kisukuma language – a striking example of amicable inter-tribal problem solving within a rural settlement.

Katoro-Buseresere emerged as a trading settlement during the 1990s. The interviewees cited the resolution of the security threat as an important step forward. In addition to the *sungusungu* militia operations, the settlement now has a court and police station.[5] One of the first signs that people had confidence in the settlement's security was when they began building residences with permanent materials, using bricks and corrugated iron roofs that were nailed down rather than merely being kept in place with the positioning of large rocks on the rooftops.

The good security situation, flourishing agriculture, and adequate water supply from seven wells and many water pumps and pipes afforded by the river nearby made Katoro-Buseresere a popular place for settlement. The weekly market grew in size from year to year as small-scale mining activities in Mwanza region expanded, boosting money circulation and purchasing power in the rural population. The settlement is now expanding very rapidly on the basis of its good transport connections to Mwanza and Bukoba as well as the Tanzanian border areas.

Meanwhile, the settlement's founding fathers, like Mzee Kalema, continue to agitate for the provision of more services including a hospital, bank, electricity supply and improvements to the water supply. They now have a post office, three primary schools and one secondary school, but these are considered insufficient for the numbers of children requiring education. While there are many people attending secondary school, so far the settlement has produced only one university graduate. There is one government health dispensary and several private clinics and pharmacies. Our informants were unwilling to even try counting the numerous places of worship, which included several Roman Catholic and Pentecostal churches as well as mosques.

Katoro-Buseresere is now a prominent trading centre with an enormous periodic market which local people proudly proclaim surpasses the availability of goods in Geita town. A livestock auction is held on Tuesdays. Every Thursday traders travel to Mwanza to get supplies in preparation for the Saturday market. Located on both sides of the main road straddling the district boundary, the market stalls are far more numerous on

---

5   Mzee Kalema relates how previously people charged with a crime had to be walked to Geita town (roughly 50 kms). Along the way, they could simply say they had to go to the toilet and disappear into the bush never to be seen again.

the Biharmulo side due to the lower district council market fees there as opposed to those of Geita district. A large clothing section abounding with *mitumba* [used clothing] and a wide variety of imported ready-made clothes for men, women and children and *khangas* from Tanzania produce a kaleidoscope of colour. Little girls' frilly dresses for parties imported from Southeast Asia are especially eye-catching. A large selection of fruit, vegetables, fresh and dried fish markets, and meat are displayed. Agricultural, household and mining tools are on hand, as well as homemade rope, woven tobacco sheets, livestock, jewellery ornaments and a few stalls of traditional medicine. There are crushing crowds of people at the Saturday market during the afternoon hours.

In addition to its Saturday market, there are now an estimated 235 permanent shops open for business throughout the week. The settlement acts as both a retail and wholesale centre. There is a highly differentiated service sector with numerous hair salons, shoeshine centres, etc. There are approximately twenty guesthouses, some imposingly built serving as centres of television entertainment provided by satellite dishes. The guesthouses primarily serve the itinerant trading population as well as miners flush with cash.

Heavy drinking and prostitution are in evidence. Unlike in rural villages, some of the drinking public can afford to buy *pombe ya kizungu* (bottled beer). Others drink *pombe ya kienyeji* (locally produced beer) including beer made from sorghum and honey. Stronger locally produced distilled drinks are officially not allowed but our informants wryly added that the police who are charged with enforcing this restriction are sometimes observed drinking it themselves. Prostitution is an income-generating activity for young women. AIDS is recognized as a problem, but the elders saw it more as an imported problem in which local households take in their loved ones who have contracted the disease elsewhere rather than a problem internal to the community as observed by the *wazee*:

> AIDS victims come back here to die but it is not a huge problem. We don't have statistics on this and we can't plan for this.

Katoro-Buseresere is favoured with good agricultural conditions and has not experienced famine in living memory despite harvest fluctuation. Our informants estimated that farmers still outnumber traders by three to one. Farming households endeavour to achieve food self-sufficiency. People normally eat *ugali* and leave rice for special occasions. Rice is now the major cashcrop which is transported to Ngara and Bukoba and then onwards to Uganda, Rwanda, Burundi and Congo. The war-torn conditions of these countries at one or another time in the recent past have been a boost to the area's commercial rice production. These days farmers are far more market savvy. They are careful not to sell all their rice at once. They hold back to get better prices from the private traders who operate in the settlement. Other food crops being sold are: beans, groundnuts, *ulezi* and cassava. Cotton production has declined because prices are considered unremunerative relative to other economic activities.

Now, however, there is a shortage of land for farming. People have to walk quite a distance from the village to fields that they rent. The wealthy people renting out land often prefer to get paid in bags of rice. There is not much buying and selling of land however. Sales take place only if someone is in financial or other distress. The elders denied that some people had become entirely landless but admitted the worrying recent incidence of many *vijana* [boys] who could not farm due to lack of access to land.

Households usually use their own members' labour to farm.[6] Only a few wealthy ones hire labour. Thus some of the *vijana* have become active in the provision of local services, notably water delivery to households around the settlement transporting plastic *debes* of water by hand carts. Others earn money working as porters in the settlement's markets and shops or operating bicycle taxis. Many male youth leave to work in regional mines, preferring this to the search for casual labour in nearby or distant towns. If they fail to find work they return to Katoro-Buseresere, which always offers a variety of money-earning activities to those willing to work. Hence, compared with many villages in the surrounding area, Katoro-Busersere is able to retain its youthful population.

The dynamism of the settlement is also reflected in a number of significant technological innovations over the last few years. Generators of four private individuals, most of them guesthouse proprietors, have been a source of power for the immediately surrounding households willing to pay guesthouse proprietors for the supply. The electrical cords are looped through trees and makeshift electricity poles and the recipient households pay the generator owner on the basis of the number of lights and appliances utilized. The government is absent from this service supply, charging no fees or taxes nor providing any safety regulations. Apart from the potential hazards from such makeshift supply, electricity availability has made possible a number of small-scale industries, notably a highly efficient peanut sheller, which was the invention of a local skilled technician.

In addition to facilitating local production, technology investment is radically changing entertainment patterns. Many of the guesthouses also have satellite dishes, which provide television. People are welcome to watch as

---

[6]   Tractors are not used in local farming because they are not suitable for rice production and the area, a former forest, has many tree roots, which would be an impediment to tractor usage. Thus tractors are only used by a few for transporting things.

long as they keep buying drinks, viewing TV as they drink their beers or sodas. Formerly, bars were dominated by conversation and music, now TV has made incursions on people's social time.

Katoro-Buseresere's residents can make telephone calls from a commercial mobile phone centre offering competing Vodaphone and Celtel services and many businessmen and government officials own mobile phones. The *wazee* were emphatic that 'farmers don't use these phones' whereas traders, government officials and other high-income people depend on them for their work and social life making it possible for them to keep in touch with their colleagues, friends and families in Mwanza, Dar es Salaam and throughout the country and beyond.

The interviewed *wazee* were very optimistic about the future of their settlement to the point of being boastful.

> Officially we are a village, however life is like the town now. Our food is very varied. We purchase most of our needs. People use charcoal and kerosene rather than firewood. We've exceeded Geita. We have no gold and yet we have this big settlement.

The settlement still has village status, but the Ministry of Lands, in preparation for town status, has surveyed it quite recently. Katoro-Buseresere's role as a service centre, rather than its agricultural output, is key to understanding its transition from a rural to an urban settlement. The settlement has deviated from the Nyerere model. Nyerere saw nuclearization of village settlement primarily in terms of an agrarian population's access to social services and parastatal marketing facilities. Katoro-Buseresere is currently expanding on the basis of being a service centre providing a wide array of recreational and consumer goods and service delights. The investment of private entrepreneurs underpins Katoto-Buseresere's economic dynamism. Some of their investment activities are buccaneering in nature: alcohol sales, prostitution, tax evasion, trading in minerals and cross-border commodities which may or may not be strictly legal – these elements were definitely not part of Nyerere's vision of rural transformation.

Nyerere's Agrarian Blueprint Reconsidered

Katoro-Buseresere is just one of thousands of settlements dotting Tanzania's vast countryside. Located in the booming Lake region mining zone, it cannot be argued that it is typical. Furthermore, it is a centre of in-migration whereas many rural settlements are experiencing net out-migration. Originating from the mid-1970s villagization programme, it has a strong Nyerere legacy, economically grounded in a peasant cotton production heyday and an *ujamaa* village farm as well as experiencing the first-hand reverberations of Nyerere's war with Idi Amin's Uganda. The settlement weathered the structural adjustment period of the 1980s then blossomed into a thriving trading settlement during the economic liberalization policies and artisanal mining boom of the 1990s.

With the advantage of hindsight, we can assess Nyerere's *kilimo* and *ujamaa* blueprint with reference to Katoro-Buseresere's present local political economy. At first glance it could be interpreted as a settlement testifying to the failure of Nyerere's vision: the population has been growing rapidly and now exceeds what could be described as rural. There are strong hints of local asset consolidation in relation to land and labour on the part of local capitalist investors. Household agricultural land shortages have appeared and youth are increasingly engaged in non-agricultural activities aligned more with the growing population of traders. Wealth accumulation is taking place with class differentiation readily in evidence. The settlement seems to have distanced itself ever further away from Nyerere's *kilimo* and *ujamaa* blueprint over the last since the early 1990s. Furthermore, there seems little evidence that its future is being consciously planned unlike the ambitious directional planning that Nyerere championed. The AIDS epidemic, taxation policies and the settlement's business and infrastructural expansion are primarily subject to the whims of free market capitalism rather than being addressed in an institutionally coordinated fashion.

However, it is telling that the *wazee* are proud of their past bumper cotton harvests, *ujamaa* pedigree and boastful about their settlement's trading success. They have no problems in reconciling their agrarian socialist past with a non-agrarian capital present and future. This may be because there are several connecting ties. First of all, agrarian forms of livelihood are still foundational to the settlement's material and possibly cultural security. Most households continue to engage to a greater or lesser degree in provisioning themselves with food. This not only helps to ensure basic food needs and economic security, it may also help to perpetuate agrarian values which bridge ethnic and class differences between residents of the settlement. Thus *kilimo* is not forsaken and, even though it is now no longer dominant in the local economy, agriculture provides a vital subsistence fallback for the poor and a common cultural frame of reference.

Second, while the settlement has grown very rapidly and is no longer a typical rural village, nor is it yet a typical town. Its residents have the best of both worlds. Both rural and urban livelihood options are available. They still have reasonable access to land and water albeit these are now increasingly market-mediated with pervasive land leasing and purchased water supplies. Nyerere's Arcadian dream and modernization goals were always in contradiction. The removal of ignorance, poverty and disease would inevitably generate population growth. Locationally concentrated populations arose from villagization, reducing access to agrarian resources and impinging on *ujamaa* ideals. In this light, Nyerere's vision has achieved contradictory success. Katoro-Buseresere's population growth, which arises to a large extent from in-migration, reflects the settlement's ability to offer welfare improvement relative to the surrounding countryside.

Third, it is certainly true that Katoro-Buseresere represents the abandonment of an egalitarian productionist model inferred in a great deal of Nyerere's *ujamaa* philosophy. The settlement's proliferating division of labour and specialization in trade and recreational services might have discomfited Nyerere were he alive today. However, this is debatable. Nyerere donned a rural mantle with his espousal of an agrarian moral philosophy but he had an urbane outlook focussed ultimately on a modern, forward-looking society rather than highly dispersed, remote, backward-looking rural communities. The national governmental structure that Nyerere designed encompassed the entire countryside, but was urban-directed. The founding members of TANU all resided in Dar es Salaam – a multi-ethnic city infused with coastal Swahili culture. Furthermore, Nyerere was a highly adept politician who knew the trade-offs involved in attaining welfare goals. It is unlikely that Nyerere would regret the economic dynamism of a near-urban, ethnically diverse settlement such as Katoro-Buseresere.

Last and by no means least, it could be argued that Katoro-Buseresere is quintessentially representative of the Nyerere legacy, a haven of peace in one of Sub-Saharan Africa's most conflict-ridden zones, the interlacustrine region of Congo, Rwanda, Burundi, Uganda and northwestern Tanzania. As previously argued, at the outset of Nyerere's long political career, he aligned himself with government on the basis of a professional bureaucracy devoid of localized interests. Nyerere stood for a cosmopolitan multi-ethnic, multi-religious identity. Interestingly, during the last years of his life he devoted much of his remaining energy to conflict resolution in the interlacustrine region as the Organization of African Unity's chief mediator. Mpangala (2004) relates Nyerere's perspective on the road to peace in the area:

> Talking to [a] journalist in 1997 Mwalimu Julius K. Nyerere explained clearly how economic backwardness and competition for scarce resources exacerbated conflicts. He was of the view that had socio-economic development in the two countries [Rwanda and Burundi] reached the level of Singapore, ethnic conflicts could have come to an end (*Daily News*, June 9, 1997). (Mpangala, 2004:15)

Nyerere's comments on Rwanda and Burundi were telling. These two countries represent Africa's most densely settled and agriculturally dependent landlocked populations. Their national economies are overwhelmingly agrarian-based economies. Nyerere highlighted the political fragility of this by contrasting them with Singapore, one of the world's most densely populated urban settlements. The inference is that *kilimo* can be as much the solution as the problem depending on the prevailing stage of population growth and level of economic development. It is highly likely that Nyerere would have approved of Katoro-Buseresere's non-agrarian trajectory. Furthermore, being a tolerant and realistic man, he may have turned a blind eye to its deviation from *ujamaa* economic principles, given that the settlement has most definitely embraced the political dimensions of *ujamaa* and ethnic harmony.

Bibliography

Bank of Tanzania 2004, *Annual Report 2003/04*, Dar es Salaam.

Bates, R. H. 1981, *Markets and States in Tropical Africa*, Berkeley, University of California Press.

—, 1988, 'Household, Hoe and Nation: Development Policies of the Nyerere Era', in Hodd, M. (ed.), *Tanzania after Nyerere*. London: Pinter Publishers Ltd.

—, 1990, *Food Insecurity and the Social Division of Labour, 1919-1985*. London: Macmillan.

—, 1992, 'Urban Bias Revisited: Staple Food Pricing in Tanzania', in Hewitt de Alcántara, C. (ed.), *Real Markets: Essays on the Political Economy of Food Pricing and Marketing Reforms*, Special issue of *European Journal of Development Research*, 82-106.

—, 1993, *Liberalizing Tanzania's Food Trade*. London: James Currey Publishers.

—, 1996, 'Deagrarianization and Rural Employment in Sub-Saharan Africa: A Sectoral Perspective', *World Development* 24 (1), 97-111.

—,. 2000, 'Peasant Theories and Smallholder Policies: Past and Present', in Bryceson, D.F., C. Kay and J. Mooij (eds), *Disappearing Peasantries: Rural Labour in Africa, Asia and Latin America*. London: IT Publications, pp. 1-36.

—, 2002a, 'The Scramble in Africa: Reorienting Rural Livelihoods', *World Development* 30(5), 725-39.

—, 2002b, 'Multiplex Livelihoods in Rural Africa: Recasting the Terms and Conditions of Gainful Employment', *Journal of Modern African Studies* 40(1), 1-28.

Chachage, C.S.L. 1995, 'The Meek Shall Inherit the Earth but Not the Mining Rights: The Mining Industry and Accumulation in Tanzania', in Gibbon, P. (ed.), *Liberalised Development in Tanzania: Studies on Accumulation Processes and Local Institutions*. Uppsala: Nordiska Afrikainstitutet.

Coulson, A. 1982, 'The State and Industrialization in Tanzania', in Fransman, M. (ed.), *Industrialisation in Africa*. London: Heinemann Educational Books.

East African Community Statistical Department, 1961-76, *East African Trade Reports*, Nairobi.

Ellis, F. and N. Mdoe 2003, 'Livelihoods and Rural Poverty Reduction in Tanzania', *World Development* 31(8), 1367-84.

Goslinga, R. 2005, *The Social Content of Credit-shaping Credit Systems: A Tanzanian Case Study*, MA thesis, School of Oriental and African Studies, University of London.

Havnevik, K. and M. Hårsmar 1999, *The Diversified Future: An Institutional Approach to Rural Development in Tanzania*, Expert Group on Development Issues, EGDI, Swedish Ministry of Foreign Affairs, Stockholm.

Iliffe, J. 1979, *A Modern History of Tanganyika*. Cambridge: Cambridge University Press.

Jamal, V. 1993, *Africa Misunderstood, or Whatever Happened to the Rural-Urban Gap?* London: Macmillan.

—, 2001, 'Chasing the Elusive Rural-Urban Gap in Tanzania', *Journal of Contemporary African Studies* 19(1), 25-38.

Jambiya, G. 1998, *The Dynamics of Population, Land Scarcity, Agriculture and Non-Agricultural Activities: West Usambara Mountains, Lushoto District, Tanzania*, Dar es Salaam: Institute of Resource Assessment and Leiden: African Studies Centre Working Paper, vol. 28.

Kaunda, K. 1985, 'A Personal Tribute', in Britain-Tanzania Society (ed.), *The Nyerere Years: Some Personal Impressions by His Friends*. London: Britain-Tanzania Society.

Komba, D. 1995, 'Contribution to Rural Development: Ujamaa & Villagisation', in Legum, C. and G. Mmari (eds), *Mwalimu: The Influence of Nyerere*. London: James Currey.

Lewis, W.A. 1978, *The Evolution of the International Economic Order*. Princeton: Princeton University Press.

Lipton, M. 1977, *Why Poor People Stay Poor: A Study of Urban Bias in World Development*. London: Temple Smith.

Madulu, N.F. 1998, *Changing Lifestyles in Farming Societies of Sukumaland: Kwimba District, Tanzania*. Dar es Salaam: Institute of Resource Assessment and Leiden: African Studies Centre Working Paper, vol. 27.

Mbilinyi, M. 2011, 'Sweet and Sour: Women Working for Wages in Tanzania's Sugar Estates', in Bryceson, D.F. (ed.), *How Africa Works: Occupational Change, Identity and Morality*. Rugby, UK: Practical Action Publishing.

McCall, M.K. 1980, *The Diffusion of Regional Underdevelopment: Articulation of Capital and Peasantry in Sukumaland, Tanzania*, Northwestern University, PhD Thesis.

Mpangala, G.P. 2004, 'Origins of Political Conflicts and Peace Building in the Great Lakes Region', Paper presented at the Origins of Instability in the Great Lakes Zone Symposium organized by the Command and Staff College, Arusha, 23 February, 2004, http://www.grandslacs.net/doc/3000.pdf.

Mungo'ong'o, C. 1998, *Coming Full Circle: Agriculture, Non-farm Activities and the Resurgence of Out-migration in Njombe District, Tanzania*. Dar es Salaam, Institute of Resource Assessment and Leiden: African Studies Centre Working Paper, vol. 26.

Mwaipopo, R., W. Mutagabwa, D. Nyange with E. Fisher 2004, 'Increasing the Contribution of Artisanal and Small-Scale Mining to Poverty Reduction in Tanzania', Report for DFID/UK, October 2004.

Mwamfupe, D. 1998, *Changing Village Land, Labour and Livelihoods: Rungwe and and Kyela Districts, Tanzania*, Dar es Salaam, Institute of Resource Assessment and Leiden: African Studies Centre Working Paper, vol. 29.

Nyerere, J.K. 1962, 'Ujamaa – the Basis of African Socialism', reprinted in Nyerere, J. K, *Freedom and Unity*. Oxford: Oxford University Press.

—, 1967, *Socialism and Rural Development*. Dar es Salaam: Government Printer.

—, 1968a, *Freedom and Socialism*, Nairobi, Oxford University Press.

—, 1968b, *Ujamaa: Essays on Socialism*, Dar es Salaam, Oxford University Press.

Ponte, S. 2002, *Farmers and Markets in Tanzania: Policy Reforms and Changing Rural Livelihoods*. Oxford: James Currey.

Pratt, C. 1978, *The Critical Phase in Tanzania 1945-1968: Nyerere and the Emergence of a Socialist Strategy*. Nairobi: Oxford University Press.

—, 1985, 'The Political Thought of Julius Nyerere', in Britain-Tanzania Society (ed.) *The Nyerere Years*. London: Britain-Tanzania Society, 20-3.

Rweyemamu, J. 1973, *Underdevelopment and Industrialization in Tanzania*. Nairobi: Oxford University Press.

Scott, J.C. 1976, *The Moral Economy of the Peasant*. New Haven: Yale University Press.

Seidman, A. 1973, 'Tanzania's Industrial Strategy', in Cliffe, L. and J. Saul (eds), *Socialism in Tanzania*, Vol. 2 *Policies*. Dar es Salaam: East African Publishing House, 96-101.

Seppälä, P. 1998, *Diversification and Accumulation in Rural Tanzania: Anthropological Perspectives on Village Economics*. Uppsala; Nordiska Afrikainstitutet.

Shivji, I. 1975, *Class Struggles in Tanzania*. Dar es Salaam: Oxford University Press.

Tan Discovery 1996, 'Final Report on a Baseline Survey and Preparation of Development Strategies for Small-scale and Artisanal Mining Programme', Dar es Salaam, World Bank/Ministry of Energy and Minerals.

Tanganyika 1961, *Commerce and Industry in Tanganyika*. Dar es Salaam: Ministry of Commerce and Industry.

Tanzania 1977-1984, *Tanzanian Trade Reports*. Dar es Salaam: Bureau of Statistics.

Tanzania Economic Trends, assorted volumes.

Treichel, V. 2005, *Tanzania's Growth Process and Success in Reducing Poverty*, Washington DC: IMF Working Paper, WP/O5/35.

World Bank 1981, *Accelerated Development in Sub-Saharan Africa*: Washington DC.

—, 2004, *World Development Indicators*, http://publications.worldbank.org/WDI/

CHAPTER FIVE

SMALLHOLDER AGRICULTURE IN TANZANIA – CAN ECONOMIC LIBERALISATION KEEP ITS PROMISES?[1]

Rune Skarstein

Background

Smallholders are the main producers of food crops in Tanzania.[1] In 1994/95, approximately 88% of the total agricultural area in Tanzania was under smallholdings, which accounted for 97.8% of total maize production, 97.3% of total paddy production, and almost all production of sorghum/millet in the country (cf. URT, 1996: 38, URT, 1997: vi-vii). For this reason, the focus of this paper is the impact of economic liberalisation on smallholder productivity.

Let me start by recapitulating the stagnation in Tanzania's agricultural production in the late 1970s and early 1980s. The first serious setback was in 1973/74 and 1974/75, associated with the villagisation campaign, but also attributed to bad weather. In 1976/77, agricultural production recovered again. But in the subsequent years, there was a persistent stagnation until 1983. In the period 1976-77 to 1982-83, the average annual growth of maize and rice production was 1.0% and 0.2%, respectively, while the agricultural GDP (crop and animal husbandry) increased by only 1.3% per year. With a population growth rate of 3.2% per annum in this period, per capita production of the two major food

[1] I am also grateful to Amit Bhaduri, Kjell J. Havnevik and Anders Skonhoft for helpful comments. Last but not least, I wish to thank Dennis Rweyemamu at the Economic and Social Research Foundation (ESRF) for his assistance in collecting data. The paper has been prepared as part of the research project "Global Models and Local Realities - African Peasants in the Age of Liberalisation". Financial support from The Research Council of Norway is gratefully acknowledged.) In this article, the term "smallholder" has the same meaning as in official Tanzanian statistics. According to the *National Sample Census of Agriculture of 1994/95* (URT, 1996), there were 3,873,000 smallholders in Tanzania Mainland. In the masika season (the great rain season), average planted area per smallholder was 0.86 ha. 9.9% of all smallholders had a planted area of more than 2 ha, while only 1.4% had a planted area of more than 5 ha. 99.9% had a hand hoe (jembe), while 9.3% had an animal operated plough. 17.6% employed temporary worker(s), while only 1.1% employed permanent wage labour. Thus, the Tanzanian smallholders operate their holdings mainly with family labour, the great majority using only hand tools.

grains declined by 2.2% and 3.0% per year, respectively.[2] Thus, production of the by far most important staple food, maize, dropped from an average of 93.5 kg per capita in 1976-77, to 82.1 kg per capita in 1982-83. On the other hand, it is notable that in the years 1983 to 1986 – which have often been considered as the worst crisis years – there was, according to official statistics, actually a strong upswing in agricultural production (cf. table 1). Maize production rose by more than 26% from the crop year 1982/83 to 1984/85, reaching a historical high of 2,093,000 tonnes, corresponding to 96 kg per capita of the population, in the latter year. In the period 1984 to 1986, both maize and paddy production increased every year; maize production rose by an average of 10.2% per year, while paddy production increased by more than 16% per year (cf. also table 1).

The stagnation of agricultural production in the late 1970s and early 1980s contributed to Tanzania's increasing dependency on large imports of the major food grains maize and rice. In the period 1972-1986, Tanzania had net imports of maize in all years except in 1978 and 1979. Total net imports of maize over the whole period amounted to 1,587,1000 tonnes, i.e. an average of 105,800 tonnes per year. In the same 15 year period, Tanzania was a net importer of rice every year, amounting to 770,000 tonnes over the whole period, corresponding to an average of more than 51,000 tonnes per year (cf. Bryceson, 1993: 239). There can be no doubt that these imports contributed to Tanzania's mounting balance of payments crisis in the 1980s.

The crop data up to 1983 stem from various publications from the Ministry of Agriculture. The data for the period 1983-1985 are from the Crop Monitoring and Early Warning Unit (CMEW), while the data from 1986 onwards are from the Agricultural Statistics Unit (ASU) within the Ministry of Agriculture. The data for 1976, refer to the crop year 1975/76, and so on.

Sources of data for the period 1976-1986: BOS (1992: 8, table 3.1), for agricultural GDP. *Tanzanian Economic Trends*, vol. 7, no. 1-2, 1994, table 12, p. 99, for production of maize and rice.

Sources of data for the period 1986-1998: World Bank (2000: 77, 92), data from ASU/MAC. An argument for using ASU data, especially from 1993 onwards, is presented in section 3 below.

However, the large imports of food grains up to 1985 were not caused by production shortfalls alone. That is indicated by the fact that net grain

---

[2]   Maize and rice/paddy are the two most important staple foodstuffs both in terms of value and weight. In 1976/77, maize contributed 43.5% to the total value and 40.2% to the total weight of consumption of staple foodstuffs. The corresponding figures for rice/paddy in second place were 13.7 and 6.3%, respectively (cf. Bryceson, 1993: 219).

Table 1: Production of maize and paddy, '000 tonnes, and growth rate of agricultural GDP, 1976-1998

| Period | Maize | | Paddy | | Annual growth, agricultural GDP, %[1] |
	Average annual production	Average annual growth, %	Average annual production	Average annual growth, %	
1976-1979	1575	+ 5.9	327	– 8.8	+ 1.1
1980-1983	1718	– 1.0	290	+ 7.5	+ 2.6
1984-1986	2081	+ 10.2	443	+ 16.5	+ 4.7
1976-1986	1873	+ 3.46[2]	356	+ 3.65[2]	+ 2.71[2]
1986-1989	2466	– 1.8	620	+ 22.4	+ 1.6
1990-1992	2261	– 4.1	511	– 20.0	+ 0.2
1993-1995	2443	+ 8.9	659	+ 16.6	+ 4.1
1996-1998	2631	– 2.3	799	+ 18.7	+ 4.1
1986-1998	2452	+ 1.12[3]	622	+ 4.95[3]	+ 2.47[3]

[1] For the period 1976-1986, crop and animal husbandry at constant 1976 prices. For the period 1986-1998, crop and animal husbandry at constant 1992 prices.
[2] Trend growth rate (fitting a least-squares linear regression trend line to the logarithmic annual values of the variable), 1976-1986.
[3] Trend growth rate, 1985-1998.

imports rose even in the period 1983-85 in spite of large production increases. In 1985, the very same year as Tanzania had a bumper harvest of maize (2,093,000 tonnes), net imports of maize also reached a historical high of 278,000 tonnes. The explanation of this contradictory development is the growth of smuggling to neighbouring countries which accelerated after the war in Uganda in 1979. The increased smuggling was caused by factors on the demand side as well as the supply side. Due to disruptions caused by the war, there was grain shortage and correspondingly very high prices in Uganda. Also in Kenya, grain prices were high due to bad harvests. On the supply side, the Tanzanian government's commandeering of a large part of the transport fleet, spare parts and fuel for the war effort caused a severe disruption of the grain purchases of the National Milling Corporation (NMC). These factors combined prompted farmers to market their maize through unofficial channels (cf. Bryceson 1993: 95).[3] It should also be noted that the average annual level of maize production was 9% higher in the "crisis years" 1980-83, than in the preceding years 1976-79 (cf. table 1).

---

[3] For the crop years 1983/84 and 1984/85, the Marketing Development Bureau estimated that as much as 75% of marketed maize and 80% of marketed rice went through parallel markets (cf. Bryceson, 1993: 96). In my assessment, these figures are exaggerated.

External Versus Internal Causes

The above considerations lead us to the heated debate on "external" versus "internal" causes of Tanzania's crisis in the 1980s. In the early 1980s Tanzanian researchers and politicians tended to emphasise external causes for the agricultural stagnation, in particular weak demand for agricultural export crops and correspondingly worsening terms of trade[4], rising interest rates in international credit markets, increased protectionism in industrialised countries, the oil price shocks in 1973/74 and 1979, the breakdown of the East African Community in 1977, the cholera epidemic in 1978, the war with Uganda in 1979.

Among "external causes" were also periods of bad weather conditions. In 1979, poor weather was reported as the cause of a bad maize harvest particularly in Arusha, which was then one of NMC's major supply regions. A few years later, a drought which affected large areas in the crop year 1981/82 and floods in parts of the country in the following year, led to extremely bad harvests with a production of only about 1650 thousand tonnes in each of those years.

Another "external cause" of Tanzania's economic troubles in the early 1980s, which was far less highlighted, was the dramatic decline in foreign aid including concessional loans, which was reduced by more than 30%, from 701.9 million US$ in 1981 to 486.9 million US$ in 1985. This reduction of foreign aid by 215 million US$, corresponded to 62% of Tanzania's merchandise exports and was 3.2 times larger than the country's merchandise trade deficit in 1986. The sharp reduction of foreign assistance compounded the crisis by leading to a drastic import compression which had a profound negative effect on the supply of implements and inputs to the agricultural sector.

The drop in foreign aid was mainly accounted for by the Federal Republic of Germany, the United Kingdom, the Netherlands, Sweden and the World Bank (cf. Havnevik et al. 1988: 124-127).[5] These cuts were related to the fact that Tanzania had refused to conclude an agreement with the IMF on structural adjustment, i.e. a programme of economic liberalisation. In October 1985 Nyerere left the presidency, refusing to stand for a new term, and in August 1986 the Tanzanian government signed an agreement with the IMF for support to an Economic Recovery Programme (ERP). It is noteworthy that as soon as Tanzania had

---

[4]   In fact, in the period 1977-1985, Tanzania's commodity terms of trade declined by 50.8%, while the income terms of trade declined by 64% in the same period (BOT, 2001: 155).

[5]   Both in absolute and percentage terms, the World Bank made the greatest cut in disbursements, from 97.9 million US$ in 1982 to 28.5 million US$ in 1985, corresponding to minus 71% (cf. Havnevik et al., 1988: 126).

adopted the ERP, which was designed by the World Bank, the Bank increased its disbursements considerably. For 1986 as a whole, World Bank disbursements totalled more than 60 million US$, or more than twice the amount in 1985 (cf. Havnevik et al., 1988: 127). In the period 1985 to 1990, foreign aid to Tanzania increased considerably every year, and in 1992, the aid inflow reached a historical peak of 1345.5 million US$, which represented an increase of 176% compared to 1985 (cf. OECD, 1990: 264; 1995: 183). The aid inflow in 1992 also represented a historical peak of 33% of the country's GDP and covered as much as 83.6% of the import bill. Against this background, it is clear that foreign aid was used both as a stick and a carrot to make the Tanzanian government enter the road of economic liberalisation.

On the other hand, without directly denying these external factors, many foreign researchers, as well as the donor community and the international financial institutions (World Bank and IMF) increasingly tended to emphasise internal causes. They argued ever more strongly that the stagnation of Tanzania's agriculture was mainly caused by wrong policies and internal economic structures suffocating the development of agriculture. Among the internal factors which were most often emphasised, was the already noted inefficiency of agricultural parastatals resulting in delayed or no payments to producers, high marketing margins and correspondingly lower share of producer prices in the final prices (cf. Ellis, 1983; 1988).[6] Other internal factors which were often referred to, were nepotism and rent-seeking by corrupt bureaucrats in the state and the parastatal sector, "financial repression" and controlled and panterritorial prices which led to "price distortions" discouraging agricultural producers from an efficient allocation of resources, and the development of an industrial sector which stagnated due to its inefficiency and import dependency and became increasingly unable to provide agricultural producers with incentive goods (cf. e.g. Bevan et al. 1989;, Collier and Gunning, 1999).

---

[6] A serious limitation of Ellis' studies in terms of explaining agricultural stagnation after 1970, is that, in addition to dealing mainly with export crops, he does not provide data from before 1970. On the other hand, with reference to data collected by Odegaard, Deborah Bryceson (1993: 239) has shown that, at least for food crops, the marketing margins, i.e. the difference between the consumer and producer price divided by the producer price, were considerably higher in the period 1964-1972 than in the stagnation/crisis period 1973-1984. For maize flour (sembe), the marketing margin was 309% in the former period and 85% in the latter period. For rice, the corresponding figures were 244 and 178%, respectively, and for wheat 212 and 199%, respectively. Neither for sembe nor rice was there any tendency of increasing marketing margins during the period 1973-1984. Both for this reason and because the marketing margins of private traders are largely unknown, the claim that, "in the Tanzanian grain market, trading costs doubled during the period of controls, and fell by over 60% once they were removed" (Collier and Gunning, 1999: 97), is in my assessment highly questionable.

It is noteworthy that the counterproductive effects of villagisation, which both the World Bank and most bilateral donors had applauded in the mid-1970s, were more rarely referred to.

After villagisation an increasingly intensive cultivation pattern developed around the villages, which could count several thousand inhabitants.[7] The average fallow period declined rapidly, while the smallholders did not have the necessary resources to conserve land by using chemical fertiliser, and walking distances to the fields increased as villagers tried to counterbalance the decline in soil fertility by cultivating areas more remote to the villages.[8] One study of five villages in Mufindi district carried out in the early 1980s, shows, "a significant and continuing fall in output per hectare of maize during the three most recent post-villagisation years. This fall in productivity does not seem to have been caused by climatic factors, because ... the excess rainfall in 1983 did not seem to have had adverse effects on crop productivity" (Kikula, 1997:78). In the years 1981-1983, the average maize yield in the five villages was 18% lower, and in 1983 as much as 25% lower than the normal yield before villagisation (Ibid., 77-80).

Economic Liberalisation

Although internal and external causes were unequally emphasised by different studies, there was considerable agreement on the diagnosis of the crisis and the identification of its main causes. Such agreement did not come about on a prescription on how to overcome the crisis. On this question there was a gulf of disagreement mainly between two groups. On the one hand there was a group, mainly researchers, who argued that the crisis problems should be solved by reforming the existing institutions and democratising society through political mobilisation from below. They would retain a high degree of economic planning and state intervention, but reform the whole public sector radically and also reduce its bureaucracy. In particular, they argued for control of foreign trade and exchange controls, for protection of infant domestic industries, for the restrengthening or revival of customary tenure rights in agriculture, for retaining panterritorial input and producer prices, and for a profound democratisation of the cooperatives, as well as society as a whole (cf. e.g. Boesen et al.,

---

[7] In 1979, there were on average about 1730 inhabitants in each of the more than 8000 villages (cf. Ellis 1982: 68). In this average are included villages with much larger populations. For example the seven villages in the northern flood plain of Rufiji District, had an average population of about 4570 in 1978 (Havnevik 1993: 79), and several villages in the country have had populations of more than 10,000.

[8] As the area of cultivated land extended around the villages, the walking distance to firewood also tended to increase. According to an ILO study, the rural household distance to firewood rose from between 0.7 and 4.2 km in 1977, to between 2.5 and 5 km in 1981 (ILO, 1981: 230).

eds., 1986; Shivji, ed., 1986; Havnevik, ed., 1987; Gibbon et al., 1993; Havnevik, 1993; Shivji, 1998).

On the other hand, in particular the IMF and the World Bank, with more or less active support from virtually all bilateral donors, claimed that the only solution to the crisis was less state and more market, which implied economic liberalisation, dismantling of a large number of parastatals and generally a dramatic reduction of the role of the government in the economy. In the view of the IMF and the World Bank, the Tanzanian system with heavy state involvement in the economy had led to grave distortions in the pricing and incentive systems. Therefore, economic liberalisation was considered necessary to liberate private economic initiative and to "get the prices right", so that they would reflect relative scarcities and ensure an optimal allocation of resources. Or, as the IMF phrased it in 1986 referring to the ERP,

> ... partial attempts at correcting a fundamentally deteriorating economic and financial situation do not succeed ... in the absence of appropriate price signals. (...) ... [T]he main emphasis of the programme is to provide to economic agents the appropriate pricing signals and to give them the necessary opportunities to act on the basis of those signals. This should provide incentives toward economic efficiency and improved allocation of scarce resources (IMF, 1986:3, 6-7).

What the IMF states here, is that "appropriate pricing signals" ensure *static efficiency*, in the sense of allocating given "scarce resources" so as to produce a maximum output in the short term. But the statement does not indicate whether "appropriate pricing signals" could also ensure *dynamic efficiency*, through an "optimal path" of technical progress and growth of land and labour productivity in the longer term, which is actually the crucial problem in Tanzanian agriculture. The World Bank's structural adjustment programmes, which aim at improving long-term dynamic efficiency, also stress the objective of "getting the prices right", apparently by assuming that static efficiency will lead to long-term dynamic efficiency.[9]

The process of economic liberalisation, which was ultimately carried out from above by the power of the international finance institutions (IFIs), had started well before Tanzania was compelled to sign an agreement with the IMF in 1986. In 1981, the government launched a National Economic Survival Programme (NESP) in an attempt to mobilise foreign exchange. In 1982 this was followed by a Structural Adjustment Programme (SAP),

---

[9] "Getting the prices right" is essential in the theory of technical change through "induced innovation" (cf. e.g. Binswanger et al., 1978). For critical discussion of this as well as static versus dynamic efficiency, cf. e.g. Bhaduri (1991); and Skarstein (2008).

which apparently intended to partially meet the demands of the IMF by dealing with the economy's structural problems. In the agricultural sector, SAP aimed at higher producer prices, improved input availability, and more efficient marketing. And as a matter of fact, in the 1984/85 budget, the government more than doubled agricultural expenditure, removed the subsidy on the consumer price of maize, and announced a substantial devaluation of the Tanzanian Shilling (cf. Gibbon et al. 1993: 52-71). In October 1982, the government launched a document on national agricultural policy (URT 1982), which contained rather detailed analyses of the development of agriculture and its subsectors, as well as agricultural extension, credit and marketing in the period 1961-1982. The recommendations in the policy document could be read as a detailed follow-up of the section on agriculture in the SAP.

However, the IMF and the World Bank were still not content, and in August 1986 Tanzania had to sign the Economic Recovery Programme (ERP) with the IMF. The election of the (in IMF's sense) more reform-friendly president Ali Hassan Mwinyi in 1985 helped to reach the agreement. The ERP and its follow-up, the ERPII, Economic and Social Action Programme (ERPII ESAP) in 1989, as well as the Tanzania Agricultural Adjustment Programme (TANAA) agreed with the World Bank in 1990, and the Enhanced Structural Adjustment Facility (ESAF) agreed with the IMF in 1991, meant decisive further steps in the direction of economic liberalisation.

By 1987, all weight restrictions on interregional food grain trade had been abolished and legal private traders had started to compete with the NMC. Panterritorial pricing was abolished, and from the late 1980s onwards, primary societies and cooperative unions (created under the new Act of 1982) were allowed to sell directly to private traders. In 1990, individual farmers were also given this option, hence competition between the parastatal/cooperative system and the private sector had become fully legalised. To begin with, the role of the NMC was reduced to a buyer of last resort and manager of the Strategic Grain Reserve (SGR). However, in 1990, the NMC was in practice abandoned, as the Government, through the Food Security Department in the Ministry of Agriculture took direct control of the management of the SGR. The NMC ceased to buy crops directly from the producers in 1991/92. The SGR is currently buying maize both directly from producers and from private traders who deliver the produce at its godowns (MAC/MDB, 1995: 18-20). In 1986-87, 36% of marketed maize was still handled through the official market. In 1988-97, this share had declined to between 10 and 20%, while private traders handled between 80 and 90% of all marketed maize (Temu and Ashimogo, 1999:142). In 1994/95, the procurement and distribution of agricultural inputs were liberalised. Agricultural subsidies are seen by the World Bank to cause economic inefficiencies, and the Bank demanded that they should be abolished altogether. For example, as will be described in section 5.2, the subsidy on fertiliser was completely removed in 1994/95 (cf. World Bank, 1994:85-92; Ponte, 1999:11, 14).

The transition from a single-tier to a multi-tier agricultural marketing system had been completed by 1990 when indicative prices for food crops were introduced. By 1992, the private sector had taken control of nearly the entire grain market (MAC/MDB, 1995:21-25). In sections 5.2 and 5.3, we will see that the impact of these changes, including the withdrawal of input and transport subsidies, was a sharp decline in the profitability of smallholder cultivation of maize, especially in the south-western part of the country. Maize production started to shift gradually back to the northern part of the country where more fertile soils allow cultivation with less dependence on chemical inputs and access to the national markets is much easier. This, in turn, resulted in an agricultural depression in the south-eastern highlands of Rukwa and Ruvuma.

In the view of the IMF and the World Bank, the rent seeking character of the state had become a major obstacle to economic development. The state therefore had to be forced to withdraw in order to open up space for an entrepreneurial private sector starved of opportunities because of the all-embracing character of the state. The government was further obliged to bring about balance in its budget which implied a dramatic reduction in its expenditures and less efforts to strengthen its revenue side. At the same time, the credit system, foreign trade and foreign exchange transactions were liberalised.

Finally, in 1995 Tanzania adopted a national land policy, which – despite the fact that all land should still be "vested in the President as trustee on behalf of all citizens" opened the door slightly for commodification of land, through the statement that, "Individuals should be allowed to obtain individual titles within an area not designed for communal uses, land conservation and other specified village or community projects" (MLH, 1995:9, 21).

In 1992 – a year when production of the main food crops dropped by 3.3% and agricultural GDP rose by only 0.5% (cf. Delago et al., 1999:160) – the World Bank started to celebrate Tanzania's economic liberalisation by asserting that, "the economy is no longer in crisis" (World Bank, 1992:1). And in 1995, the IMF stated that, "With the support of the international community ... the authorities [of Tanzania] are trans- forming perhaps one of the most regulated economies in Africa into one of the most liberalized. More could be done, but a lot has been achieved" (IMF, 1995:1). We will consider to what extent these assertions can be defended by an actual upswing in Tanzanian agriculture in the wake of economic liberalisation.

The Growth Performance of Tanzanian Agriculture in The First Decade of Liberalisation

We have already referred to the optimistic predictions of the World Bank and the IMF: with economic liberalisation, including "free prices" and removal of input and output subsidies, agricultural producers would respond to "price incentives", and start to specialise, accumulate and innovate. And indeed, good agricultural harvests – owing to good weather conditions – in 1987 to 1989 allowed the IFIs, as well as bilateral donors and the Tanzanian government to proclaim that their new agricultural policy was a success, although maize production also fell in that period compared to 1986. In the official rhetoric, the immediate positive response of the agricultural producers was linked to the new marketing arrangements, especially for food crops, and the restored availability of incentive goods. However, from 1989 to 1994, production of the main food crop maize, as well as the growth of agricultural GDP suffered a serious setback (cf. also table 1).[10]

There are several and partly conflicting statistics on agricultural production in Tanzania, issued by different government agencies. This has led to a discussion on which data source is the most reliable (c.f. e.g. Bhaduri et al., 1993: 87-90; Ponte, 1999:15 21; Delgado et al., 1999:99-106). It is beyond the scope of this paper to enter this discussion. Suffice it to say that the two most important data sources are the Crop Monitoring and Early Warning Unit (CMEWU) and the Agricultural Statistical Unit (ASU), both within the Ministry of Agriculture and Cooperatives. The CMEWU figures are derived from pre-harvest forecasts, while the ASU figures are post-harvest estimates. On a year-to-year basis, the difference between the series from these two sources has been considerable for some years, but over the longer run they are almost equal. It should also be noted that until 1994, the two series relied on the same agricultural reporting system.[11] However, I agree with Ponte, as well as Delgado et al. that – since the

---

[10] As noted in footnote 1), maize is by far the most important staple food in Tanzania. In 1998, maize production was almost three times larger than the production of paddy measured in GDP contribution. Maize accounted for 22.8% of agricultural GDP, while paddy accounted for 8%, millet/sorghum contributed 4.6% and wheat only 0.5% (cf. Delgado et al., 1999:145).

[11] I disagree with Ponte (1999: 18-19) when he, using data for 1986/87-1990/91, implies that CMEWU has systematically overestimated production. As a matter of fact, the CMEWU data for the period 1986-1998 yields a trend growth rate for maize production of only 0.2% per year, compared to 1.12% per year derived from the ASU data (cf. data in Delgado et al., 1999:148 and table 1 above).

mid-1990s – the data issued by ASU is the most reliable, and "should be considered the 'official' government estimates" (Delgado et al., 1999:106). The statistics from ASU are therefore the basis of the production figures as well as of the growth rates of agricultural GDP for the period 1986-1998 presented in table 1.

As table 1 shows, neither the average annual production of maize nor rice was higher over the whole period 1986-1998 than in the years 1986-1989. Although paddy production showed a clearly positive trend in the 1990s, it should be noted that it was first of all marked by strong fluctuations mainly due to changes in rainfall and floods. For example, in 1985 it was only 276,000 tonnes, and then soared by more than 50% to 418,000 tonnes in the following year. In 1996, it reached 807,000 tonnes and then dropped by 32% to 550,000 tonnes the year afterwards (cf. Delgado et al., 1999:148). On the other hand, the growth of production of the main food grain maize of only 1.12% per year over the period 1985-1998 was alarmingly low in view of a population growth of 3% per year in the same period according to FAO statistics (FAO 2000). In the years 1993-1995, the average annual maize production of 2,443,000 tonnes was only 19.5% higher than the estimated average production in the "crisis years" 1983-1986, of 1,945,000 tonnes, while population had grown by almost 30% between the two periods (cf. table 1 and Havnevik et al., 1988:67).

In their report commissioned by the World Bank, Delgado et al. conclude that, "Overall agricultural performance in the post-reform period has been respectable but not outstanding. We estimate that agricultural GDP grew 3.5 % per year over 1985-90 and 3.3 % over 1990-98, for an average rate of 3.3 % over the entire period ..." (Delgado et al., 1999:134).[12] In my assessment, this characterisation is highly disputable. In their calculation of the growth rate of agricultural GDP between 1985 and 1998, Delgado et al. use only two observations. In their "base" year 1985, the agricultural GDP was exceptionally low (therefore the increase from 1985 to 1986 was as much as 14.5%), and in the end year 1998 it was exceptionally high (with an increase from 1997 to 1998 of 15.3 %), cf. Delgado et al. (1999:160). This choice of endpoints also gives an upward bias to the estimates for the sub-periods 1985-90 and 1990-98.

If, on the other hand, 1986 is chosen as "base year", the average annual growth rate of agricultural GDP over the period 1986 to 1998 turns out to be less than 2.5% per year. This demonstrates the arbitrariness of using only endpoints when calculating growth rates. For this reason I have used all 14 observations and estimated the annual trend growth rates of maize and paddy production and agricultural GDP from 1985 to 1998. As table

---

[12] In June 2000, this report was published as a World Bank country study, cf. World Bank (2000).

1 shows, the trend growth rate of maize was only 1.1% per year, while that of agricultural GDP was a modest 2.5% per year, which means that in per capita terms, especially maize production but also the agricultural GDP declined considerably over the period, by 22.5% and 5.5%, respectively.[13]

It turns out that neither the growth rate of maize production nor the growth rate of the agricultural GDP was higher in the post-liberalisation years than in the "crisis years" 1976-1986, cf. table 1. In other words, if "agricultural performance in the post-reform period has been respectable but not outstanding", that characterisation applies even better to the "crisis years" 1976-1986. This becomes even clearer when we consider the development of agricultural productivity. Table 2 below shows that labour productivity of maize production (measured in kg per economically active person in agriculture), as well as production per capita of the total population, was lower in all sub-periods of 1990-1998 than in any of the sub-periods of 1976-86. Moreover, while the trend growth rates of these two

Table 2: Labour productivity and production per capita of maize and the five major food crops, 1976-1998

	Maize		Five major food grains[1]	
Period	Labour productivity[2]	Kg per capita of total population	Labour productivity[2]	Kg per capita of total population
1976-1979	203.9	91.6	343.2	154.2
1980-1983	201.0	88.1	346.3	151.8
1984-1986	218.9	95.6	372.2	162.5
Growth 1976-1986,%per year[3]	+ 0.66%	+ 0.25%	+ 1.08%	+ 0.66%
1987-1989	230.6	100.3	363.6	158.2
1990-1992	198.7	85.8	313.6	135.4
1993-1995	197.7	84.1	330.2	140.4
1996-1998	200.3	83.8	320.7	134.1
Growth 1985-1998, % per year[4]	- 1.94%	- 2.35%	- 1.39%	- 1.80%

1) Maize, paddy, wheat, sorghum and millet, accounting for 71% of the value of total staple food consumption in 1976/77 and 55% of total food crops contribution to GDP in 1992 (cf. Bryceson, 1993:219; Delgado et al., 1999:145).

2) Production in kg per economically active person in agriculture.

3) Trend growth rate 1976-1986 (fitting a least-squares linear regression trend line to the logarithmic annual values of the variable), 11 observations.

4) Trend growth rate 1985-1998, 14 observations.

Sources of production figures: cf. table 1.

Source of population figures: FAO (2000).

---

[13] The population growth rate over the period in question was 3.0% per year (FAO, 2000).

indicators were positive in the period 1976-1986, 0.66% and 0.25% per year, respectively, they were negative in the period 1986-1998, by as much as -1.94% and -2.35% per year, respectively.

It may be argued that the productivity figures for maize could be misleading because the crop composition of agricultural output may have changed after economic liberalisation. In table 2, I have therefore also included figures for the five major food grains which accounted for between 60 and 65% of total food crop production in Tanzania in recent decades. But the picture remains the same. In all sub-periods of 1990-1998, labour productivity as well as production per capita of the entire population was lower than in any of the sub-periods of 1976-1986. Moreover, for the five major food grains, the trend growth rate of labour productivity was 1.08% per year in the period 1976-1986, but negative, −1.39% per year, in 1986-1998. The trend growth rate of production per capita of the total population was also negative in the latter period, −1.80% per year, as against +0.66% per year in the period 1976-1986 (cf. table 2).

Moreover, the decline in labour productivity for the five major food grains, as I have measured it in table 2, cannot be entirely explained by a change in the composition of total food output. In 1985/86-87/88, the major five food grains accounted for an average of 61.4% of the total tonnage of crops, while other food crops (cassava, sweet potatoes and pulses) accounted for 33.9%, and export crops (tobacco, cotton, cashew and pyrethrum) 4.7%. In 1995/96-97/98, the major five food grains accounted for 59.7%, other food crops 35.2% and export crops 5.1%.[14] Almost the whole change in the composition of food crops was due to a strong rise of 83% in the production of sweet potatoes, from an annual average of 279,000 tonnes in 1985/86-87/88 to 511.000 in 1996/97-97/98 (while the rest of the difference was made up by cassava). But this change may well be due to underreporting of sweet potatoes as well as cassava in the former period. The conclusion is that in terms of food grain production and productivity, the performance of Tanzanian agriculture has declined considerably after economic liberalisation, and in all the years 1990-1998 it was poorer than even in the "crisis years" 1980-1983.

An important aspect of technical progress in agriculture is improved or more intensive use of land which leads to increased yields, i.e. increased production per ha of cropped area. However, an increase in land productivity will have a positive impact on labour productivity only to the extent

---

[14] Calculated from data in URT/MAC, *Basic Data – Agriculture and Livestock Sector*, editions from 1990 and 2000. For lack of data, I have not included (cooking) bananas in other food crops, while tea has been excluded from export crops because it is a typical estate crop.

that it is not neutralised or even outweighed by a declining land/labour ratio. A rise in land productivity may be caused by increasing land shortage and a corresponding decline of the land/labour ratio, which compels the producers on small holdings to intensify cultivation, while their labour productivity falls. This is the central theme of the debate on the "inverse relationship" between size of holdings and land productivity (cf. Boserup, 1965; Bharadwaj, 1974; Dyer, 1991;1998).

From table 3, which shows estimated maize and wheat yields for the period 1986 to 1998, it appears that the trend of land productivity (yields) for maize is much the same as the trend of labour productivity shown in table 2. Table 3 also shows that the average maize yield (ASU figures) was lower than in 1986-87 in all subsequent periods except 1996-97. A comparison of the figures in tables 2 and 3 leads us to the conclusion that the declining labour productivity – at least for the major food crop maize – in Tanzanian agriculture is the combined result of a declining land/labour ratio and declining land productivity.[15]

One probable reason for this development may be that owing to high population growth in rural areas, smallholders have been forced to culti-vate increasingly less fertile land, while lacking the means to improve yields on those lands. However, the decline of wheat yields (on parastatal NAFCO farms), which is also shown in table 3, cannot be given such an explanation.

Possible causes

Did changing rainfall play a role?

In Tanzania, only 6% of the crop growing holdings use irrigation, and only 2% of total planted area is under irrigation. Rivers are the most common source of irrigation, leading the water to the fields through furrows, prac-tised mainly in Kilimanjaro, Arusha, Mbeya and Tanga. Much of the irri-gated land area belongs to large scale farms (URT/MAC 1999: 18; URT/MAC 2000: 44; URT 2001: 4). In other words, almost all smallholder agriculture is rain-fed. Therefore, it is no surprise that several studies suggest that changing weather conditions are the major cause of *short-term* fluctuations in agricultural output.[16]

---

[15] Average labour productivity in agriculture can be expressed by the identity (Y/L) (Y/A)×(A/L), where Y is agricultural production, L is labour and A is cultivated area. Thus, a falling land/labour ratio, A/L, will reinforce the fall in labour productivity, Y/L, caused by declining land productivity (yields), Y/A.

[16] For a survey of the literature on this issue, cf. e.g. Hella and Kamuzora (1999).

Table 3: Maize and wheat yields, 1986-1998

Year(s)	Crop area		Yields, kg per hectare		
	'000 hectares		Maize		Wheat
	Maize	Wheat (NAFCO)	ASU data	CMEWU data	NAFCO data
1986-87	1530.2	24.2	1603.2	1496.1	1505.0
1988-89	1671.9	25.3	1480.8	1634.9	1830.0
1990-91	1739.9	26.4	1313.2	1380.3	1540.0
1992-93	1728.5	26.0	1312.5	1317.3	1500.0
1994-95	1687.8	26.3	1493.8	1396.7	983.2
1996-97	1650.7	26.4	1624.8	1400.1	1268.1
1998	2088.0	n.a.	1285.9	1285.9	n.a.
Growth, 1986-1998, % per year*	+ 1.01%	+ 0.79	- 0.31%	- 1.24%	- 4.14%

* Trend growth rate (fitting a least-squares linear regression trend line to the logarithmic annual values of the variable). For maize, 13 observations (1985/86-1997/98). For wheat, 12 observations (1985/86-1996/97). In the table, 1986-87 refers to the crop years 1985/86 and 1986/87, and so on.

Estimates of cropped area for maize, which have been made by the Crop Monitoring and Early Warning Unit within the Ministry of Agriculture, are probably rather inaccurate for single years, but more reliable in showing the trend over time.

Source of crop area figures for maize: URT/MAC (1992: 33; 1998: 16; 2000: 14).

Source of production figures for maize, cf. table 1.

Source of cultivated area and yields for wheat (both for NAFCO farms): Kapunda (1998: Appendix B).

We have already noted that a bad maize harvest in parts of Tanzania in 1979 was caused by poor weather, while drought in large areas in the crop year 1981/82 followed by floods in parts of the country in the following year were reported to have resulted in bad harvests. Even after economic liberalisation, low agricultural production in some years has been caused by bad weather. In the years 1992-93, drought and uneven rains in large parts of the country were probably an important cause of exceptionally low maize yields, down to an average of 1177 kg per ha in 1992. However, such short-term variations do not indicate *longer-term* trends over time. The question therefore remains, whether *a declining trend of rainfall over time* may have led to a fall in the growth rate of maize production from the period 1976-1986 to 1986-1998 (table 1). In other words, may a long-term trend in rainfall explain that labour productivity in the production of maize as well as the five major food grains rose modestly in the former period but declined considerably in the latter period (table 2), and that maize yields declined over the entire period 1986-1998 (table 3).

Table 4: Rainfall: Annual averages in millimetres and coefficients of variation (CV)

Name of station (region)	1976-86		1987-1998		1964-2000	
	Mean	CV[1]	Mean	CV[1]	Mean	CV[1]
Amani (Tanga)	1914.0	0.185	1789.6	0.229	1839.5	0.216
Arusha	928.8	0.361	809.7	0.280	839.5	0.343
Bukoba (Kagera)	2096.5	0.082	1972.5	0.112	2054.3	0.119
Dodoma	547.9	0.171	603.2	0.218	568.3	0.216
Kigoma	1039.6	0.138	919.6	0.138	975.3	0.184
Mbeya	926.5	0.184	945.3	0.239	964.3	0.237
Moshi (Kilimanjaro)	985.0	0.223	866.9	0.299	877.3	0.290
Mtwara	1105.2	0.129	1034.0	0.274	1083.7	0.210
Mwanza	1000.5	0.170	1151.3	0.198	1082.8	0.200
Songea (Ruvuma)	1156.2	0.181	988.7	0.236	1113.2	0.210
Tabora	958.2	0.202	851.5	0.323	917.1	0.243
Total averages[2]	**1150.8**	**0.393**	**1084.8**	**0.386**	**1119.6**	**0.391**

1) Standard deviation divided by annual mean in the period.
2) Average of regional means and CV of regional means in each period.
Source of data: Directorate of Meteorology, Ministry of ommunications and Transport, DSM. I am indebted to Dennis Rweyemamu at The Economic and Social Research Foundation (ESRF), Dar es Salaam, for providing the data, as well as to professor Ashok Parikh) at the University of East Anglia for having carried out the statistical computations underlying this table.

Table 4 shows rainfall data from stations in 11 regions, covering the periods 1976-1986 (before liberalisation), 1987-1998 (liberalisation period), as well as the whole period from 1964 (when the Tanzanian Union was established) until 2000. It appears from the table that average rainfall declined at eight of the eleven stations from 1976-86 to 1987-98. But only in Moshi was the change in rainfall between the two periods statistically significant at a 5% level. Also the annual average of all the eleven stations declined slightly, by 66 mm or 5.7%, from 1976-86 to 1987-98. Table 4 shows that the annual average for the sub-period 1976-86 is above the average for the long period 1964-2000, while the average for 1987-1998 is slightly (3%) below the long-period average. With regard to variability over time, table 4 shows that for ten of the eleven stations, the coefficient of variation (CV) in the period 1987-1998 is marginally higher than or equal to that of the preceding period. The exception is Arusha, where the CV declined significantly from 1976-86 to 1987-1998. Finally, table 4 shows that the CV between the stations was slightly higher in the former than in the latter period, which indicates that rainfall in Tanzania did not become more regionally uneven from 1976-86 to 1987-98.

With regard to the trend over time, a study covering the period 1960-1996, based on data from two meteorological stations in Morogoro and 16 other stations randomly selected from all over the country (15 regions), found no significant change in rainfall either over time or between the regions.

Also the number of raindays in each year showed no trend over time (cf. Hella and Kamuzora, 1999). This finding is broadly confirmed by our own analysis. For the period 1976-86, a trend was statistically significant only for two regions, with positive trend for Mtwara and negative trend for Mwanza. For the period 1987-1998, there was only one significant (positive) trend, for Kigoma.

The general conclusion is that – with the possible exception of the Mwanza station – there have been no noteworthy changes of rainfall either over time or with respect to regional pattern. Therefore, we cannot expect rainfall to have caused the change in agricultural productivity from 1976-86 to 1987-98. It is a bit surprising that regional data on maize yields for the years 1985-98 (for which such data is available) showed no significant relation to rainfall in the corresponding regions and years.[17]

However, the above results do not exclude the possibility that slightly poorer rainfalls *in combination with other inputs*, in particular fertiliser use, may have had a negative impact on yields in the period 1985-1998. Unfortunately, data on fertiliser use to control for this possibility is not available, but an experiment carried out in Ikuwala and Llambiole districts in Iringa Region, 1995-1998, may illustrate the point.

That experiment showed that change of rainfall from about 500 to about 1000 mm per year had no noteworthy effect on maize yields at a low use of fertiliser. For example at Ikuwala, a use of nitrogen fertiliser of 40 kg per hectare resulted in about 2500 kg maize per ha at any rainfall between 600 and 1000 mm per year. With soil and water conservation practices but no use of fertiliser, the maize yield was 1800 to 2000 kg per ha at amounts of rainfall varying from 600 to about 1000 mm per year (cf. MacDonagh et al., 1999: esp. fig 4a). In other words, at a low use of fertiliser there seems to be hardly any substitutability, but only complementarity between fertiliser use and rainfall.

On the other hand, the Ikuwala experiment showed that the effect of an increase in fertiliser use was quite significant at rainfalls between about 600 and 1000 mm per year. An increase in nitrogen fertiliser use from 40 to 140 kg per ha raised the maize yield from about 2500 to almost 4000 kg per ha (approximately 50% increase) at a rainfall of about 600 mm per year, and from about 2500 to more than 5000 kg per ha (approximately 100% increase) at a rainfall of about 1000 mm per year (ibid). Below an annual rainfall of 500 mm, the yield effect of increased fertiliser use

---

[17] I am indebted to professor Ashok Parikh for having carried out the statistical computations. Another study (Bilame, 1996) gave a similar result, finding that good weather had a negative but entirely unimportant effect on total maize production in the period 1970/71-1983/84, but a small positive effect in the years 1984/85-1994/95 (Bilame, 1996:47ff).

became rapidly smaller with less rainfall. This means that smallholders in marginal (semi-arid) areas are exposed to the risk that there may be little or no yield effect of fertiliser use due to failing rains. Conversely, at rainfalls well above 500 mm per year, the effect of a change in rainfall appears to be considerable only at fertiliser use that is far above the levels in Tanzania after 1990.

Did removal of fertiliser subsidy play a role?

In Tanzania, chemical fertiliser is used mostly in the growing of maize, tobacco, coffee and cotton, with more than 70% of total fertiliser consumption used on maize in 1994/95 (Hawassi et al., 1999: 76). The proportion of agricultural holdings using fertiliser reached a historical peak of 27% in 1991/92, declining to approximately 15% in 1994/95, and only about 10.5% in 1997/98. In the early 1990s, the average use was estimated at somewhat more than 20 kg per ha of planted area (World Bank, 2000:39; MAC/NBS, 2000:21, 73; World Bank, 1994:77-78). Only four regions – Ruvuma, Iringa, Mbeya and Tabora – accounted for more than half of total fertiliser use in Tanzania in 1997/98 (MAC/NBS, 2000:21, 74).

Fertiliser consumption has experienced two growth periods since the early 1980s. From a low of about 80,000 tonnes in 1981/82 it increased every year to 140,000 tonnes in 1986/87. In 1987/88 it dropped to less than 120,000 tonnes due to insufficient supply, and then rose in the subsequent years to about 150,000 tonnes in 1986/87 and further to almost 200,000 tonnes in 1994/95. There can be little doubt that an important reason for this development was the heavy subsidy. In the period from 1976 to 1984, the subsidy reduced the final price by about 50%. After 1984, the World Bank has estimated that there was an implicit subsidy reaching almost 80% of the final price in 1988/89 (World Bank, 1994:79-80; Hawassi et al., 1999:73).

As part of the structural adjustment programme, the government started to phase out the subsidy in 1990/91 (70%), reducing it to 55% in 1991/92, 40% in 1992/93, 25% in 1993/94, and zero in 1994/95 and onwards (cf. World Bank 1994: 79-80). Panterritorial input and output prices as well as the fertiliser subsidy were removed on advice from the World Bank and the IMF. The Bank's main argument for abolishing the subsidy was that, "Government interference in the fertilizer market *constrains supply* by both parastatal and private sector suppliers" (World Bank, 1994:91. My italics). In view of this argument it is ironical that fertiliser use fell steeply after removal of the subsidy, to only 63,000 tonnes in 1998/99, which was lower than in any year since 1973, "mostly because of decreased use on maize" (World Bank, 2000:42; cf. also MAC, 2000:153).

That a high price is an important cause for decreasing fertiliser use, was clearly indicated by the *Integrated Agricultural Survey 1997/98* (MAC/ NBS, 2000:73) which reported that 89.5% of all agricultural holdings in Mainland Tanzania did not use fertiliser. Among these holdings, 75% responded that the reason was either "too expensive" fertiliser (39.1%), or that fertiliser was "not available" (35.9%), cf. table 5. The survey showed interesting differences between regions which deserve some further discussion.

The Southern Highlands (Iringa, Mbeya, Rukwa and Ruvuma regions) account for the major share of fertiliser use in Tanzania. This pattern of regional distribution of fertiliser use began to develop in the late 1970s. The combination of stable rainfall and altitudes above 1500 metres made the Southern Highlands suitable for hybrid maize, and within a decade a green revolution took place in these regions (cf. Rasmussen, 1986). The result was a steep increase of maize production in the Southern Highlands while production stagnated or declined in the rest of the country. That the Southern Highlands became the "granary of Tanzania" is indicated by the fact that the NMC's purchases of maize from these regions as a share of its total purchases rose from an average of 33% in 1974/75-75/76, to 86% in 1982/83-83/84 (cf. Rasmussen, 1986:202; Bryceson, 1993:233-234).

When panterritorial pricing was the practice and subsidies were applied, the Southern Highlands consumed more than 50% of all fertiliser in Tanzania. With the abandoning of these practices, the pattern of fertiliser consumption changed dramatically. The cooperatives had no longer any responsibility to supply remote areas with fertiliser and give credit for such deliveries, while private traders found it too costly to transport fertiliser to those areas. Moreover, the price of fertiliser in the more remote areas became so high that it was no longer profitable to use it in maize production. For example, in 1998/99, the price of ammonia sulphate in Kilimanjaro was up to 12% higher, while the price of triple superphosphate was 65% higher than in Tanga Region, although Kilimanjaro cannot be considered a remote area.

Table 5: Percentage share of holdings reporting reasons for not using fertiliser, 1997/98

	Too expensive	Not available	Other reasons, incl. lack of credit
Mbeya Region	52.2	12.0	35.8
Iringa Region	66.6	7.7	25.7
Rukwa Region	48.2	28.2	23.6
Ruvuma Region	67.4	15.1	17.5
Tabora Region	41.1	36.6	22.3
National average	39.1	35.9	25.0

Source: Estimated from data in MAC/NBS (2000:73).

This is probably the reason why, especially in the remote typical maize producing areas, a higher proportion of holdings than the national average report "too expensive" as the reason for not using fertiliser, cf. table 5.

Table 5 shows that the highest shares of holdings reporting "too expensive" are in regions where maize is the dominant crop, viz. Mbeya, Iringa and Ruvuma. It is noteworthy that Ruvuma which has been most specialised in maize production, had the highest share of 67.4%. On the other hand, Rukwa, where both maize and tobacco are important, had a lower share of holdings reporting "too expensive", while Tabora where tobacco growing is dominant, had the lowest share of the regions in the table, at about the national average. That the high price was the main reason for reduced or no use of fertiliser, was confirmed by a comprehensive field study in Mbinga district in south-western Ruvuma, comprising 150 smallholders randomly selected in 15 villages. According to that study, 87% of the sampled farmers indicated high prices after subsidy removal as the main reason for applying fertiliser below the recommended rates. In the study area, the average intensity of fertiliser application in the growing of maize was reduced from 74.96 kg nitrogen per ha in 1992 to 59.94 kg per ha in 1996 (Hawassi et al. 1999: 77-79). In a field study in Songea, Stefano Ponte observed a similar trend: average fertiliser use per acre in maize production declined from 61 kg in 1986/87 to 44 kg in 1994/95 (Ponte, 2002:89).

Regional data on fertiliser consumption indicates that the intensity of use has continued to fall after 1996. Iringa and Ruvuma regions which consumed almost 65,000 tonnes of fertiliser in 1990/91, used a mere 20,000 tonnes in 1998/99. By contrast, Tabora's fertiliser consumption rose from less than 18,000 tonnes in 1990/91 to 31,000 tonnes in 1998/99 (MAC, 2000:153). In other words, while total fertiliser consumption in Tanzania has declined dramatically since the mid-1990s, there has also been a sharp change away from typical maize growing regions to typical tobacco growing areas, which implies a change in fertiliser use away from maize, especially in the Southern Highlands, and towards use in tobacco growing.

The World Bank claims, without referring to any evidence, that the fall in fertiliser consumption has not affected maize production negatively: "... the impact on production of fertilizer-using crops has been negligible, suggesting either inadequate application or wastage in use" (World Bank, 2001:53). This claim is not supported by available evidence. In particular Bilame's study showed a significant and considerable negative correlation between the price of fertiliser and maize output in the period 1984/85-1994/95 (Bilame, 1996).

Accordingly, there is reason to expect that the sharply reduced use of fertiliser in the growing of maize has already had a negative impact on overall maize yields in Tanzania (cf. table 3), which signals the decline of the Southern Highlands as the "granary of Tanzania".[18] This process is reinforced by the fact that private traders, due to high transport costs, do not find it profitable to collect maize in remote areas, especially in Mbeya, Rukwa and Ruvuma. Therefore, the World Bank's finding is not surprising: "The regional composition of maize production shows that between 1987-89 and 1996-98 maize output has declined by 13-19 percent in the three more remote regions of the southern highlands (Mbeya, Ruvuma, and Rukwa), while expanding in Iringa, Dodoma and other regions closer to Dar" (World Bank, 2000:53).

The Bank's finding is consistent with the field study from Mbinga district, which provides ample evidence that complete removal of the fertiliser subsidy had significantly reduced maize yields and output in the study area (cf. Hawassi et al., 1999: 72;80-81). Also the general trend in maize yields and production in Tanzania suggests that the rise of fertiliser prices and the dramatic fall in fertiliser use has had a negative impact which may be reinforced in the coming years as soil nutrients are being gradually depleted.

On the other hand, we may assume that marketed output of a crop depends not only on the fertiliser price, but rather on the ratio between the producer price of the relevant crop and the fertiliser price. In table 6, the development of this ratio from 1985 to 1998 is shown for the four most important food crops in Tanzania.

Table 6 shows that the ratio of crop producer price to farmgate fertiliser price has declined by between 74% for maize and 47% for wheat from 1985-89 to 1998. According to estimates made for the World Bank, the decline in the ratio of producer maize prices to inputs prices (seed, fertiliser pesticides), led to a reduction of the real return per "man-day" of maize production from 2,496 TShs at 1998/99-prices in 1992 to 501 TShs in 1998, in other words an 80% reduction (Delgado et al., 1999:95).[19] The field study in Mbinga district in Ruvuma in 1996 found that it was not profitable to use any fertiliser at the current fertiliser and maize prices given the responsiveness of maize yield to fertiliser input

---

[18] Against this background, it is not surprising that the Tanzanian government, against the advice of the IMF and the World Bank, reintroduced the transport subsidy on fertiliser (of TShs 2 billion) to Ruvuma, Mbeya, Iringa and Rukwa regions in its budget for 2003/04. (Cf. paragraphs 70 to 72 in the Budget Speech by the Minister of Agriculture for the Fiscal Year 2004/2005, in Swahili.)

[19] In a note to the table from which these figures are drawn, is the following clarification: "Assumptions are: hand-hoe technology, involving 123 man-days of family labour, with a yield of 1,500 kg/ha. ..." It is well known that almost all hand-hoe work in Tanzanian agriculture is done by women. Therefore, "person-days", or even "woman-days", would be more appropriate terms than "man-days".

Table 6: Ratios of average crop producer prices to farmgate fertiliser prices 1985-1998

	1985-89	1990-94	1995-98	1998	% change from 1985-89 to 1998
Maize	1.40	0.83	0.37	0.36	− 74.3
Paddy	2.23	1.39	0.56	0.60	− 73.1
Wheat	1.58	1.87	0.92	0.84	− 46.8
Millet/sorghum	1.05	1.15	0.85	0.54	− 48.6

Source: World Bank (2000: 46)

(Hawassi et al., 1999:82). However, the declining ratio of producer price to fertiliser price was not only due to rising fertiliser price, but also a relative stagnation in the producer prices for maize (as well as for other food crops).

The role of deregulated producer prices

A main argument for economic liberalisation was that deregulation of prices and free competition in the marketing of inputs as well as crops would result in "correct" input prices, but also higher and "correct" producer prices, which would in turn spur producers to increase efficiency, produce more, and make investments to raise land and labour productivity. Table 7 shows the development of real producer prices from 1981 to 1999.

For all crops reported in table 7, there was a rise of the producer price in the early 1990s, which peaked around 1993-94. But since the mid-1990s, the real producer prices of all crops have declined. It is noteworthy that the by far most important staple crops, maize and rice, have experienced the largest decline in producer prices compared to the 1980s.

With regard to declining marketed production, the short to medium term fluctuations of producer prices in a deregulated market are most probably at least as important as the long-term trend. In Tanzania, as in other sub-Saharan countries, the market demand for staple grains, in this case maize, is highly inelastic, with an (absolute) value of price elasticity considerably lower than unity. As a consequence, without intervention in the market, rather modest changes in supply lead to quite large price changes.[20] Before the deregulation of prices in 1990, such variations were modified through the government's price setting. The agricultural producers were informed at planting time of the procurement prices for the next harvest. There could be considerable price changes from one year to the next, but there

---

[20] The first to spell this out clearly was, as far as I know, Michal Kalecki in his article on "Costs and prices" (1943), where he distinguished between cost-determined prices in industry and demand/supply-determined prices in primary production (Cf. Kalecki, 1971:43-61).

Table 7: Real producer prices for main food crops, 1981-1999. TShs per kg at 1998/99-prices[1]

Year	Maize	Paddy	Wheat	Millet	Beans
1981-1985[2]	140	232	195	117	334
1986-1990[2]	149	250	170	109	369
1990/91	106	212	473	279	471
1991/92	279	370	495	289	508
1992/93	298	491	525	365	533
1993/94	256	424	497	376	712
1994/95	181	254	452	484	797
1995/96	165	216	423	538	571
1996/97	138	245	362	245	475
1997/98	117	195	272	175	431
1998/99	118	151	228	175	317

1) Nominal prices deflated to constant 1998/99 prices using the National Consumer Price Index.
2) Official procurement prices (before deregulation of prices in July 1990). Reference is to fiscal years (1 July to 30 June) which largely coincide with crop years.
Source: World Bank (2000:26).

was no uncertainty among smallholders about the producer prices of the next harvest.

This may explain Bilame's finding that before liberalisation there was a positive correlation between the real producer price and maize production, while this correlation was found to be negative in the liberalisation period (Bilame 1996). After liberalisation, a high price reflects a situation of deficient supply, while a low price reflects a bumper harvest. Such price variations will, in turn, affect the production plans of surplus producing smallholders. When prices are low in one harvesting season, smallholders tend to make plans for lower marketed output of the crop in question in the next season, and vice versa. This is supported by Bilame's finding of a negative correlation between maize production in one year and production in the preceding year. Thus, in a deregulated agrarian economy, the behaviour of producers will also tend to reinforce the volatility of prices. In the absence of price stabilisation measures, strong price volatility and stagnation of marketed output will therefore be a basic feature of the Tanzanian maize market, as well as of other deregulated sub-Saharan markets for food grains.

Before deregulation there was no change of producer prices during a particular crop year, implying that the smallholders would not make losses by selling their crops immediately after harvest. By contrast, after deregulation, producer prices have shown a considerable seasonal variability, being lowest just after the main harvest (masika season) and highest before the next main harvest. As can be seen in table 8, in the years 1994-1998, the

Table 8: Highest and lowest monthly producer and consumer prices of maize

Year	Producer prices.		TShs per kg	Consumer prices.		TShs per tin*
	Highest price (H)	Lowest price (L)	H:L	Highest price (H)	Lowest price (L)	H:L
1992	58.30	44.91	1.30	1195.1	945.2	1.26
1993	66.01	39.98	1.65	1354.1	794.3	1.70
1994	128.95	49.90	2.58	1458.2	1104.5	1.32
1995	71.50	49.12	1.46	1695.2	1144.5	1.48
1996	101.76	54.11	1.88	2159.0	1259.5	1.71
1997	120.77	84.96	1.42	2531.3	1795.1	1.41
1998	116,70	61.04	1.91	2924.4	1471.4	1.99
Average 1994-98	107.94	59.83	1.80	2153.6	1355.0	1.59

* One tin is approximately 20 kg.
Source of producer prices: URT/MAC (2000:39)
I am indebted to Dennis Rweyemamu at The Economic and Social Research Foundation (ESRF) for having compiled for me the data on consumer prices from the files at the Marketing Development Bureau (MDB).

highest monthly producer price of maize was on average 1.8 times higher than the lowest producer price in the same year. The seasonal pattern of consumer prices is much the same, with the notable exception of the year 1994.[21] This is well in accordance with experience from other sub-Saharan countries where producer prices have been deregulated. For example, in Zambia and Malawi the producer prices before a new harvest are generally about 2 times or more higher than towards the end of the preceding harvest (cf. Øygard et al., 2003).[22]

---

[21] A main reason for the discrepancy in 1994 may be that domestic production covered only 71% of domestic demand in 1993/94, implying a gap of about 750,000 tonnes, or 39% of domestic demand. Also in 1996/97, domestic demand exceeded production by 350,000 tonnes (cf. Kapunda, 1998:52). It is unclear to me how and to what extent especially the gap in 1993/94 was covered. According to the MDB, only 61,150 tonnes of maize were imported in 1994 (MAC/MDB, 1995:30). On the other hand, the Strategic Grain Reserve reduced its stocks (which mainly include maize) by only 57,000 tonnes from 1993/94 to 1994/95 (MAC, 2000:128). Probably, a considerable share of maize imports in 1994 was in the form of flour and therefore categorised as food in the data on imports. From 1992 to 1994, food imports rose by 61.9% at constant 1994 prices (deflated by the food component of the NCPI). As a consequence, food imports as a share of total imports rose from 3.3% in 1992, to 6.2% in 1993, and 8.5% in 1994. From 1994 to 1995, food imports at constant prices declined by 69%, reducing the share of food in total imports to 2.9% (cf. BOT, 1998:64 and 76). In any event, large imports of maize or maize flour will affect domestic consumer prices strongly.

[22] On the other hand, I miss evidence for Collier's and Gunning's claim (1999:97) that, "The coefficient of variation of Tanzanian maize prices in regional centers doubled between 1964 and 1980, and sharply declined again once the market was liberalised."

The low price elasticity of maize is the major cause of seasonal price variability. However, in a deregulated market, the price variability is reinforced by speculative behaviour among traders, as well as consumers. A rising price, which may be triggered by a bad harvest, will result in increased revenue both to each individual trader and the traders as a whole. Traders will therefore tend to withhold grain from the market, i.e. postpone sales, when the price is rising. On the other hand, relatively wealthy consumers will tend to hoard staple grain in such a situation, if they have the facilities to do so. The combined effect of these two behaviours is a continued and reinforced price rise. Conversely, a declining price, which may be caused by a bumper harvest, will make traders reluctant to buy crops from the smallholders in expectation of an even lower producer price, while selling out their stocks in order to avoid losses. In such a situation, consumers will postpone purchases as much as possible. Both behaviours will result in a continued and reinforced fall of the price.

The seasonal price variability is reinforced by "forced commerce" (cf. e.g. Bhaduri 1986). For lack of money as well as storing facilities -- in other words because of their poverty – many smallholders, among them a large number of deficit producers, sell so much of their crop (at low prices) at harvesting time that they do not have enough food grain to last until the next harvest. Later on they therefore have to buy food grain (at high prices) – often with expensive credit – in order to survive.[23] Forced commerce implies a serious income loss to the smallholders and a corresponding income gain to private traders. Government control of producer prices and public buffer stocks (buying above market prices at harvest time, selling below market prices in the months before the next harvest) have so far proved to be the most effective means to alleviate this problem (cf. e.g. Gabre-Madhin et al., 2003).

However, so far there is no public storage system in Tanzania that can work as an effective buffer stock, and seasonal storage is largely left to the smallholders themselves. In 1997/98, about 60% of all agricultural holdings reported storage of maize. Among those holdings which did store maize, 68% reported that the duration of storage was less than six months, and 44% reported that the storage was in sacks at home (MAC/NBS, 2000:51, 75-76). Their lack of adequate storage facilities forces the smallholders to sell the surplus of their crop at harvest time, when prices are at their lowest. Moreover, the private storage that does exist, implies a considerable losses, because much of the crops which are stored on the holdings, is eaten by rats or destroyed in other ways.

---

[23] This is not at all a question of market efficiency, but a question of how a market *necessarily* works within a particular structure of production.

Concluding Remarks

The advocates of economic liberalisation – in particular the IMF and the World Bank, but also bilateral donors – promised that economic liberalisation would provide a strong stimulus to Tanzanian agriculture, resulting in increasing yields, increased labour productivity, rising agricultural production and higher incomes. Available data show that, as far as food crop production is concerned, this promise had not been fulfilled by the end of the 1990s. Even compared to the "crisis years" 1979-1984, labour productivity, yields and production per capita of food grains had stagnated or declined.[24]

The experience of liberalising Tanzanian agriculture should indicate that introducing "free markets" and "getting the prices right" is not at all the right means for triggering transformation and growth in a predominantly pre-capitalist agriculture which is not even surrounded by a developed capitalist environment. Economic liberalisation has not spurred Tanzanian smallholders to specialise, improve technology and increase land and labour productivity. By contrast, several studies have shown that, instead of fostering specialisation, economic liberalisation has increasingly forced the smallholders to seek income diversification outside their holdings in order to reduce risk and secure their livelihood, while at the same time leading to "subsistence fallback" (cf. e.g. Seppälä, 1998; Havnevik and Hårsmar, 1999; Bryceson, 1999; Ponte, 2002:133-158).

The phenomena of "subsistence fallback" and "income diversification" are two sides of the same coin. On the one hand, the vagaries of the market, the declining ratio of crop prices to input costs, in many cases even lack of any marketing possibility, has increasingly led smallholders to produce agricultural crops only for their own consumption, i.e. subsistence fallback. On the other hand, the agricultural households seek cash incomes outside their holdings, in petty trade, petty transport, beer brewing, etc. Some neoclassical economists note that income diversification is not consistent with specialisation: "In diversifying to cope with shocks, the household sacrifices the gains of specialization in favour of spreading risk over multiple income generating activities" (Collier and Gunning, 1999: 77). But they do not acknowledge that the rising income diversification, as well as subsistence fallback, is the outcome of the economic liberalisation they are advocating. In other words, instead of fostering specialisation in smallholder agriculture, as its proponents promised, economic liberalisation in Tanzania has resulted in exactly the opposite.

---

[24] In the longer run, this, of course, leads to reduced surplus production by smallholders and possibly mounting food shortages. In late 2003, the Science and Development Network reported that, "Tanzania is facing a shortage of 350,000 tonnes of food this fiscal year and has waived all import duties on food" (Deodatus Balile, "Tanzanian parliament blocks government on GM seeds", www.scidev.net/ 28 November 2003). For comparison, Tanzania's annual net imports of food grains averaged 321,000 tonnes in the "crisis" years 1980-1982 (cf. Bryceson, 1993:239).

As opposed to liberalisation, prices of agricultural output and inputs should be considered and used as policy instruments and not left to be determined solely by market forces. The recent Asian experience points to the extensive role of government in both stabilising and supporting prices as a means of encouraging and sustaining technology adoption among smallholders (cf. Gabre-Madhin et al., 2003). As Gabre-Madhin et al. have emphasised, "The alternative to the free market-based transformation strategy is that of a market-based stabilization policy to support agricultural transformation. By placing the burden of ensuring stability on governments and not markets, it transfers risk away from producers, who are least able to bear it" (ibid., 35).

In order to transform Tanzania's smallholder agriculture, there is a strong need for government involvement, among other things in the construction of rural roads, irrigation systems and storage facilities, in the establishment of institutions providing cheap agricultural credits, as well as an agricultural insurance system which can protect the smallholders in years of crop failure. Farmers cooperatives are needed first of all to give the smallholders bargaining power in the input, output and credit markets. Government support appears to be necessary for facilitating the establishment of such cooperatives, and it is indispensable for agricultural extension services, experimental stations and agricultural colleges, and not least for improved primary education. In other words, as the Asian experience shows, what is needed is not state withdrawal from the market, but an accountable and determined developmental state. In my assessment, these issues are not adequately addressed in the government agricultural policy document of 2001, which seems to believe that agricultural transformation can be promoted by giving more room for private agribusiness, while the government emphasises poverty reduction in smallholder agriculture.[25]

The following acronyms are used in the reference list:

BOT – (Central) Bank of Tanzania

BOS – Bureau of Statistics (Dar es Salaam)

DSM – Dar es Salaam

---

[25] The *Agricultural Sector Development Strategy*, "proposes further modifications to permit private agribusiness to expand investments in primary production directly or through partnerships with smallholders, input distribution, produce marketing, and agro-processing. (...) The overarching Government objective is poverty reduction and this calls for strategies that are capable of raising the incomes and living standards of a large portion of the rural population in the relatively near future. (...) At the same time, the macroeconomic reforms rule out the possibility of profligate government expenditure or subsidies and limit the role of the Government to policy formulation, the establishment of a regulatory framework, and the provision of public goods and safety nets for the most vulnerable in society" (URT, 2001:vii).

FAO – Food and Agriculture Organisation of the United Nations

GOT – Government of Tanzania

ILO – International Labour Organization

IMF – International Monetary Fund

MAC – Ministry of Agriculture and Cooperatives (Dar es Salaam)

MDB – Marketing Development Bureau (now within MAC)

MLH – Ministry of Lands, Housing and Urban Development (Dar es Salaam)

NBS – National Bureau of Statistics (the new name of BOS, cf. above)

URT – United Republic of Tanzania

References

Bevan, D., P. Collier and J.W. Gunning 1989, *Peasants and Governments - An Economic Analysis*. Oxford: Clarendon Press.

Bhaduri, Amit 1986, "Forced Commerce and Agrarian Growth", *World Development*, vol. 14, no. 2, pp. 267-272.

—, 1991, "Economic Power and Productive Efficiency in Traditional Agriculture", in Gustafsson, B. (ed.), *Power and Economic Institutions*. Hants: Edward Elgar Publishing, pp. 53-68.

Bhaduri, Amit, Laurean Rutayisire and Rune Skarstein 1993, *Evaluation of Macroeconomic Impacts of Import Support to Tanzania*, Report no. 4/93, Centre for Environment and Development, University of Trondheim.

Bharadwaj, Krishna 1974, *Production conditions in Indian agriculture*. Cambridge: Cambridge University Press.

Bilame, O.S. 1996, Performance of maize production during structural adjustment programmes in Tanzania, MA thesis, University of Dar es Salaam.

Binswanger, Hans P. et al. 1978, *Induced Innovation*. Baltimore/London: John Hopkins University Press.

Boesen, Jannik, Kjell J. Havnevik, Juhani Koponen and Rie Odgaard (eds) 1986, *Tanzania - crisis and struggle for survival*. Uppsala: Scandinavian Institute of African Studies.

BOS (1992), *Agriculture Statistics 1989*, DSM.

Boserup, Ester 1965, *The Conditions of Agricultural Growth*. Chicago Aldine Publishing Co.

BOT 1998, *Economic Bulletin for the Quarter ended 31ˢᵗ December 1997*, vol. 27, no.4.

—, 2001, *Economic and Operations Report for the Year ended 30ᵗʰ June, 2001*, Dar es Salaam, November.

Bryceson, Deborah Fahy 1993, *Liberalizing Tanzania's Food Trade*. London: James Currey.

—,1999, "African rural labour, income diversification and livelihood approaches: A long-term development perspective", *Review of African Political Economy*, no. 80, pp. 171-189.

Collier, Paul and Jan Willem Gunning 1999, "Explaining African Economic Performance", *Journal of Economic Literature*, vol. 37, pp. 64-111.

Delgado, Christopher L., Nicholas Minot and Claude Courbois 1999, *Agriculture in Tanzania since 1986: Follower or Leader of Growth?* Revised version, November. Washington DC: International Food Research Institute.

Dyer, Graham 1991, "Farm size - farm productivity re-examined: Evidence from rural Egypt", *The Journal of Peasant Studies*, vol. 19, no. 1, pp. 59-92.

—,1998, "Farm size and productivity - A new look at the old debate revisited", *Economic and Political Weekly*, June, pp. A-113-A116.

Ellis, Frank 1982, "Prices and the transformation of peasant agriculture: The Tanzanian case", *IDS Bulletin*, vol. 10, no. 4, Sept. 1983.

—,1983, "Agricultural Marketing and Peasant-State Transfers in Tanzania", *Journal of Peasant Studies*, Vol. 10, No. 4, pp. 214-242.

—,1988, "Tanzania", in: Charles Harvey (ed.), *Agricultural Pricing Policy in Africa - Four Country Case Studies*, MacMillan, London, pp. 67-104.

FAO 2000, *The State of Food and Agriculture - Country Time Series*, FAOSTAT Diskette, FAO, Rome.

Gabre-Madhin, Eleni, Christopher B. Barret and Paul Dorosh 2003, *Technological change and price effects in agriculture: Coneceptual and comparative perspectives*. MTID Discussion paper no. 62, International Food Policy Research Institute, Washington D.C. April 2003.

Gibbon, Peter, Kjell J. Havnevik and Kenneth Hermele 1993, *A Blighted Harvest: The World Bank and African Agriculture in the 1980s*. London: James Currey.

Havnevik, Kjell J. (ed.) 1987, *The IMF and the World Bank in Africa*. Uppsala: Scandinavian Institute of African Studies.

—, 1993, *Tanzania - The Limits to Development from Above*. Uppsala and Dar es Salaam: Nordic Africa Institute and Mkuki na Nyota Publishers.

—., F. Kjærby, R. Meena, R. Skarstein and U. Vuorela 1988, *Tanzania - Country Study and Norwegian Aid Review*. University of Bergen: Centre for Development Studies,

—, and Mats Hårsmar 1999, *The Diversified Future - An institutional approach to rural development in Tanzania*. Swedish Foreign Ministry: Expert Group on Development Issues, EGDI.

Hawassi, F.G.H., N.S.Y. Mdoe and F.M. Turuka 1999, "Efficiency in fertilizer use among smallholder farmers in Mbinga district", *AGREST Proceedings*. Sokoine University of Agriculture, pp. 72-86.

Hella, J.P. and F.T. Kamuzora 1999, "Climate Change and Agricultural Planning beyond the 21st Century: A Case Study of Morogoro District", *AGREST Proceedings*, pp. 230-215.

ILO 1981, *Basic Needs in Danger*, draft report, ILO, Addis Ababa.

IMF 1986, *Statement by the IMF Representative*, paper presented at the meeting of the Tanzania Consultative Group, Paris, 10-11 June.

—, 1995, *Statement by the IMF Staff Representative*, paper presented at the meeting of the Tanzania Consultative Group, Paris, 27-28 February.

Kalecki, Michal 1971, *Selected essays on the dynamics of the capitalist economy 1933-1970*. Cambridge: Cambridge University Press.

Kapunda, Stephen 1998, *The impact of agricultural parastatal reform on agricultural development and food security in Tanzania*, Revised Final Report of the FAO Sub-Regional Representative for East and South Africa, DSM June 1998.

Kikula, Idris 1997, *Policy Implications on Environment - The case of villagisation in Tanzania*. Uppsala: The Nordic Africa Institute.

MacDonagh, J., R.H. Bernhard, J.R. Jensen, J.P. Møberg, N.E. Nielsen and E. Nordbo 1999, *Productivity of maize based cropping systems under various soil-water-nutrient management strategies*, SASA Centre for Research on Sustainable Agriculture in Semi-Arid Africa, The Royal Veterinary and Agricultural University, Copenhagen November 1999.

MAC 2000, *Tanzania agriculture: Performance and strategies for sustainable growth*, Dar es Salaam, February 2000.

MAC/MDB 1995, *1993/94 Industry Review of Maize, Rice and Wheat*, Marketing Development Bureau, MDB, Dar es Salaam.

MAC/NBS 2000, *Integrated Agricultural Survey 1997/98*, DSM May 2000.

MLH 1995, *National Land Policy*, DSM.

OECD 1990, *Geographical Distribution of Financial Flows to Developing Countries 1985-1988*. Paris: OECD.

—, 1995, *Statement by the IMF Staff Representative*, paper presented at the meeting of Ponte, Stefano 1999, "Trading Images: Discourse and Statistical Evidence on Agricultural Adjustment in Tanzania (1986-95)", in Peter G. Forster and Sam Maghimbi (eds), *Agrarian Economy, State and Society in Contemporary Tanzania*, Aldershot: Ashgate, pp. 3-25.

Ponte, Stefano 2002, *Farmers and Markets in Tanzania*. Oxford: James Currey.

Rasmussen, Torben 1986, "The green revolution in the Southern Highlands", in Boesen, Jannik et al. (eds), *Tanzania - crisis and struggle for survival*. Uppsala: Scandinavian Institute of African Studies, pp. 191-205.

Seppälä, Pekka 1998, *Diversification and Accumulation in Rural Tanzania*. Uppsala: Nordic Africa Institute.

Shivji, Issa G. (ed.) 1986, *The state and the working people in Tanzania*. Dakar: CODESRIA.

—, 1995, *Statement by the IMF Staff Representative*, paper presented at the meeting of 1998, *Not yet democracy: Reforming land tenure in Tanzania*. IIED/HAKIARDHI/Faculty of Law, University of Dar es Salaam.

Skarstein, Rune (2008), "Explaining productivity change in underdeveloped agriculture – Is there a theory of induced innovation?" draft paper, Department of Economics, NTNU, November.

Temu, A.E. and G.C. Ashimogo 1999, "Economic reform in Tanzania: Impacts on maize production, marketing, prices and food security", *AGREST Proceedings*, Sokoine University, Morogoro, pp. 137-145.

URT 1982, *The Tanzania National Agricultural Policy*, MAC, Dar es Salaam.

—, 1995, *Statement by the IMF Staff Representative*, paper presented at the meeting of 1996, *National Sample Census of Agriculture 1994/95, Tanzania Mainland - Report Volume III: Planted Area, Crop Produc-*

tion, Yield Estimates, Agricultural Inputs and Related Characteristics, Dar es Salaam, April.

—, 1995, *Statement by the IMF Staff Representative*, paper presented at the meeting of 1997, *The Census of Large Scale Farming 1994/95, Tanzania Mainland*, Dar es Salaam, April.

—, 1995, *Statement by the IMF Staff Representative*, paper presented at the meeting of 2000, *The Economic Survey 1999*, The Planning Commission, Dar es Salaam, June 2000.

URT 2001, *Agricultural Sector Development Strategy*, Government of Tanzania, Dar es Salaam, October.

URT/MAC 1992, *Basic Data - Agriculture & Livestock Sector 1985/86-1990/91*, MAC, Dar es Salaam.

—, 1998, *Basic Data - Agriculture and Livestock Sector 1991/92-1997/98*, MAC, Dar es Salaam.

—, 1999, *Expanded Survey of Agriculture 1995/96 - Tanzania Mainland. Main Report*, Dar es Salaam, March.

—, 2000, *Basic Data - Agriculture and Livestock Sector 1992/93-1998/99*, MAC, Dar es Salaam.

World Bank 1990, *Policy Framework Paper, Tanzania 1989/90 to 1991/92*, SecM90-83, Washington DC.

—, 1991, *Tanzania Economic Report. Towards Sustainable Development in the 1990s*, Vol. 1: Main Report, Report No. 9352-TA, Washington DC.

—, 1992, *A Vision for Sustained Growth in Tanzania*, paper presented at the Tanzania Consultative Group Meeting, Paris 29-30 June.

—, 1994, *Tanzania - Agriculture*, A World Bank Country Study, Washington DC.

—, 2000, *Agriculture in Tanzania since 1986 - Follower or leader in growth?* World Bank Report No. 20639, Washington DC.

—, 2001, *Tanzania at the Turn of the Century - From Reforms to Sustained Growth and Poverty Reduction*, A Country Study, World Bank, Washington, DC.

Øygard, Ragnar et al. 2003, *The maze of maize: Improving input and output market access for poor smallholders in Southern Africa region - The experience of Zambia and Malawi*, typescript, NORAGRIC, Ås, June.

CHAPTER SIX

GENDER DIMENSIONS OF LAND CONFLICTS: EXAMPLES FROM NJOMBE AND MASWA DISTRICTS IN TANZANIA

Aida C. Isinika and Khamaldin Mutabazi

Introduction

Land conflicts are a common phenomenon in many parts of Africa, partly because of the unique nature of the African land tenure system. In Tanzania for example, both customary and statutory land tenure systems are officially recognized and they operate concurrently, which sometimes fuels conflicts. This discussion focuses on conflicts which arise under the customary land tenure system due to its dominance in the country. In most cases, such conflicts become more prevalent where there is land shortage due to population pressure, expanding urban boundaries or competing new opportunities for investment. Also conflicts may arise due to institutional deficiencies or changes in the administration of land as happened in Tanzania following the villagization process during the mid-1970s (URT, 1994). Most of the land conflicts, which are documented in the literature, do not address aspects of gender. This paper attempts to raise this discussion.

In Tanzania, the majority of the people, especially in rural areas, derive their livelihood from farming, which means land is their most important productive resource, whether they own it or they simply have use rights. Consequently, land conflicts involve ownership and use rights. When such conflicts involving land arise women often become very vulnerable.

The laws governing the administration of land in Tanzania are highly influenced by historical developments in this respect. In 1895 the German administration introduced a shift in the customary land tenure system when all land in German East Africa was presumed to be un-owned and declared to be crown land vested in the German Empire. Ownership of land was defined by conveyance and leasehold. Natives only had use rights for land they occupied. Subsequently, prime agricultural land was alienated and allocated to white settlers (URT, 1994; Mwanda, 2001; Marwa, 2003). After the First World War, the British administration sought to develop Tanganyika as a peasant plantation economy. They enacted the Land Tenure ordinance No. 3 of 1923, also known as the Land Ordinance Chapter 113. This land ordinance purported to uphold the natives' interests over land by mentioning this in a non-binding preamble to the ordinance. The Governor held land in trust on behalf of natives. German conveyance and leasehold titles were converted to freehold titles, providing granted rights of occupancy to foreigners and deemed right of occupancy to natives. The former had documentary evidence while the latter did not. Therefore, customary land rights were not really secure under this law.

Since the radical title was still vested in the State, alienation of native land continued as determined by the Governor. In an "attempt" to further protect the natives' rights the rights of occupancy were redefined in 1928 providing statutory recognition of customary titles or deemed right of occupancy as opposed to granted rights of occupancy (URT, 1994). In 1950 the land ordinance was further amended, requiring "consultation" with native authorities before alienation of land. Following the East African Royal Commission (1953 – 55), the colonial government passed another government paper in 1958 emphasizing individual, exclusive, secure and unlimited tenure in order to promote efficient land use and enhance access to credit. However this could not be implemented since TANU activists vehemently opposed it, as strongly argued in Mwalimu Nyerere's paper "*Mali ya Taifa*" or "National Property" (Nyerere, 1958 cited in Sungusia, 2003), and independence was just around the corner.

Immediately after independence, in 1962 Government Paper No. 2 was published, which intended to change the land tenure. It has been argued that apart from substituting the President for the Governor as trustee over land the only other notable change was the conversion of all freehold titles to leasehold of up to 99 years (Sungusia, 2003, Gondwe, 1986). There were other changes in government policy and structure, which had a direct bearing on the land tenure. These include: nationalization of property in 1967 (Arusha Declaration), villagization in 1974 – 76, decentralization in 1972, urbanization, which often extinguishes customary land rights of surrounding villagers, and economic liberalization from the mid 1980s. Some of these changes had accompanying legal provisions. Others however, such as land appropriation under the villagization programme did not, and were therefore simply guided by government and sometimes party directives. The Villages and Ujamaa Villages Act of 1975 only provided for registration of villages. All these changes and particularly the change in land tenure emanating from villagization fomented many conflicts whose intensity increased over time, especially following the liberalized political environment after 1985 (URT, 1994; Tibaijuka *et al.*, 1993; Riwa, 1999).

Since Tanzania embarked on economic liberalization in 1986 there have been deliberate efforts to induce land reforms so that the prevailing land tenure is consistent with the ongoing economic transformation. Consequently a number of steps have since been taken to guide the land reform process. First, in order to address the increasing number of land conflicts, a Presidential Commission of inquiry into land matters (hereafter called the Land Commission) was established in 1991 to, among other things, review policies and laws, which were then in force and make recommendations for their improvement (URT, 1994). Meanwhile, the same government in 1992 enacted the regulation of land tenure act, which extinguished customary land rights in villages before operation *vijiji* of 1974/76. This however, did not extinguish the conflicts. The reform process continued, a new land policy was presented to and accepted by the Parliament in 1995 based on which two new land laws were enacted in 1999. Some of the Land Commission's recommendations were ignored by the Land Policy and the subsequent land laws (Koda, 2000). Land Act number 4 of 1999 covers general land while Land Act number 5 of 1999 addresses land that falls within village boundaries. The latter is specifically intended to cover customary law. Under this law security of customary tenure is assured by issuance of a customary land certificate, thereby giving equal status to both granted and deemed rights of occupancy. Some people argue however that such equality cannot exist since village land can be transferred into general land by order of the President (Mwanda, 2001).

Both the land policy and the land laws sought to improve the ownership rights of women under statutory law. However, the same policy and laws also recognize ownership and administration of land under customary law, which is the most dominant in rural areas. In 1992 it was estimated that about 82% of the land in Tanzania was administered under customary law (Tibaijuka and Kaijage, 1995). It is widely known that these laws do not work in favor of women, especially in as far as ownership and transfer rights are concerned. For this reason it was proposed by Tibaijuka et al., (1993) that the gender dimension needed to be put in to the research agenda to examine the extent to which different customs and traditions around the country were capable of accommodating the rising demand for the recognition of women's right in land.

Consistent with this proposal, the current paper therefore examines whether the changing policy and institutional framework enabled women to assert their rights over land as granted under the law. The study looks at the nature and trend of land conflicts in two ethnic groups, which offer slightly different use and transfer rights to women under customary tenure. The study assumes that as women become more aware of their rights, and the institutional framework is available to support their claims, there will be an increasing trend of land related conflicts between women and men within clans.

The Land Tenure-Gender Discourse

Land tenure is defined as a bundle of rights that a person may possess with respect to a piece of land. Such rights prescribe what the person can or cannot do on the land including means of access, disposal and exclusion. Restrictions on these rights impinge on one's security of tenure on that piece of land, while unrestricted continuous use and disposal rights enhance them. Customary land tenure separates use and proprietary rights (Malton, 1994).

Much has been written and said about the skewed nature of land tenure systems with respect to gender in most African countries. Most of the land is owned and administered under customary law, where land is often transferred through the patriarchy, even among matrilineal ethnic groups (Van Donge, 1993; Mwanda; 2001, Mzandah, 2000). In Tanzania, the customary laws of inheritance, which are codified under the local customary law, place women in the third degree after the oldest son who falls in the first degree and other younger sons who fall in the second degree. According to this law, daughters of a deceased person can only inherit family land if they are the only surviving member of the family. Even then, a woman can only occupy and use the land until her death, without powers of transfer. Many of the studies on land and gender in Tanzania are dominated by examples from Kagera, Kilimanjaro region (Rwebangira, 1996). There are also studies from Rungwe district in Mbeya region which give various examples of male dominance in land tenure. This does not reflect the diversity which prevails within the African land tenure system (Dobson, 1954; Tibaijuka *et al*, 1993). For example a study that was done in several villages of Iringa region in Tanzania revealed that daughters and widowed women could inherit land from their deceased parents and husbands respectively (Ashimogo et al., 2003).

Meanwhile, the literature on land tenure provides many examples to show that although women often only have use rights over land, as long as population pressure is low, such land tenure provides them with use rights that may be quite robust, to the extent that many of them may not bother to pursue new opportunities which give them more advantage using customary or statutory law. The robustness of the land tenure rights of women with regard to land varies widely among different ethnic groups (URT, 1994, Tibaijuka et al., 1993; Dobson, 1954). Koda (2000) for example concludes that the land tenure security of women in Msindo village (Same district) is not as it is portrayed in the mass media or in academic debates.

In Moshi district, where land tenure is supposed to be highly patriarchal, Shauri (1996) found that in Mabogini village where the population was multiethnic, being constituted of migrant laborers who had previously worked in the Tanganyika Plantation Company TPC (Ltd) with sugarcane, women could inherit, sell or bequeath land, demonstrating the capacity of customary land tenure to adapt to changing social, economic and technical realities (URT, 1994).

Gender related campaigns, which have been organized by the government as well as local and international NGOs such as the Land Rights Research Institute (LARRI) also known as HAKIARDHI in Kiswahili, Tanzania Gender Network Project (TGNP), Tanzania Women Lawyers' Association (TAWLA), Tanzania Media Women Association (TAMWA) as well as local civil society institutions have also had some positive impacts on improving the level of awareness regarding women's land rights. Such initiatives have been assisted by a more favorable legal environment, including the bill of rights, which is enshrined in the constitution, standing for equality and the right to own property (Mzandah, 2000). Although the transformation of attitudes and institutions may be slow and not so obvious sometimes, it is happening nonetheless, be it in small strides. The study cited earlier, Ashimogo (op. cit.), was also done in Kilombero district in Morogoro region, where more than 85% of the parents in two villages (Idete and Mbingu) reported having changed their attitudes in favor of supporting bequeathal of land to their daughters. Similar sentiments have been reported in Kigoma region (BACAS, 1999). Koda (2000) also reports an increasing tendency of parents to offer equal land inheritance rights to both daughters and sons, as reported by 48% of the respondents on account of equality but also because daughters are said to be more supportive to their aging parents and grand parents. Koda reports further that in Msindo village, daughters are often bequeathed land as presents to avoid restrictions imposed by customary and statutory inheritance laws.

As stated earlier, customary land tenure is the most dominant in Tanzania, and it has proved to be capable of adapting to changing socio-economic conditions (URT, 1994; Van Donge, 1993). This view is also true in other African countries where it has been established that indigenous land tenure arrangements are dynamic and they have historically adapted to economic and technological changes, inclining towards simplification as individuals and households acquire increasing rights of exclusion and transfer (Migot-Adholla, Place and Oluoch-Kosura, 1994). Therefore, understanding the positive attributes of this system of land use, ownership and transfer, which work in favor of women and other disadvantaged groups, is an important step towards informing the review process of both the land policy and the land laws. In this paper land conflicts are used as a proxy of both the presence of land pressure, which leads to increasing insecurity of land use and ownership rights.

The Land Commission (URT 1994) reported at length about the nature and causes of land conflicts in Tanzania, many of which were attributed to the administrative and conflict resolution institutions. Other studies have also reported on the frequency of land conflicts, which sometimes lead to unrest (Tibaijuka et al., 1993; URT, 1994; Runyoro, 1999; The Guardian Newspaper (T), 2000). Most of the conflicts which are reported in the literature as well as in the media involve ethnic groups, neighboring farmers, crop farmers and livestock owners or pastoralists, local communities and external investors. Almost without exception, the plight of women within such conflicts is subsumed and discussed under the umbrella of the larger group within which women are found, even though such conflicts further jeopardize the status of women in as far as their land rights are concerned. Some of them may even be rendered landless (Neef and Heidhues, 1994).

The government of Tanzania is currently undergoing decentralization, whereby some, particularly those previously falling under the regional offices, powers are increasingly devolved to Local Government Authorities (LGAs). Departments within the regional offices have been streamlined into lean secretariats, organized into clusters. The Regional Land Officer now falls under the cluster for Economic Services. Officers within a cluster have an advisory role to LGAs for their respective technical area. Before the new land laws came into force in 2001 (which is applicable for the period under study), the administration of land in Tanzania fell under the Ministry of Lands Housing and Urban Development.[1] Under the Minister, there was a Commissioner for land who is the main land administrator. The regional land officer was in charge of land administration within his region. Likewise the district land officer played this role at the district level. The team officers at both levels consisted of land officers, planners, valuers and estate managers. Below the district, land was administered by the Village Council.

Before 2001 the settlement of land conflicts used the existing legal institutions, starting from the primary court, which had concurrent jurisdiction in land matters other than granted right of occupancy. Primary courts could also hear cases involving short term rights of occupancy held for not more than five years. Appeals from this level were sent to the District Courts, followed by the High Court and finally to the Court of Appeal. However, the Presidential Commission found that organs of the executive arm of the government from the village up to the ministry as well as the ruling party were more heavily involved in settling land disputes than

---

[1] Currently the Ministry of Land and Human Settlement.

the judiciary (URT, 1994). This was attributed to the inaccessibility and painfully slow pace of proceedings within the judiciary, corruption and the tendency of the executive to amass powers for itself.

Following recommendations of the Presidential Land Commission, under the new land laws, the institutions for land administration and conflict resolution have been revised for separation of power and to enhance efficiency as well as promote fairness. The Commissioner for Land is still in charge at the national level, followed by the District Council and then the Village Government. A separate line of institutions have been established for adjudication of land conflicts as stipulated in the Court (Land disputes settlement) Act of 2002. At the lowest level, there is the Village Land Council. Appeals are forwarded upwards to the Ward Tribunal, the District Land and Housing Tribunal, Land Division of the High Court and the Court of Appeal of Tanzania (URT, 2002).

The participation of women in these institutions has been ensured under the law. For example, it is provided for that the Village Council shall consist of seven members, of whom three shall be women. The quorum of a meeting of the village Land Council shall be four persons, of whom at least two must be women. Likewise the composition of the Ward Tribunal shall not be less than four or exceed eight people of whom three must be women and the quorum shall be one half of the total members. Members of the District Land and Housing Tribunal are appointed by the Minister after consultation with the Regional Commissioner. The district tribunal comprises a chairman plus not more than seven assessors, three of whom shall be women (URT, 2002; Mbise, 2002). Although this formal machinery for land administration and adjudication is in place, most of the land is still held under customary tenure. Therefore, informal customary institutions play a major role both in the administration of land and in conflict resolution.

It is to be expected that as women become marginalized in the ownership and use of land, as a result of land pressure and land market dynamics, some of them will take legal recourse to restore their customary rights, which govern most of the land they use. Their awareness of the prevailing land policies and laws therefore becomes important for them to pursue such rights. This paper examines how women have used the legal system (despite its weaknesses as reported in URT, 1994) to protect or restore their land rights according to customary law. The study was done in two steps. First, data was collected from case records at primary courts and district appeal courts in Njombe and Maswa districts (Annex 1) for the period 1990 – 2003, when the land reform process was publicized in various media. Information that was collected from primary courts included: the village where the land in conflict is located, area of land under conflict, year when the case was filed, sex of the plaintiff and defendant, relationship between them, the nature of the land conflict and the ultimate ruling on the case. Case stories of selected examples were also compiled to illustrate salient features of the land tenure system.

The data from primary and district appeal courts was complemented with survey data, which was done in each of the two districts. The objective of the survey was to document the local land tenure system through discussion with key informants. The survey also provided a means to obtain more information on the meaning and implications of some of the issues which were encountered in court case records. Data from the household survey contained information on a number of variables including, ethnic group of respondents, sex, whether or not they had migrated, where from and reason for migration, their level of education and their main occupation. In addition there was also information on land ownership including size of land owned, means of acquisition, proprietary rights on land, any history of conflict over land, relationship between conflicting parties, how the case was resolved, or handled, information about land market and many others. Table 1 reports on the courts and villages from which information was collected.

Table 1: Sources of Data

District	Source of Data	Number of Cases or Records
Njombe		
	Makambako primary court	24
	Mtwango primary court	5
	Wangin'gombe primary court	29
	Njombe primary court (also handled cases from Lupembe primary court, which was closed temporary at the time)	20
	Njombe district appeal court (all appeal cases were from Mtwango primary court)	3
	Sub-total Njombe court cases	81
	Mtwango village household survey	43
Maswa	Malampaka primary court cases	40
	Bukangilija village household survey	28

Source: Own survey data

Description of Customary Land Tenure

It has already been stated customary land tenure in Africa is not homogenous. Accordingly, the land tenure systems of the Wabena and Wasukuma ethnic groups or tribes have some unique characteristics, which distinguish them from others. Some of these features give specific advantage or disadvantage to women in terms of land ownership and use rights. These are briefly described here in order to provide a better understanding of the land conflicts, which are presented later.

Njombe district is located in the Southern Highlands of Tanzania. It is one of six districts within Iringa region. (Annex 1). According to the census of 2002, the population of Njombe was 419,115, being 47% men and 53% women. The Bena tribe is the most dominant accounting for over 95% of the population. Maize is the main crop, providing food as well as cash income. Actually, Njombe is one of the leading maize producing areas in the country. The district is also important for the production of Irish potatoes. Other crops include beans and sunflower. Tea and coffee are also produced in some parts of the district. There is high potential for producing temperate fruits but this potential is yet to be fully exploited. The production of cut flowers is also just emerging.

Maswa district is located in Shinyanga region (Annex 1). In 2002 the district had 204,402 people, of whom 48% were men and 52% women. The Sukuma tribe was the most dominant accounting for over 90% of the total population in the district. The gender balance of the population in the two districts was close to the national average, which according to the year 2002 census stood at 48.9% men and 51.1 % women (URT, 2002). Up to the 1980s, cotton was dominant as a cash crop. The main food crops included sorghum and millet, due to their drought resistance. However, in recent years farmers' preferences have shifted in favor of maize and paddy rice as dual-purpose crops serving both as food and cash crops. Rice production is done in the lowland by flooding excavated and bunded fields known as *majaluba*.

Although both Wabena and Wasukuma are patrilineal, they differ somewhat in terms of the use and transfer rights which are granted to women for clan and family land. The land tenure system of Wasukuma is probably closer to the typical case, which is often reflected in the literature, where women often have use rights but they are not allowed to transfer land through bequeathal, gifts or sale. Land is typically owned by the clan, community or family (Dobson, 1954). In the past, society offered equal access (to households or clans) to uncultivated land for grazing, water supplies for domestic use, firewood, manure and collection of building materials such as thatching grass and poles. But, ownership of cultivated fields and water holes was recognized and vested in the individual or family (Birley, 1982). However, population pressure and changes in land tenure which were brought about by villagization are slowly transforming land tenure towards more individual ownership. For example natural resources within the traditional fodder banks, locally known as *Ngitiri* are now being sold (building poles, thatching grass) or rented out (grazing rights) (MNRT, 1996 and 2003). For this reason, some of the people, who own large herds of cattle, have been forced to move to other regions in search of pasture and water, where they have created recurrent conflicts between themselves and crop farmers (Mungo'ng'o, 1998).

Women among the Wasukuma basically have use rights over land and in terms of inheritance, they are heirs of the third degree as exemplified by the following inheritance case, which was filed at Malampaka primary court.

> The plaintiff (a woman) requested the court to give her the right to own 45 acres of land, which belonged to her late farther. Members of the clan wanted to take the land away from her because as a woman, she could not inherit land. The court ruled in her favour. Another case involved a brother of a deceased man who contested that the widowed wife d not inherit clan land. The widow won because she was able to prove that the land had been bought by the couple and not inherited from the clan as claimed.

These two cases represent examples of how limits on women's customary land ownership are transforming in the face of a more favorable policy and legal environment.

The customary land tenure of the Wabena is also guided by usufuctuary rights of occupancy. However, here women enjoy more use and transfer rights, since they can inherit land from their parents as well as bequeath it to their offspring. As is the case for the Wasukuma, grazing land is used communally, but most of the land under crop production is owned by clans or individual families. According to Friis-Hansens (1987), in some parts of Njombe district villagization did not significantly change the land tenure system. In Ngamanga village for example only 100 acres of land were expropriated for the village farm. The remaining 95% of the land was still cultivated privately. The extent to which land was redistributed depended on a number of factors including the proportion of households which had been reallocated and the powers assumed by the local leadership in as far as redistributing land was concerned. Such a situation was however not typical in areas dominated by annual crops (Tibaijuka et al., 1993). In many other parts of the country, especially in Arusha region (URT, 1994) and in some parts of Mwanza region (Katemi & Mlelwa, 1994), villagization brought havoc as far as land tenure was concerned since land was reallocated without due consideration to customary land rights. Consequently, the misallocation of land under villagization has been the cause of many land conflicts across the country involving entire communities and families (URT, 1994). Some of these problems are still manifested in the conflicts affecting men and women today.

Among Wabena the land, which a young couple uses for crop production comprises land from the husband's clan as well as land which the wife brings from her clan. This land tenure also applies for the Wahehe, another ethnic group residing in Mufindi, Iringa and Kilolo district of Iringa region. Young men and women are given by their parents a piece of the family or clan land (*lilungulu*) to till in order to meet their personal needs from when they are teenagers (about 16 – 18 years old). A woman continues to use that land even after marriage (Ashimogo et al., 2003). The young couple may add to their stock of land by clearing new land (if the land frontier is still open) or they may buy from other villagers. Children belonging to this couple will have the right to use the family land even after their parents' death. This implies, women are implicitly allowed to bequeath their clan land to their children, who in terms of lineage belong to their husband's clan as depicted in Figure 1. This means the assertion by Mung'ong'o (1998) that inheritance of land and *vinyungu* gardens has always been to sons and daughters are expected to be provided for by the families they marry into is not entirely correct. However, if a married woman did not have children, the clan land she had been using would revert to members of her clan and not to her husband's clan, implying limited transfer rights.

In this regard, it is obvious that when society was still closed, marriage interaction was limited to within neighboring villages. Therefore, land circulated in and out of clans without causing any threat. However, as outsiders enter into the village scene and begin to intermarry with local women, the equilibrium of clan land becomes distorted. This is illustrated by an example from Uhekule village, also in Njombe district, where following villagization, the village government gave equal access to village land to both men and women. But, this right had to be withdrawn after it became evident that some men from outside the village used marriage only as a ploy to gain access to village land. In Maposeni village, which is in neighboring Ruvuma region, single unmarried women were allocated less land than men or widowed women on the ground that they would eventually marry and in some cases move out of the village (Mwanda, 2001).

Court case stories that were collected from Njombe district reflect the prevailing customary land tenure system. For example:

Figure 1: Circulation of land under the Bena customary land tenure

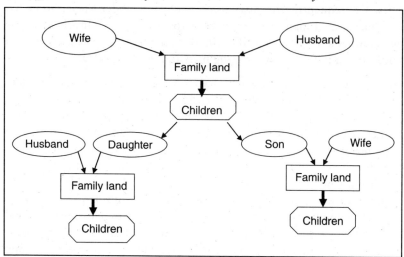

One case was filed at Makambako primary court in 2001, where the plaintiff (a man) was reclaiming his mother's land, which was confiscated by another brother following the death of the plaintiff's mother, thus indicating that women could bequeath land to their children. Another case was filed at Mtwango primary court in 1998, where the plaintiff (a woman) was fighting for land she had inherited from her late father, but which was then being confiscated by her uncle (father's brother). Yet another case was filed at Njombe primary court in 1998 where clan members refuted the right of a woman to sell land she had inherited from her father, and subsequently sold it to another women (the defendant), without seeking clan members' approval. Later, the plaintiff (a man) plus other male clan members, wanted to restore clan land by buying it out from the defendant. The court ruled in favor of the defendant arguing that the sale was lawful on the basis of customary law.

Increasingly, statutory law has been used to enhance the rights of women to gain full ownership of land, even in tribes where such rights are restricted (Mwánda, 2001; Riwa, 1999). Nonetheless, in some cases the same courts have used customary law to reaffirm the superior rights of men, ruling that the courts do not have jurisdiction to change customary law, rather it is the community itself, which can change its own laws (Riwa, 1999).

While the customary land tenure of Wabena provides women with some advantages it does not mean that men, under the influence of the patriarchal social system, do not try to usurp the customary lands rights of women as illustrated by the following court case stories.

A case was filed at Wangin'gombe primary court in 1990, where the plaintif, (a woman) filed a case on behalf of her two sisters, accusing their brother (defendant) who prevented them from using family land. The two sisters could not continue using their late husbands' clan land because they were refused inheritance by other clan members as wives under the levitate system. In this case, the land in dispute belonged to the late mother of the three sisters and brother. The court ruled in favor of the sisters on the basis of customary law. Another example involves an appeal case that was filed at Njombe district court, where a brother from Mtwango village appealed against a primary court decision, which granted his sister the right to own land she had inherited from their parents. The court reaffirmed the sister's right on the basis of customary as well as statutory law.

Sometimes women may lose their late husband's land if they remarry and they did not bear any children with the deceased husband.

In a case that was filed at Makambako primary court in 1997, the plaintiff (a man) was claiming land from the widow of his late uncle after she remarried. However, the plaintiff lost the case. According to the law, widowed women acquire occupation rights in the deceased landed property by virtue of their children's rights (Mwanda, 1999).

Based on the differences in land tenure between the Wabena and Wasukuma, it would be expected that women in Njombe district are more likely to claim their rights as plaintiffs in land disputes involving clan land. In order to test this hypothesis, analysis was done using both the court case records and household survey data. Results from these analyses are presented next.

Analysis for Evidence

The two data sources complement each other. As reported earlier, information for the survey was collected from 42 and 28 households in Njombe and Maswa districts respectively. Respondents were asked to recall land disputes which had been brought before local institutions as well as courts. As expected the sample of respondents reflect the dominance of the Wabena (98%) and Wasukuma (96%) in the two districts respectively. In Njombe the sample had 57% male respondents and 43% were female. In contrast, male respondents dominated in Maswa being 89% compared to only 11% women. Married women in Njombe were more forthcoming to be lead respondents or even contributed to some of the responses in the presence of their husbands. In Maswa district however, wives were often not as forthcoming, saying that interviewing the husband sufficed.

Land conflicts often increase as land becomes scarce. The intensity of pressure on land was assessed using two indicators; (i) the level of development of land markets and (ii) the frequency of land disputes. The results clearly show that the land market is more developed in Mtwango village in Njombe compared to Bukangilija village in Maswa. The participation of non-natives in buying land was much higher in Mtwango, being reported by 46% of the respondents compared to only 4% in Bukangilija. It seems that in Mtwango more people have experience with renting rather than buying since more of them could report on the latter than the former. The price of land as presented in Table 2 is also indicative of the more vibrant land market in Mtwango as reflected by a higher mean price. However, the land market is more differentiated in Maswa, as reflected by more categories of land types that are sold. The value of land for paddy and in some cases for cotton is quite high. It should also be noted that in some cases grass fodder reserves (*ngitiri*) have been rented out for as much as one hundred thousand shillings (Tshs 100,000) for a period of time, ranging from a few days up to several months depending on the agreement between the buyer and seller.

Respondents expressed mixed feelings about the rising market for land. The majority of the respondents (over 88%), both men and women, were concerned that these developments would lead to landlessness, which would deepen the level of poverty, bring tenancy and food insecurity. However, 67% of the men in Mtwango village pointed out that the developing land markets had improved the ease of converting land into liquid assets, which could be reinvested elsewhere or used to solve other impending problems. But, only 4% of the male respondents in the same village said the market had made it easier to acquire land. In Maswa, only 8% of the male respondents said it was now much easier to acquire land through purchase, reflecting the dominance of an agrarian society, with farming as the main economic activity. Therefore outright sale of all family or clan land is not common.

In contrast, 67% of the women respondents in Njombe and 33% in Maswa did not perceive any benefit of the market for land (Table 3). This is probably because women are less likely to participate in the land market as buyers due to lower income relative to men. This attitude by women could also reflect the precarious condition they find themselves in where there is pressure on land, which often leads to marginalization of any rights they may be granted under customary or statutory law. Ironically it is in Maswa, where there is less pressure on land and less participation of outsiders in the land market, that the most concern for landlessness was raised. This however may be a reflection of more secure customary tenure granted to women in Njombe district.

Table 2. Land sale and rental prices

Category of land trans- action	Number of respondents	Minimum	Maximum	Mean	Standard deviation
Land rent Bukangilija (Maswa)	37	7,500	15,000	9,959	1,043
Land sale (suitable for paddy- majaruba)	28	20,000	100,000	52,143	23,465
Land sale (suitable for cotton)	28	15,000	150,000	48,929	25,689
Land rent (suitable for paddy)	28	4,000	20,000	10,321	4,456
Land rent (suitable for cotton)	28	5,000	15,000	7,286	2,522
Land rent (fodder bank – ngitiri)	28	2,500	100,000	18,552	26,529

Source: Own survey data

Regarding the ongoing land reforms, it is relevant to note that more than 60% of the respondents were not aware of the ongoing land reforms. Nonetheless the majority of the men in Mtwango were at least aware that land belonged to the state (government) and they only had the right to land as long as they used it. Women in both Mtwango and Bukangijila were not aware of this fact.

In both districts, less than 25% of the male respondents were informed that titling could enhance their security of tenure as purported by the government and other proponents. According to professor Issa Shivji, this is yet another ploy by the government to further alienate villagers land through privatization and globalization. There have been efforts by the government to promote registration and titling of land in Tanzania, especially after 1982. However, such efforts have completely failed due to high cost and an inadequate administrative set up. As a consequence, it is customary land tenure which often governs most land sales. Therefore, the emerging land market is largely unregistered and is likely to remain so for some time to come. This may explain

Table 3. Attitudes towards land markets

Effects of and attitudes on land markets	Per cent of respondents from:			
	Mtwango		Bukangijila	
	Male	Female	Male	Female
Positive				
No positive outcome	29	67	24	33
Improves liquidity of land assets	67	33	8	-
Makes acquisition of land easy	4	-	8	-
Negative				
Increasing landlessness	92	94	88	100
Increasing land scarcity	-	-	12	-
Those who sell land will lose if they do not reinvest	8	6	-	-
Awareness on land reforms				
Unaware	67	66	64	67
Land belongs to state (government)	71	28	8	33
Security of land tenure is enhanced by titling	12	-	24	-

Source: Own survey data

why the villagers in this survey could not perceive any relationship between titling and security of tenure. Also, where the pressure on land is still low, customary land tenure offers quite robust security of tenure (Migot-Adholla et al., 1994, URT, 1994). But, as indicated in Figure 2, there is an increasing trend of land conflicts in both districts, reflecting rising land pressure.

According to the household data, there was an upsurge of land disputes in both districts after 1992, which could be a reflection of the awareness created by the media regarding the land reform process. The same data also shows that men are more likely to appear in land conflicts both as plaintiffs and defendants (Mutabazi and Isinika, 2005). This is clearly supported by court case records as shown in figures 3 and 4, which are based on dominance analysis, a method that is increasingly used to determine whether one group dominates another in terms of intensity, gap or any other chosen parameter from probability or frequency analysis (CFA, 2002; Van der Berg, 2003). If the cumulative stochastic or percentage curves do not intersect within the relevant range, then dominance of one group exists for the period under discussion.

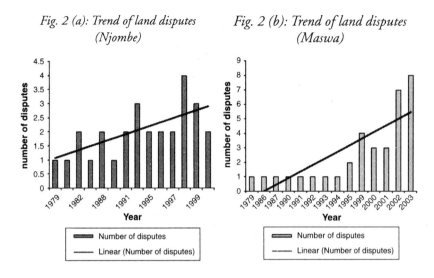

Fig. 2 (a): Trend of land disputes
(Njombe)

Fig. 2 (b): Trend of land disputes
(Maswa)

Further analysis of the records shows that most of the land disputes
were between villagers, who were not necessarily relatives, belonging
to the same clan. Such cases represented 78% in Njombe and 52%
in Maswa (Table 4). Koda, (2000) similarly found that in about 43%
of the land conflicts in that study the aggrieved parties were neigh-
bors and 95% of the conflicts involved disagreement over boundaries.
In the current study, cases that involved a female plaintiff against a
brother or another male member of the clan accounted for only 4%
of all the cases in Njombe. In Maswa however, this proportion was

*Figure 3: Dominance analysis of plaintiff and defendant by sex:
Njombe district*

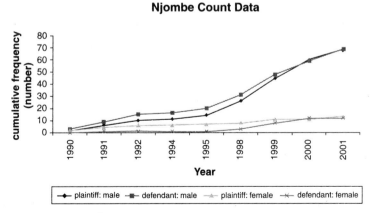

Source: court Case Records

Figure 4: Dominance analysis of plaintiff and defendant by sex:
Maswa district

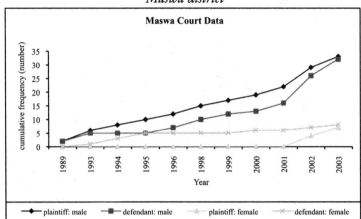

Source: Court Case Records

higher being 27.5% (including cases that involved divorced couples and a neglected wife).

As the data indicates, the proportion of women who filed cases in formal courts was fewer in both districts, being only 16 and 17% of all the plaintiffs in Njombe and Maswa respectively. In the case of Njombe, women were more likely to win a case they file (62%) compared to men (29%). The percent of men and women who lost was not very different in this district. However, about 46% of the cases which were filed by men were dismissed. In the case of Maswa, in terms of percentage, women were quite as likely to win a case as men, which is consistent with similar findings based on household data (Mutabazi and Isinika, 2005), where many of the cases that were recalled by respondents had been settled through local institutions (outside the court system). What stands out in the case of Maswa is the high proportion of cases that were withdrawn (35%) especially by women, representing 57% of all the cases that were filed by them. This is consistent with findings reported by Koda (2000) that more women than men prefer clan committees, probably because they are less aware of formal organs for conflict resolution or because they are less likely to afford the more costly formal proceedings, which are associated with delays and humiliation (Van Donge, 1993).

Policy Implications

From this discussion it is obvious that differences exist between the two ethnic groups (the Wabena and Wasukuma) in terms of the customary ownership and transfer rights that are granted to women. Nonetheless,

Table 4. Sex of Plaintiff and Relationship with Defendant

S.N.	How plaintiff relates to defendants	Njombe				Maswa			
		Sex of Plaintiff				Sex of Plaintiff			
		Male	Female	Total	%	Male	Female	Total	%
1.	Villagers (neighbouring farms)	54	10	63	78	20	1	21	52
2.	Male clan members (relatives)	3	0	3	4	6	2	8	20
3.	Brothers	6	0	6	7	3	0	3	8
4.	Male clan member (plaintiff) & widow (defendant)	1	0	1	1	-	-	-	-
5.	Female (plaintiff) & male clan member (defendant)	0	1	1	1	-	-	-	-
6.	Sister & brother	1	1	2	3	-	-	-	-
	Sisters	0	1	1	1	-	-	-	
7.	Male immigrant and native villager	1	0	1	1	-	-	-	-
8.	Villager (plaintiff) & village leaders (defendant)	3	0	3	4	-	-	-	-
9.	In-laws	-	-	-	-	4	0	4	10
10	Divorced couple	-	-	-	-	0	2	2	7
11.	Co-wives	-	-	-	-	0	1	1	2
11.	Neglected wife	-	-	-	-	0	1	1	2
	Total	69	13	81	100	33	7	40	100
	Percent	85	15			83	17		

Sources: Court records from Njombe and Maswa districts

Table 5. Sex of plaintiff versus outcome of case (Njombe)

Outcome of case	Sex of Plaintiff					Total	
	Male		Female				
	Number	%	Number	%		Number	%
Won	20	29	8	62		28	35
Lost	13	19	2	15		15	18
Case dismissed	31	46	2	15		33	41
Agreed to share	1	2	0	0		1	1
Case still pending	3	4	1	8		4	5
Total (Number/percent)	68	100	13	100		81	100
Percent	84	-	16	-		100	-

Source: Court records from Njombe district

the cultural advantage, which seems to be apparently more favorable to women in Njombe district in terms of land tenure does not mean that they have been spared the whims of a patriarchal society. It has been argued by Agola (1999) that in addition to customary land laws, there are several other laws which discriminate against women. For example, under the law governing inheritance of immovable property, based on the provisions of local customary law of 1963, Agola cites Fimbo as identifying seven rules that are not favorable to women. The marriage law also has such sections. Even the recent land laws have many shortcomings, including upholding customary law, some of which may not be supportive to women.

These findings imply that enhancing the rights of women over land requires another step, which should entail the combination of actions by different stakeholders including:

- Raising the awareness of both women and men about the new land laws and their rights as prescribed therein. In fact, the demand for information on the new land laws including the institutional and legal implications to the general public is very high, especially in rural areas (Isinika and Shao, 2005). In some districts, such as under the Land Management Programme (LAMP) (in Babati, Kiteto, Simanjiro and Singida) or in Tabora under the Village Land Management (VLUM) programme, there are structured training programmes for this purpose. This however is not the case in all districts, especially where there are

Table 6. Sex of plaintiff versus outcome of case (Maswa)

Outcome of case	Sex of Plaintiff				Total	
	Male		Female		Number	%
	Number	%	Number	%		
Won	6	18	1	14	7	18
Lost	8	24	0	0	8	20
Case dismissed	3	9	0	0	3	8
Case withdrawn	10	30	4	57	14	35
Case transferred back to primary court	2	6	0	0	2	5
Case transferred to village/community elders	1	3	0	0	1	3
Case still pending	3	9	2	29	5	13
Total (Number)	33	100	7	100	40	100
Percent	83	-	17	-	100	-

Source: Court records from Maswa district

no donor funded development projects. This calls for political will on the part of the governments (both central and local) to ensure that this important piece of information regarding the Land laws of 1999 reaches everybody in the country, especially in rural areas where their livelihoods so intimately depend on land.

• Efforts should also be directed at organizing awareness and sensitization programmes to initiate a process of change within communities in terms of attitudes and institutions to enhance the transformation of customary laws that are not favorable to women or other disadvantaged groups. As has already been shown, such changes are already happening in respect of bequeathal of land to daughters in some parts of the country. Supporting local institutions including NGOs and CBOs, which have effectively played this role in the past would help to enhance the transformation process. However, this must be carefully done so that external organizations only facilitate the process of change, which should emanate from the communities themselves.

• The law does not discriminate against women to acquire land through sale. Therefore, improving the economic power of women, especially women headed households, would enhance their ability to access land through this option as well.

These are given just as examples of initiatives that can be supported or initiated. There is a lot of room for localized innovation and variation which can be instituted to meet objectives of enhancing women's land rights, ownership and use. This is the challenge to all those who purport to promote equitable sustainable development.

Conclusion

Land conflicts have often been discussed without considering, or with an insignificant emphasis on the gender perspective. This paper highlights examples from court case records and field surveys that were done in Njombe and Maswa districts to assess whether under the changing political, administrative and legal environment, women would be more inclined to assert their land rights as provided under customary and statutory laws. The empirical evidence shows that although there is a trend in this direction, women require an additional push in order to assert their rights. It is therefore proposed that awareness and sensitization campaigns should continue, coupled with more structured training program to educate the general public on the institutional and legal implications of the new land laws. This task is for both government and other institutions, which should be adequately supported in order to fulfill this important role at this point in our history, when the economy is being transformed towards dominance of the private sector with emphasis on individual as opposed to communal property.

References

Agola, Laurent 1999, "Effectiveness of the law relating to inheritance of landed property in Tanzania Mainland". University of Dar-es-Salaam. Third year compulsory research paper in partial fulfillment of the Bachelor of Law Degree.

Ashimogo, G.C., A.C. Isinika and E.D. Mlangwa 2003, "Africa in Transition Microstudy – Tanzania". Afrint research report. Published in Djurfeldt, G. et al. (eds) 2005, *The African Food Crisis*. London: CABI.

BACAS 1999, "Production systems in Kigoma region. Final report." A consultancy report submitted to UNDP development coordination and micro-project in Kigoma region.

Birley, Martin H. 1982, "Resource management in Sukumaland, Tanzania", *Africa* 52 (2), pp. 1-29.

CFA- Centro Franco - Argentino 2002, *Inequality in economic development.* http://www.delta.ens.fr/bourguignon/buenosaires_cfa_c1.pdf

Dobson, E.B. 1954, "Comparative land tenure of Ten Tanganyika Tribes", *Journal of African Administration.*

Friis-Hansen, Esbern 1987, *Changes in land tenure and land use since villagization and their impact on peasant agricultural production in Tanzania: The case of the Southern Highlands.* Centre for Development Research. Copenhagen. CDR Research Paper No. 11; Institute of Research Assessment (IRA), University of Dar es Salaam, Research Paper No. 16.

Gondwe, Z S. 1986, "Agricultural policy at the crossroads", *Land Use Policy* 31-36.

Isinika, A.C. and G.C. Ashimogo 1998, "Promoting efficiency and equity in land markets: Some relevant lessons for Tanzania". Paper presented to the 2nd Scientific Conference of the Agricultural Economics Society of Tanzania (AGREST) 29-31 July, Morogoro, Tanzania.

Isinika, A.C. and I. Shao 2005, "Traditional Irrigation Programme Evaluation Report". Report submitted to the Traditional Irrigation and Environmental Programme (TIP).

Katemi, Alphonce and Richard Mlelwa 1994, "The impact of villagization on land tenure in Tanzania. The case of Sengerema district". University of Dar es Salaam. Compulsory research paper, LL.B third year, 1993/94.

Kamazima, Michael 2001, "Problems facing land tenure systems in Tanzania". University of Dar es Salaam. A research paper.

Koda, Bertha Omary 2000, "The gender dimension of land rights in Tanzania. A case study of Msindo village, Same district". A thesis submitted in fulfillment of the requirement for the PhD degree (Development Studies) of the University of Dar es Salaam.

Malton, P. 1994, "Indigenous Land Use Systems and Investment in Soil Fertility in Burkina Faso", in Bruce, J.W. and S.E. Migot-Adholla (eds), *Searching for Land Tenure Security in Africa.* Iowa: World Bank, Kendal/Hunt Publishing Company.

Marwa, Phanuel Maridadi 2003, "Management of village land under the village land act, 1999: A case study of Kyoruba and Nyabitocho villages in Tarime". University of Dar es Salaam. A research paper submitted for the partial fulfillment of the requirements for the Bachelor of Law (LL.B) degree.

Mbise, Emilian G. 2002, "New land dispute settlement system in Tanzania". A paper presented at the conference of the Resident and District Magistrates, Morogoro, Tanzania, on 27-29 November, 2002.

Migot-Adholla, S.E., F. Place and W. Oluoch-Kosura 1994, "Security of tenure and land productivity in Kenya", in Bruce, J.W. and

S.E. Migot-Adholla (eds.), *Searching for Land Tenure Security in Africa.* Iowa: World Bank, Kendal/Hunt Publishing Company.

MNRT 1996, Hifadhi Ardhi Shinyanga (HASHI)/ICRAF, Agroforestry Project Evaluation Report.

—, 2003, Baseline Study in the Wami-Mbiki, Uyumbu, and Ipole Pilot WMAs in Morogoro, Mvomero, Bagamoyo, Urambo and Sikonge Districts, Volume 1: Methodological Report.

Mung'ong'o, C.G. 1998, "Coming full circle: Agriculture, non-farm activities and the resurgence of out-migration in Njombe district". ASC Working Paper 26/1998.

Mutabazi, K. and A.C. Isinika 2005, "Land relations in agrarian societies of Tanzania: Local realities and reflections for land reforms". A paper presented at an regional annual conference of soils science in East Africa in Arusha Tanzania, March 2005.

Mwanda, Neema 2001, "The place of customary land rights in the village land act and the land act of 1999". University of Dar es Salaam. A third year research paper in partial fulfillment of the requirement for the award of the degree of Bachelor of Law (LL.B) degree.

Mzandah, Habiba 2000, "Gender and Property Ownership in Land. University of Dar-es-Salaam". A research Paper submitted for partial fulfillment of the Bachelor of Laws Degree 1999/2000.

Neef, A. and F. Heidhues 1994, "The Role of Land Tenure in Agroforestry: Lessons from Benin", *Agroforestry systems* 27 (2):145-16.

Rwebangira, Magdalena 1996, *The Legal Status of Women and Poverty in Tanzania.* Research Report No.100. Uppsala: the Nordic Africa Institute.

Shauri, Vincent Daniel 1996, "Village titling and its legal ramifications in the development of rural land tenure in Tanzania". University of Dar es Salaam. A dissertation submitted in partial fulfillment of the requirements for the degree of Master of Law.

Sije, George 2000, "Customary land rights in Tanzania". University of Dar es Salaam. A third year research paper in partial fulfillment of the requirement for the award of the degree of Bachelor of Law (LL.B) degree.

Sungusia H.G. 2003, "The Nyerere doctrine of land value and the enactment of the Land Act (1999)". University of Dar es Salaam. Course Work Paper II.

TGNP 1998, "Gender Platform". Tanzania Gender Network Project Newsletter, Vol 3 (2), January-March, 1998.

The Guardian Newspaper (T) 2000, "Cattle Clashes, the case of Tanzania". [http://www.edcnews.se/Research/TanzaniaCattleclash.html]   site visited on 25/8/2005.

Tibaijuka, A.K., F. Kaijage, F. Mgongo and A. Nshala 1993, "The Implications of the regulation of land tenure (established villages) act, 1992 for peasant land tenure security and natural resources management and conservation in Tanzania." Land Tenure Studies Group. University of Dar es Salaam.

Tibaijuka, A. and F. Kaijage 1995, "Land Policy in Tanzania: Issues for Policy Consideration". Paper prepared for the National Conference on Land Policy Organized by the Ministry of Lands, Housing and Urban Development, Arusha, 16-19 January, 1995.

Riwa, Hellen S. 1999, "Implications of the new land bill on customary land tenure and ownership by women". University of Dar es Salaam. A research paper presented to the Faculty of Law in partial fulfillment of the requirements for the LL.B. degree 1998/99.

Runyoro, Victor Apollo 1999, "Land use conflicts: Case of Ngorongoro conservation area in Arusha region". A paper presented at the Land Policy debate workshop hed at Sokoine University of Agriculture, Morogoro, Tanzania on 19-20 February, 1999.

United Republic of Tanzania (URT) 1994, *Report of the Presidential Commission of Inquiry into Land Matters. Volume 1, Land Policy and Land Tenure Structure.* Ministry of Lands, Housing and Urban Development, Government of the United Republic of Tanzania and the Nordic Africa Institute, Uppsala, Sweden.

—, 2002, The Courts (Land Disputes Settlement) Act, 2002.

Van Donge, Jan Kees 1993, "Legal insecurity and land conflicts in Mgeta, Uluguru mountains, Tanzania", *Africa* 63(2).

Van der Berg, S. 2003, "Poverty in South Africa – An analysis of the evidence". Department of Economics, University of Stellenbosch. http://www.sarpn.org.za/documents/d0000727/P801-Poverty_SA_vdBerg.pdf.

Annex 1 Location of Study Area

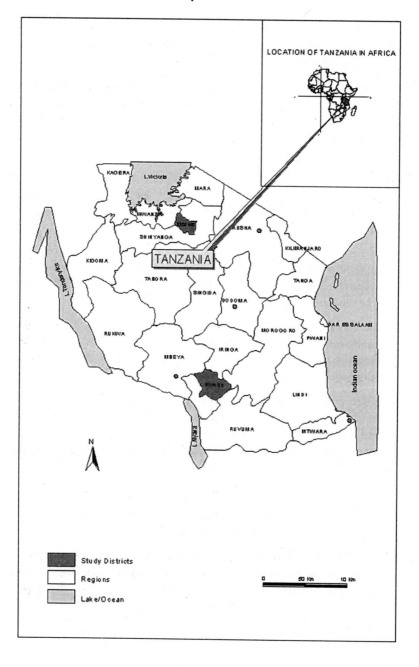

Annex 2 Formal Institutions for Land administration and Conflict Resolution in Tanzania

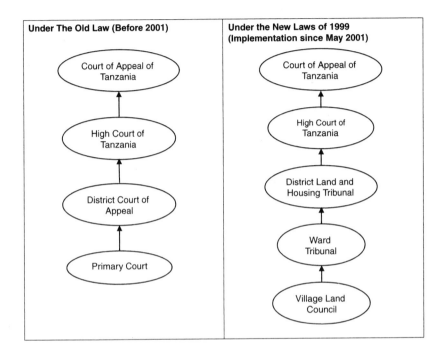

CHAPTER SEVEN

DYNAMISM OF NATURAL RESOURCE POLICIES AND IMPACT ON FORESTRY IN TANZANIA

Gerald C. Monela and Jumanne M. Abdallah

Background

Forest resources: Natural and plantations forest

Tanzania is endowed with extensive forest and woodland resources but there has been inadequate reliable data about the coverage of these forest and woodlands. Whereas the Ministry of Natural Resources and Tourism (MNRT) in 1998 calculated the forest and woodland coverage to be about 33.5 million hectares (ha), FAO (2000) estimated 38.8 million ha while the World Bank (2002) refers to about 40 million hectares. This implies the exact forest and woodland coverage is between 30 and 40 million ha or between 32% and 43% of Tanzania's total land area. About 13 million ha of forests and woodlands have legal status as gazetted Forest Reserves, of which about 2 million ha are gazetted as Local Government Forest Reserves. Forest Reserves account for about 37% while non-reserved forests and woodlands account for 57% and the remaining 6% falls under National Parks. Furthermore, reserved forests and woodlands are categorized into productive forests which occupy about 76% and protective forests covering about 22% of the forest reserve area of which 2% meets both productive and protective functions (Iddi, 2002a).

Tanzania has about 16 industrial plantations with a total of about 80,000 ha of both hard and softwood species. The main species include *Cupressus lusitanica*, (which has been seriously affected by aphids), *Pinus patula*, *Tectona grandis* and some Eucalyptus species. The plantations are found in different locations in the country. A recent World Bank report (2002) shows the private sector owns and manages about 55,000 ha (69%) of forest plantations including about 6,000 ha of wattle (*Acacia mearnsii*) mostly owned by the Kibena Wattle Company in Njombe district and about 8,000 ha of teak (*Tectona grandis*) most of which is owned by the Kilombero Valley Teak Company (KVTC), whereas Iddi (2002b) indicates that about 80,000 ha of forest plantations are operated by the private sector mostly as woodlots ranging from 50 ha to over 1,000 ha. These are owned by individual households, villages and Community-Based Organizations (CBOs) such as youths and women. Over 24,000 ha of privately owned plantations (30%) in Tanzania are found in Mufindi district in the Iringa Region. It is the only district where forestry activities are second to agriculture in terms of income generation (Mufindi District Profile, 2006).

Forests are imperative for the welfare of both the rural and urban Tanzanian population especially the poor and the marginalized. Most of the people rely directly or indirectly on the forest resources for their livelihoods. Forests provide employment opportunities to between one million and ten million people. Meanwhile, forest products contribute approximatly USD 14 million (10-15%) of the country's recorded export earnings. Through fuelwood and charcoal, forests provide 95% of Tanzania's energy supply. Approximately 75% of construction materials come directly from forests. In addition, forests provide essential indigenous medicinal and supplementary products to 70% of Tanzania. Therefore, the manner in which forests are managed – or mismanaged – would have profound implications for the country's future (CIFOR, 2004).

This paper discusses transitions in Tanzania's forestry sector and its importance both in terms of forestry practices on the ground and regarding policy and legal aspects. The paper shows and discusses transitions in forest management, which among other things advocate collaborative management between the forest sector and communities, in the management of forests. The paper further shows that the Forest Policy of 1998 is designed to address most of the problems affecting the forest sector.

Institutional transition and impacts in forestry

Formal forest management and conservation in Tanzania dates back to the German colonial period. Formal management of forests was introduced to avert unsustainable and destructive forest utilization through uncontrolled harvesting and encroachment from agriculture. But others have argued that this was a move to alienate native land. The first forest reserve was gazetted in 1906 (Ahlback, 1986). Mountain forests were considered to have high biodiversity-rich forest and to be of key significance for watershed protection. They were among the first areas reserved under the German and British colonial regimes. In 1922, the British also made all land the property of the state (URT, 1994; Ylhäisi, 2003). Thus the colonial period marked the beginning of major changes in forest management in the country through the introduction of state owned forests. Kajembe and Kessy (1999) also argue that the emergence of the colonial state marked a major challenge to traditional forms of governance in managing natural resources. It seems the colonial forest management regimes undermined local people's capacity for sustainable forest management, leaving local communities with few rights over the resources they purportedly owned. It is argued that the stringent regulations of the colonial governments in East Africa have had negative effects; such as discouraging tree planting and conservation by the local people (Kajembe et al., 2000a).

Following the Arusha Declaration in 1967, Tanzania went through a major social revolution. The policy of *Ujamaa*[1] required the state apparatus to control all major means of production and exchange; abolishing the exploitation of man by man in an attempt to eliminate social classes; and reducing the income gap between the rich and the poor as well as between urban and rural areas in the country. The policy also required that economic development should be based on self reliance, implying that development be carried out by the people using available resources, including forests (Kihiyo, 1998). During this period, a high proportion of the rural population was regrouped into centralized 'ujamaa' villages for the purpose of accelerating development. *Ujamaa* villages were publicized as places where people would live and work for the benefit of all. The period of 1968-1972 was the height of the *ujamaa* policy. All over the country, government and political leaders were busy encouraging establishment of *ujamaa* villages and a larger proportion of rural government budgets and services were directed to this campaign.

However, such large-scale resettlement programmes did not match with forest conservation practices. For example, there were several big programmes initiated through *Ujamaa Vijijini*[2] such as the 'Tobacco Complex' in Tabora, Iringa and Ruvuma regions financed by the International Development Agency (IDA) of the World Bank. These programmes required clear felling of big tracts of forests.[3] Specific steps were taken in the 1970s to nationalize the remaining forests. The Government, though the Forest Division, managed the forests and wood based industries which were controlled by a government parastatal, the Tanzania Wood Industries Corporation (TWICO) (Kihiyo, 1998). By the 1980s Tanzania was the world's second poorest country in terms of GDP per capita. At the same time, its natural resource base became noticeably threatened.

In order to address a deteriorating economic situation during the 1980s, Tanzania tried its own structural adjustment programmes. These included the National Economic Survival Program (NESP) in 1981 and the Structural Adjustment

---

[1] *Ujamaa* is a Kiswahili word which means communalism, sometimes referred to as African socialism, see also chapter 2.

[2] *Ujamaa vijijini* means communalism or socialism in villages.

[3] *For example, in the Urambo scheme 28 households requested to establish an Ujamaa village. The request was approved by village authorities and about 700 ha of natural forests were clear felled and the land laid out for tobacco cultivation.*

Program (SAP) in 1983. The main objectives of SAP were: to bring about sustainable economic growth, restore a sustainable balance of payments position, reduce budget deficit, cut down inflation, reform government trade policies and provide incentive to farmers so that production was stimulated. The reform targeted parastatal restructuring and privatization (Kihiyo, 1998). Generally, structural adjustment programs attempted to correct economic imbalances and improve efficiency of developing and transitional economies; thereby setting the stage for further development. The IMF, World Bank and other bilateral donors have financed structural adjustment policies in Tanzania for about 15 years since the mid-1980s. Yet these programs have not improved the quality of life for the majority of citizens.

Per capita income and basic human welfare indicators fell during this time period (1980 -1990). For example, per capita GDP has fallen to the 1960 level and primary school enrolment rates plunged below 50 percent from an average of 80 percent during the 1980s. Indirectly, structural adjustment in Tanzania has increased rates of environmental degradation. Agricultural input prices have risen, forcing farmers to adopt soil mining and other unsustainable farming practices. Meanwhile, the government has reduced funding on reforestation (Reed, 1996). This means, none of the reforms that followed the socialist period made any impact on the basic forest practices. Moreover, lack of resources during the reform period (1986 – 1995) hindered smooth enforcement of regulations. Consequently, most of the forest areas became open access resources where nothing was managed and anyone could use the resources as they pleased without constraints.

During the 1970s and 1980s there was a widespread perception in Tanzania (though a somewhat narrow and inaccurate one) that the high and accelerating rates of deforestation in some areas were primarily being driven by demand for woodfuel and construction timber. In order to cope with these dynamics, and take a comprehensive and strategic view of the sector, the government launched the Tanzania Forestry Action Plan for the period 1990–2008. In addition, the World Bank-assisted Tanzania Forest Resources Management Project (FRMP 1992–99) was formulated to implement the Action Plan, and to generally improve forest management in the country. The project aimed, as a first step, to strengthen the institutions responsible for developing forest and land policies, as well as regional and district forestry services in selected areas (World Bank, 2002). This project managed to introduce a new system of royalty collection by the regional forest services, closing several loopholes in the system, and resulted in relatively increased revenue collection. For example in the four pilot regions of Tabora, Shinyanga, Singida and Mwanza, revenues increased from Tsh. 90.7 million in 1992 to Tsh. 227.9 million in 1996 and then to Tsh. 299.2 in 1998, a 30 % increase within 6 years or 5 % increase per year at a time when the annual inflation rate was below 5 %, thus representing revenue increase in real terms.

Since 1998 Tanzania has revised the National Forest Policy. The accompanying National Forest Act No. 14 was approved in 2002. Both aim at addressing the challenges to managing Tanzania's forest resources as a national heritage on an integrated and sustainable basis so as to optimise their environmental, economic, social and cultural values. The Government of Tanzania realised that a more comprehensive approach was needed to ensure sustainable forest management in the country. Also recognising the broad and cross-sectoral linkages between forestry and other sectors, the National Forestry Programme (NFP) was developed and approved in November 2001, taking into account macro-economic and social policy developments that relate to land-based resources and use, including land, the environment, water, energy and agriculture. The NFP is an instrument for implementing the National Forest Policy. The goal of the National Forestry Programme is to promote the conservation and sustainable use of forest resources to meet local, national and global needs. The NFP aims to achieve this through fostering national and international partnerships to manage, protect and restore forest resources and land production. All these emphasize the need for involving communities as an integral part of a new way to manage forests, which is also firmly enshrined in the Land Act of 1999 and the new Forest Act of 2002. However, the main constraint is lack of capacity to implement and achieve these strategic objectives, particularly in the four focus areas of the policy implementation namely: (i) forest land management, (ii) forest based industries and products, (iii) ecosystems conservation management, and (iv) institutions and human resources for participatory forest resource management. Human capital and financing are particularly deficient. For example, in most Local Governments, the forestry sector is seriously under-staffed and under-equipped, lacking essential resources for monitoring. Therefore, while decentralization and devolution of power have involved political relegation of functions and finances to Local Governments, less has been done at the ground level to ensure that community competencies in terms of empowerment, pluralism and building of social capital are developed for effective implementation of PFM programmes.

The challenge at this point is: to what extent and under what conditions is true decentralization possible? For effective decentralization there should be devolution of power and empowerment of the target beneficiaries. Devolution of power is the principle that decisions should be made at the lowest possible level where competencies exist. Meanwhile, empowerment entails basic elements that include; (i) access to information, (ii) inclusion and participation, (iii) responsiveness and accountability, and (iv) local organization capacity. Many of these aspects are lacking in rural communities, especially as they relate to management of natural resources. This has in most cases caused problems due to the inherent characteristic of the powerful to prevent the powerless from sharing or having their own power in order to increase their access to natural resources and other forms of capital (physical, human, financial, and social) in order to enhance their livelihoods.

Since 2002, the Ministry of Natural Resources and Tourism (MNRT) is implementing the Forest Conservation and Management Project with support from the World Bank, the Government of Denmark and the Global Environmental Facility (GEF). The main objective is to support forest management institutional change, and improve service delivery, by providing resources to strengthen the capacity for administration, and management of the Tanzania Forest Service (which will be established). The other objectives are to improve revenue collection from forests and woodlands and improve service delivery mechanisms for a participatory forest management.

The main purpose of establishing the TFS is to improve the delivery of public services as they relate to forestry and the forestry sector at large. It is hoped that an independent or semi-autonomous Forest Service will provide efficient and better services in a business-like environment. The establishment of TFS is led by a nine member Agency Implementation Team (AIT) under the guidance of the President's Office Public Service Management (PO-PSM) with technical backstopping from relevant institutions (including consultants from time to time). The process to establish TFS, *inter alia*, has made the following achievements: (i) TFS key documents have been finalized, these include the Business Analysis (BA), Strategic Plan (SP), Business Plan (BP), Framework Document (FD) and the Establishment Order (EO) (ii) a peer review process has been initiated and (iii) an evaluation report on short-listing of consultants has been resubmitted to the Ministerial Tender Board (MTB). Initiatives to recruit the Chief Executive have restarted. Despite such progress however, some stakeholders are raising concerns that the process of implementing the TFS is very slow.

Forest governance

The governance of forest resources involves administration and management of forests and woodlands, which currently fall under various regimes and involve different management approaches. Under the current land laws, forests and woodlands may fall under general lands (formally called public lands), or on privately owned land. Forests fall under three main categories. There are family forests, those belonging to the central and local governments as well as community forests. Forests under general lands basically denotes an open access resource with no clear tenure structure or formally guaranteed user rights and hence no incentive for systematic and sustainable forest management (FAO, 1999). Open access resources are available to anyone and therefore unlikely to elicit investment in maintenance or sustainable utilization (Bromley, 1992). Family forests that come from natural regeneration or preservation of existing trees (such as *ngitiri*[4] in shinyanga and *Malungulu*[5] in Iringa), are managed by households or clans. Such family forests are generally overseen by influential elders guided by traditional beliefs which have some conservation elements. These norms, practices and beliefs include for example restriction on farming near water sources or very steep slopes, and restricted harvests of some tree species because of medicinal or ritual purposes. Although these practices are being revived and operating well in some areas of Shinyanga region (Monela et al., 2000), in most others areas they are under threat due to increasing pressure on land.

The Village Land Act of 1999 recognizes customary land rights within general lands and family hold. Before 1999 customary rights did not have legal backing. Even now, however, changes in statutory law regarding customary land rights have not significantly changed people's perceptions and practice regarding land use because people perceive their customary land rights to be quite secure. Thus forests under customary rights are susceptible to alienation by the government at any time. Consequently, there is little incentive for effective conservation. Ongoing forest harvesting in general land, without taking into account replacement capacity, leads to the depletion as well as complete disappearance of most forest on general lands. This phenomenon occurs in family forests as well because most of family forests in Tanzania lack legal ownership, which is an incentive for sustainable management and utilization (Abdallah and Sauer, 2007).

Forest reserves fall under central and local government management, where utilization of any kind by communities is generally forbidden. The local villagers are not involved in the management of these forests. However, both the central and local governments are seriously under-staffed having limited facilities to police and manage these reserves, which has triggered degradation especially in the form of deforestation. On the other hand, forests formulated under the Community Based Forest Management approach such as village land forest reserves (VLFRs) are owned by the community as a whole. This type of forest is declared a reserved forest area by the Village Council acting on the recommendation of the Village

---

4   Ngitiri are basically fodder reserves, full of regenerated trees.
5   Malungulu are family or clan farms on a fallow rotation cycle.

Assembly. The VLFR is the major arrangement by which the Community Forest Management (CBFM) is implemented. These forest areas are designated by the village government in relation to agricultural production ('utilization zones') and/or resource protection according to the village sustainable management objectives as defined for each forest in the forest management plans. Such management plans are required by the 2002 Tanzanian Forest Act No. 14 (Abdallah and Sauer, 2007).

In addition to forests that fall under local and village governments, which are managed through the District Councils, the MNRT through the FBD is directly managing 16 industrial plantations and about two million hectares of Catchment Forest Reserves. In most cases the FBD has inadequate numbers of staff in the regions and very few at the district level. Therefore, the FBD operates through the DFOs who administratively are answerable to the Local Government Authorities (LGAs). The MNRT has overall responsibility for the development of the forestry and beekeeping sector thus it formulates policies and supervises their implementation. However, there are other government structures responsible for overseeing the implementation of activities in the sector. For instance, at the local level, implementation of the policy becomes the responsibility of the Prime Minister's Office - Regional Administration and Local Government (PMO-RALG), which has the mandate to coordinate and oversee the functions performed by Regional Secretariats and Local Government Authorities.

The Forest and Beekeeping Division (FBD) provides overall policy guidance and technical support. It is also the responsibility of the FBD to undertake law enforcement through monitoring and supervision in order to ensure compliance of laws and accompanying regulations. District Forest Officers (DFOs) are in charge of all forestry matters in the districts with technical guidance from FBD. Furthermore, the latter also facilitates training of technical and professional cadres. This includes organizing in-service training for DFOs and the paraprofessionals who undertake regular extension services to farmers. Such capacity building is done through tailor-made short courses and study tours ranging from one week to three months. In general however, there is inadequate capacity for effective forest governance in Tanzania since district forest offices are understaffed and under-equipped as alluded to earlier, which has contributed to the high rate of deforestation and degradation.

For example, the country's natural forest and tree resources on the general land face massive degradation and deforestation, at a rate of 91,200 ha annually (FAO, 2000; Shayo, 2006). Unsustainable extraction of scarce tree species is widespread. Government's effort to gain an upper hand in the battle against illegal logging and trading of illegally sourced timber has thus far proved to be ineffective. For instance, the Government's requirement that suppliers of timber should ensure that their products have been legally sourced and produced is not reflected in tender documents. Also the complex structure of the hardwood timber supply chain is not clearly understood, therefore complicating monitoring mechanisms that have been set to curb illegal timber timber (Milledge and Kaale, 2005).

Collaborative Forest Management: paradigm take-over

The government during the 1990s realized that both central and local governments had failed to provide adequate protection and management of the forest estates, which led to increased deforestation and degradation of state controlled forests at alarming rates (Kajembe and Mgoo, 1999). The major reason behind the negative state of management was the declining government capacity to protect the forests in terms of finances, low human resources due to retrenchment of staff during economic reforms (1980-1995) and general attitude of communities towards state property as not belonging to them. The current forest policy (MNRT, 1998), therefore clearly shows the need for the government to involve local communities in managing these forest resources as a step towards sustainable forest management.

Under collaborative management of state owned resources like catchment forest reserves, the local people would become involved while also realizing some benefits through user rights and access to some forest products and services. In developing this collaborative system, it was hypothesised further that the local people might become the strongest and most effective managers of natural forests at the same time lowering transaction costs. This paradigm shift, is taking place all over the developing countries. In Tanzania it is called Participatory Forests Management (PFM). It entails two major emphases namely Joint Forest Management (JFM) and Community Based Forest Management (CBFM). The JFM is designed to bring about cooperation between local community and formal government organs in managing forest resources that belong to governments (local and central government). Meanwhile, the CBFM is designed to empower communities as potential managers of their own forest resources. It is therefore envisaged to transfer most of the so called general land forests into community management responsibility (Wily, 1995).

Under the CBFM approach local communities are both owners and duty bearers, reaping all the benefits accrued from the resources. Although the importance of the community forest was felt early in the 1980's (Kajembe, 1994), CBFM started making news in Tanzania in the mid 1990's particularly following the success stories from Duru-Haitemba and Mgori Forest reserves (Wily, 1995). To date both community and Joint Forest Management are mushrooming all around the country. Apart from those success stories there are a number of forests that are at various stages of JFM or CBFM development. These include the Gologolo, Kipumbwi and Amani Nature Reserve, as well as Chome forest in Tanga region, Ufiome in Manyara region, Nkweshoo in Kilimanjaro region, Kitulanghalo in Mahenge district, and Kimboza within the Uluguru Mountains in Morogoro region (Kajembe and Kessy, 1999). There are also Gangalamtumba and Kidundakyave in Iringa region (Abdallah and Sauer, 2007).

Kajembe et al. (2000b) revealed that CBFM at Duru-Haitemba had a positive impact on the resource base and people's livelihoods – the forest is healthier than before and people are satisfied with the products they collect from the forests. Empirical evidence elsewhere in the country (see Luoga et al., 2006a; Luoga et al., 2006b) also indicated that, there were very few signs of human disturbance, and there was increased stocking in forests under JFM. The increase in stocking can be attributed to reduced fire occurrences, controlled grazing and reduced illegal harvesting of trees as a result of effective protection under JFM strategy. Participatory Forest Management is a key strategy to realize an equitable forestry management system in Tanzania. Participatory Forest Management offers an important potential in all forest type to realize improved livelihood benefits on a local scale. A recent pilot study has demonstrated that annual village income under this type of management may increase by up to US$ 653, which is quite significant in a rural context. The Forestry and Beekeeping Division (2006) reported that JFM and CBFM in some places led to improvements in forest condition – including factors such as improved water flow from water sources or streams, reduced illegal activities, and boundary consolidation due to a reduction in agricultural encroachment. Despite the progress which has been made and benefits that have been realized from PFM in Tanzania (WRM, 2002), there are widespread feelings that collaborative management is failing to meet the required expectations in the country. Some of the problems limiting the potential of PFM are narrated below.

Participatory Forest Management constraints

While many villages are participating in PFM across the country, relatively few have formalized their forest management plans in line with the policy and legislation, which require entering into management agreements with people who depend on public forests for their livelihoods, on condition that they must have approved the forest management plans and by-laws. This requires the communities to have an approved management plan or signed a Joint Management Agreement for the part of the forest, which falls within their village land. Moreover, the capacity of field forestry extension staff and communities needs be to be improved in order to facilitate a process of participatory management in a manner that is appropriate to stakeholders' needs. Monitoring and evaluation plans are often lacking. Due to diverse interests among forest users, there is a strong need to develop a system of monitoring and evaluation that captures and manages data from a variety of stakeholders. However, the capacity to collect, analyse, interpret and manage data is inadequate. Thus *lack of agreements and management plans* poses a threat to PFM in Tanzania.

The second constraint relates to *high implementation costs of PFM initiatives*, which hamper its introduction to many parts of the country. Due to such high costs and the time it takes to transfer management right to non-government stakeholders, currently only 1% of the total forest reserve area is under this form of management. It is estimated for example that a single PFM may even take up to 4-years to realize, and cost between USD 50,000 and 100,000 to implement, depending on the size and the location of the forest. Clearly more work is needed to improve the economic efficiency of the PFM process and to streamline the actual implementation process.

Lack of alternative sources of livelihoods for people living near forests poses yet another constraint. The FBD (2006) revealed that revenues reported from areas under JFM - particularly in catchment forests -, remained particularly low. One important source of revenue from village forest management are fines levied by the Village Council on those caught undertaking unauthorized activities in the forest. However, as law enforcement efforts by local communities increase and as illegal activities drop, revenue from fines decreases. This sometimes acts as a disincentive to local forest management as fines often represent one of the only sources of revenue to local communities from catchment forests. Promotion of income generating activities should go hand in hand with the PFM awareness programme.

Agriculture is the principal land use in Tanzania and remains the major livelihood source of poor people, employing about 80 % of the population in the country and particularly the rural poor (MNRT, 1998). It is also the mainstay of the country's economy, contributing 50 % of the GDP compared to only a 3 % contribution of forestry. Agriculture is probably the single most powerful human activity with significant influence on the environmental quality of particularly forest resources, even those under PFM. Over the last three decades, rapid population growth has resulted in land scarcity in high potential areas. Many small-scale farmers cannot afford high prices of inorganic fertilizers and this has contributed to a decline in crop production, and off-farm activities such as forest products harvesting are becoming the only resort for most rural poor. The expansion of agricultural activities in semi-arid areas is through shifting cultivation, and using inappropriate farming practices has increased deforestation and land degradation.

Deforestation and land degradation especially in arid and semi-arid lands are on the increase all over Tanzania. Information on the extent of deforestation is vague. The widely quoted figure for deforestation is 130,000 – 150,000 ha cleared annually (MNRT, 1998). A figure appearing in the literature and relating to the early 2000s, is 91,200 ha per annum (FAO, 2002). While the global impact of increasing deforestation is still shrouded in uncertainty, there is consensus on major causes of deforestation. According to MNRT (1998), the principal direct agents of deforestation include agricultural expansion along with inappropriate agricultural practices. There are also problems related to overgrazing, bush fires, excessive fuelwood gathering, commercial logging and industrial development. Environmental degradation is taking place mainly in the unreserved forestland. These direct agents of environmental degradation have a number of underlying factors or causes, which include: population growth and rural poverty, market and policy failures, state and international asymmetry of trade and increased demand for natural resources.

The marginalization of rural poor is also a problem. In some PFM projects often the interests of women are often forgotten. In addition, conversion of general lands into JFM or CBFM restricts access to land and other natural resources by women (Rani, undated) and other users as well. Women are often excluded from community organizations or committees that manage natural resources, even when the projects are intended to benefit them (IFAD, undated). Realities that could work against CBFM or JFM include, among others, difficulty in recognizing the most appropriate community members for programme participation, such as men or women (Little, 1994). Another challenge that relates to marginalization is the stratified nature of communities. The interests of some actors are not adequately represented in JFM and CBFM initiatives.

Lack of political will at the centre to give powers to communities and grassroots organizations is also a challenge to community based forest management initiatives. It is important to note that benefits accruing locally must be significant if the community is to take the trouble of establishing and enforcing the rules about resource use. This begs the question on whether community based forest management programmes and projects have sufficient value to stimulate community participation. This remains an unresolved puzzle! Rural communities are undergoing rapid social, economic, and political change, as the development and modernization process spreads and deepens. Even if effective and viable user groups exist or can be put in place today, it is not clear if these will survive and persist in the face of modernization pressures. More needs to be known about the institutional context in which users now find themselves and the type of support, which will increase the probability of sustainable management of our forest resources (Kajembe *et al.*, 2000a).

The *low educational level* is also an underlying cause of deforestation and degradation. Most rural communities in Tanzania remain ignorant of existing options for their empowerment under the revised Forest Policy of 1998, Forest Act of 2002 and National Forest Programme. This is one major limiting factor preventing communities from buying into PFM and forest management initiatives in general. A community awareness programme that consolidates all stakeholders inputs needs to be introduced, to ensure village communities fully understand: (1) the different forms of community participation, (2) the true value of timber resources, (3) rights and potential community benefits, (4) risks and responsibilities involved, and (5) the legal procedures for achieving community participation. The benefits from participation could include financial returns as well as reduced vulnerability, which is the ability or inability (as the case may be) to recover from shocks.

Lack of alternative sources of energy causes another serious threat to environmental sustainability. About 90 % of total energy consumption (biomass, petroleum, electricity and coal) is from fuelwood compared with only 14 % in South Africa. Statistics show that more than 78 % and 14 % of all the households in the country use firewood and charcoal respectively as sources of household energy, with annual requirement estimated at 46 million m^3 (MNRT, 1998). The majorities of urban households depend on fuelwood, charcoal and paraffin for their energy needs. For example, in 1993 urban woodfuel consumption (mostly as charcoal) was reported at 5.4 million m^3 or 13.6% of the national total (Nindie and Mbise, 1995). By 1999 the total was about 40.4 million m^3 but by 2002 urban consumption had risen to 13.4 million (Kaale and Sawe, 2001). This situation among other issues threatens sustainability of all forest resources even those under participatory management.

A review of the energy sector in Tanzania shows that the country has considerable amounts of alternative energy resources such as hydroelectricity, natural gas, solar energy and coal. These however do not play an important role in rural energy supply and most urban households because they are poorly developed with relatively high running costs. For instance, hydroelectric power is said to be playing an increasing role for the community compared to other sources of energy, but only 10 % of its total potential has actually been developed. Moreover, the coverage of electricity is only 10 % in urban and less than one percent in rural areas. Even in urban areas there are significant numbers of districts still not connected to the national grid. Regions with the lowest electricity coverage are Coast, Lindi,

Mtwara, Ruvuma, Singida, Rukwa and Kigoma, which constitute 35% of all regions in the country. Moreover, electricity services and related infrastructure are largely poor in urban and desperate in rural areas, but also use of electricity for cooking is reported by only 1 % of households in the country. This is probably because the electricity tariff of 45.05 Tsh/Kwh charged by Tanzania Electricity Supply Company (TANESCO) for domestic use is the highest in the SADC region (Mwandosya et al., 1997; Ubwani, 2003). TANESCO is a monopoly public organization, responsible for producing and distributing electricity throughout the country. The high price of electrical appliances adds to the problem, most of them being unaffordable to many households and agro-based industries. Thus, firewood, which is regarded as free, still provides a cheap alternative that is perceived to be accessible in the foreseeable future, thereby reducing the incentive, at all levels, to pursue alternative energy sources. Under these circumstances, even if all forests in Tanzania are placed under either JFM or CBFM, harvesting woodfuel and charcoal in a sustainable manner remains a surmountable challenge. Another challenge is how to develop viable alternative energy sources and make them accessible to society.

The problem of *poor institutions and limited human capacity* has been discussed earlier and remains a challenge which needs to be surmounted. Extreme shortage of institutional capacity is evident especially at the local government level. A critical shortage of manpower is a common feature in all Local Government Authorities (LGAs). It therefore is almost impossible to ensure implementation of existing forest laws and provide adequate monitoring of forest management activities. For example in 2002 there were only two qualified foresters for the entire Rufiji district, which has some 100, 000 ha of reserved forest and several hundred thousand hectares of unreserved forest (Milledge and Kaale, 2005). Moreover, most of the staff at checkpoints and revenue collecting offices are not trained in forestry and not conversant with species identification, forest policy and law. Poor basic office facilities, and poor equipment, low wages and long working hours all contribute to low morale amongst staff, hence leading to corruption even in places where PFM is operating.

Forest officials belong either to local, central or village governments. However, there are no memoranda of understanding or sharing of benefits and responsibilities amongst the employees of village/district/central governments. In reality incongruent objectives and poor linkages between different institutions and stakeholders is a recipe for creating obstacles to effective participatory forest management. Government revenue collections from joint forest management resources are generally weak because of poor institutional linkages and lack of trained manpower. Timber revenue is collected only if harvesters and transports of timber happen to pass through checkpoints. In most cases traders bypass the checkpoint or collude with forest officials to under-invoice or evade payment of fees. Common practices to avoid fee payment include misclassification of timber, under-declaration of volumes, and transporting wood as planks, semi-processed furniture parts, off-cuts or as wood chips.

Inadequate judicial mechanisms at village, LAG and regional levels impose additional constraints for PFM activities in Tanzania. While local governments can bring court cases under legislation pertaining to the environment, experience shows that repeatedly, such cases are postponed for years because there are no qualified judiciary staff to hear environment related cases. In addition, no formal instrument exists to hear such cases. The competence of the law enforcers, especially in the rural areas is also insufficient and lacks efficient monitoring capacity as alluded to earlier.

All the good programmes developed by the government and local communities require *financing*, which *remains a major constraint*. Although it is envisaged that the sector will continue to receive donor assistance at least in the short and medium term, donor assistance in the forestry sector is declining. Presently there are over 40 donor-supported projects in the country, including PFM initiative activities, involved in the management of forest resources under the central and local governments. Fragmented projects have led to a heavy management and monitoring burden on FBD while also creating overlaps and inefficient in resource use. The Government is now developing a Sector Programme Approach, inspired by the Sector-Wide Programme (SWAP) for donor assistance under basket funding. It is expected that this will reduce the multitude of administrative roles and paperwork involved in programme management.

Although this arrangement intends to encourage donors to negotiate and develop larger technical assistance packages, optimizing the use of scarce human and financial resources, while increasing ownership, commitment and reducing overlaps, it also implies that the PFM activities will now have to compete equally with other projects in the country to access funds from one basket. The forest sector in Tanzania has not yet fully exploited innovative new financing mechanisms, which can be used, particularly in financing the production of non-tangible forest services such as biodiversity conservation amenities and watershed conservation. Initiatives such as the Eastern Arc Conservation Endowment Fund, GEF, Kijani Initiatives, Kilombero CDM, are among the few emerging examples which have managed to secure alternative funding. These are all still in their infancy, but quite promising at this stage. Many stakeholders in the forestry sector should be ready to learn from their achievements and problems.

Conclusion and Recommendations

The preceding analysis attempted to determine some of Tanzania's trajectories in terms of forestry development, policy options and resulting legal aspects. The development of the forestry sector in Tanzania compares to similar findings in other poor countries where there have been periods of growth (in terms of the resource, related institutions and people's welfare), only to fizzle out after a while. Most of the forestry and related policies which were adopted immediately after independence, neither improved the quality of forests in the country, nor the lives of most citizens. Even the policies, which were pursued during the transition to a market economy from mid-1986, did not match with sustainable forests management practices. In Tanzania, structural adjustment has increased rates of environmental degradation by for instance increasing agro-input prices. Lack of resources hindered smooth enforcement of regulations, and then most of the forest areas became open access resources where nothing was managed and anyone could use the resources as they pleased without constraints.

The mergence of these trajectories led to a situation where villages and all the other administrative layers of the government moved in the same direction, providing mutual support for each other towards promoting, supporting and implementing participatory forest management. Although the Tanzanian experience with PFM shows a promising future for a conservation pattern which takes into account power relationships and control over forests, while increasing citizen participation at the community level, there are widespread feelings that collaborative management is failing to meet the required expectations of various stakeholders. This paper recommends that efforts should be directed to address constraints emanating when implementing collaborative management. In tandem to this, there should be serious efforts and strategies to develop alternative energy sources, as well as other livelihood options and make them accessible to communities, especially the poor among them.

Reference

Abdallah, J.M. and J. Sauer 2007, " Forest diversity, tobacco production and resource management in Tanzania", *Forest Policy and Economics* 9 (5) 421–439 ISSN 1339-9341.

Ahlback, A. J. 1986, "Industrial plantation forestry in Tanzania – Facts, problems and challenges". Ministry of Natural Resources and Tourism, Forestry ,and Beekeeping Division, Dar es Salaam.

Bromley, D.W. 1992, "Property rights as authority systems: The role of rules in resource management", *Journal of Business Administration* 20(1-2):453-470.

CIFOR 2004, "Forests for people and environment". CIFOR Annual Report 2004.

FAO 1999, *The State of the World's Forests, 1999.* Rome: FAO Information Division, 154 p.

—, 2000, *A strategy for sustainable forest management in Africa.* Proceedings of international workshop on community forestry, Rome, Italy.

—, 2002, *Forest Genetic Resources,* No. 30. Edited by Palmberg-Lerche, C., Iversen, P. A., Sigaud, P., Rome.

FBD 2006, "Participatory Forest Management in Tanzania - Facts and Figures" . Extension and Publicity Unit of the Forestry and Beekeeping Division of the Ministry of Natural Resources and Tourism, Dar es Salaam, July 2006.

Iddi, S. 2002a, "Community participation in forest management in the United Republic of Tanzania", in *Defining the way forward: Sustainable livelihoods and sustainable forest management through participatory forestry.* Proceedings of the second international workshop on participatory forestry in Africa. Arusha, Tanzania, 18–22 February pp. 59–67.

—, 2002b, "Community Involvement in Forest Management: First Experiences from Tanzania: The Gologolo Joint Forest Management Project: A Case Study from the West Usambara Mountains". In the Proceedings of the International Workshop on Community Forestry in Africa. April 26 –30, 1999. FAO/FTPP/GTZ/Republic of Gambia, Banjul, pp. 153-162.

IFAD (undated), "Why Women Should Be Included in Village Natural Resource Management". Rome.

Kaale, B.K. and E.N. Sawe 2001, *Wood Fuel Strategy Options.* TaTEDO report presented to the Ministry of Natural Resources and Tourism (website http://www.see-net.co.tz/www.see-net.co.tz).

Kajembe, G.C. 1994, "Indigenous management systems as a basis for community forestry in Tanzania: A case study of Dodoma urban and Lushoto Districts". *Tropical Resource Management Paper Series,* no. 6. Wageningen Agricultural University, the Netherlands

Kajembe, G.C. and J.F. Kessy 1999, "Joint forest management in Urumwa Forest Reserve, Tabora, Tanzania: A process in the making", in Virtanen, P. and M. Nummelin (eds), *Forests, chiefs and peasants in Africa: Local management of natural resources in Tanzania, Zimbabwe and Mozambique,* University of Joensuu, Finland. Silva Carelica, 34:141-58.

Kajembe, G.C. and J.S. Mgoo 1999, "Evaluation Report on Community-Based Forest Management Approach in Babati District: A case of Duru-Haitemba Village Forest Reserve". Orgut Consulting AB, Stockholm (Unpublished).

Kajembe, G.C., J.N. Duwamungu and E.J. Luoga 2000a, "The impact of community-based forest management and joint forest management on forest resource base and local people's livelihoods: Case studies from Tanzania". *Commons Southern Africa occasional paper series,* no. 8.

Kajembe, G.C., V.B.M.S. Kihiyo, A.Y Banana, W. Gombya-Sembajwe and. P. Ongugo 2000b, *Community participation in the management of protected forest areas in East Africa: Opportunities and challenges.*

Kihiyo, V.B.M.S 1998, "Forest policy changes in Tanzania: towards community participation in forest management". The World Bank/WBI s CBNRM Initiative Sokoine University of Agriculture.

Little, P. 1994, "The Link between Local Participation and Improved Conservation: A Review of Issues and Experiences", in Western, D. and R. Wright (eds), *Natural Connections: Perspectives in Community-Based Conservation.* Washington, DC: Island Press, pp. 347-372.

Luoga, E.J., P.O. Ongugo, G.C. Kajembe, D.K. Shemwetta, D. Silayo, G. Sigu and J.W. Njuguna 2006a, "Linking Mount Kilimanjaro Forest Resources to physical, socio-political and institutional factors: A cross border comparative analysis". IFRI policy brief.

Luoga, E.J., G.C. Kajembe and B.S. Mohamed 2006b, "Impact of Joint Forest Management on Handeni Hill Forest Reserve and Adjacent Communities in Tanga, Tanzania".

Milledge, S.A.H. and B.K. Kaale 2005, *Bridging the Gap:Linking timber trade with infrastructural development in Southern Tanzania — Baseline data before completion of Mkapa Bridge.* TRAFFIC Network.

MNRT 1998, *Forest Policy of Tanzania.* Dar es Salaam: Government Printer, 56p.

Monela, G.C., G.C. Kajembe, A.R.S Kaoneka and G. Kowero 2000, "Household livelihood strategies in the Miombo woodlands of Tanzania", *Tanzania Journal of Forestry and nature Conservation,* Vol. 73.

Mwandosya, M.J., Luhanga, B.E. and M. Mahanyu 1997, "Current status and the regulatory framework of electricity in Tanzania", in Mwandosya M.J., F.M. George and P. Young (eds), *Competition policy and utility regulation.* Dar es Salaam, Tanzania.

Mufindi District Profile 2006, *Strategic Plan for Mufindi District Council –Iringa Tanzania.*

Nindie, R.M. and H.A. Mbise 1995, "Sources of Energy: Wood Fuel Consumption in Tanzania and Impact on the Environment", in Njau, G.J. and E.K. Mugurusi (eds), *Towards Sustainable Environment in Tanzania.* Environment Division, Dar es Salaam.

Rani, K.U. (undated), "Empowering Women Through Natural and Social Resource".

Reed, D. 1996, *Structural Adjustment, the Environment and Sustainable Development.* London: Earthscan, pp. 107-127.

Shayo, H. 2006, "Forestry governance in limbo in Tanzania". London South Bank University. *RICS research paper series*, Vol. 6 No. 5.

Ubwani, Z. 2003, "Experts Seek Power Tariff Changes in Tanzania". [http://www.nationaudio.com/News/EastAfrican/060999/Regional/ Regional45.htm] site visited on October 15.

Wily, A.L. 1995, "Collaborative forest management. Village and Government: A case of Mgori forest reserve".

World Bank 2002, "Tanzania: Managing forest resources", *Infobrief*, no. 72.

WRM 2002, "Tanzania: Community-based forest management as a way forward for conservation", *Bulletin*, no 58.

Ylhäisi, J. 2003, "The tortuous path toward better resource management on a national scale". The University of Helsinki.

CHAPTER EIGHT

TRENDS IN CORRUPTION DURING
THE MKAPA ERA – WHO WANTS TO KNOW?

Brian Cooksey

Introduction

The period 1995-2005 covers the years of the 'Third Phase' government of President Benjamin Mkapa. It is widely accepted that President Mkapa inherited a state apparatus from the 'Second Phase' government of President Ali Hassan Mwinyi characterised by high levels of 'official' corruption and the misuse of foreign aid.

While continuing with the policies of economic liberalisation and political democratisation initiated by the Second Phase government, President Mkapa pledged to eradicate the corruption that threatened to undermine the legitimacy of the ruling party and the government. This paper examines the record of the Third Phase government in reducing corruption in Tanzania, and tries to come to some conclusions on the current situation.

A number of constraints make it extremely difficult to come to firm conclusions. First, there are large gaps in the available literature, particularly regarding the nature, extent and impact of political corruption. Second, given the informal nature of corrupt transactions, it is virtually impossible to quantify trends. Third, although in recent years the various components of governance have been 'unbundled', the governance component called 'corruption' remains curiously 'bundled'. All this means that the conclusions drawn from the analysis are likely to be strongly influenced by the interests and ideological preferences of the author.

Why do I ask 'who wants to know'? Both aid recipients and donor agencies are gearing up for further large increases in aid transfers. Naturally, both want to hear the good, not the bad, news. Increasingly, aid agencies use trends in governance and corruption control to justify aid disbursements and debt relief.

Donors and the Government of Tanzania draw selectively on the empirical governance/corruption record. Recent history is quickly forgotten on both sides when it comes to justifying the next round of aid. In part, power inheres in the ability of both sides to dominate the development discourse on the basis of a selective reading of the historical record. If you read the left hand columns in *Appendix 1, Figures 1 and 2*, you may find enough 'good news' to justify more aid to Tanzania. If, on the other hand, you read the right hand columns, you are more likely to conclude that the Tanzanian government is seriously under-performing on most governance indicators, making further increases in aid a risky proposition. Though there are many gaps in our knowledge, there is no firm evidence from the governance/corruption literature that could be used to justify further increases in development assistance to Tanzania.

The chapter draws on a review of the record of the Mkapa presidency on governance and anti-corruption.[26]

Governance and corruption, poverty and growth[27]

The quality of governance influences the rate and depth of social and economic development.[1] In the aid and development literature, corruption is conceptualised as a core component of governance. Analysts differ in the relative weight they attribute to corruption and other aspects of governance in determining development outcomes. Corruption undermines governance, but does not necessarily prevent growth or poverty reduction. Some countries with high levels of official corruption achieve high levels of growth and poverty reduction, others do not. Most of the 'others' are in sub-Saharan Africa (SSA).

There are a number of possible explanations for the concentration of low growth and high poverty levels in SSA. Apart from 'governance' issues, analysts look for explanations *inter alia* in history, geography, politics and economics. For example, some stress the long-term negative impact of the slave trade, colonialism and imperialism.[28] Others highlight the geographical isolation of much of SSA, and the effects of climate on soils and disease vectors, malaria in particular.[29] A third group highlights the nature of patronage and 'neo-patrimonialism' in African politics.[30] Yet others stress unfair trading relations, agricultural subsidies, tariff and non-tariff barriers in OECD countries.[31]

---

[26] Cooksey 2005, B., Report commissioned by the Governance Working Group and financed by the Royal Norwegian Embassy, Dar es Salaam. In **Appendix I**, I summarise the main findings from the report.
[27] This section draws on Cooksey 2005b:xiii-xiv.
[28] For example, Walter Rodney (1972).
[29] For example, Sachs (2005).
[30] For example, Chabal and Daloz (1999).
[31] For example, Oxfam (2002).

There is merit in considering all possible explanations for SSA's particular status in the global pecking-order. However, it is likely that governance and corruption constraints account for a significant, though variable, proportion of African countries' poverty and relative economic stagnation. My review suggests that both the low quality of governance and high levels of corruption continue to seriously undermine Tanzania's development prospects. The progress made to date in corruption control (see below) is a drop in the ocean compared to the magnitude of the problem.

Trends in governance and corruption in Tanzania[32]

In recent years, analysts have attempted to distinguish corruption control from other aspects of governance. The World Bank Institute has pioneered this work, commissioning studies and collating information from numerous international surveys to measure changes in various governance indicators. Corruption control, voice and accountability, government effectiveness, the rule of law, political stability and regulatory quality have been 'unbundled' for this purpose. In most cases, surveys record perceptions rather than more 'objective' indicators, though personal experiences may also be documented. **Table 1** shows trends in the six WBI governance indicators for Tanzania over the period 1998-2004.

Table 1: Tanzania governance indicators (1998-2004)

Governance indicator	Change (%)
Corruption control	+24.5
Voice and accountability	+2.4
Government effectiveness	+0.9
Rule of law	–9.5
Political stability	–27.4
Regulatory quality	–28.0
Average of all indicators	–4.6

Source: Adapted from Cooksey 2005b:48 and WBI (2005)[8]

According to the World Bank Institute, Tanzania's performance in corruption control during 1998-2004 has been creditable; in terms of voice and accountability and governance effectiveness there has been no significant change; as regards rule of law there has been a slight deterioration; and political stability and regulatory quality have deteriorated markedly (**Table 1**). When averaged out, 'governance' in Tanzania has *not changed significantly* in the recent past.

---

[32] World Bank Institute (2005).

The positive trend in corruption control is confirmed by the research summarised in *Appendix 3,* which compares Tanzania's performance with a number of other African countries on Transparency International's Corruption Perception Index for the same period (1998-2004). Tanzania's CPI score has improved steadily during this period both in absolute terms and compared to a number of other African countries. The rest of this paper takes these six governance indicators and provides further evidence from my review, summarised in *Appendix 1.*

Unbundling corruption and 'corruption control' (*Appendix 1, Figure 1*)

The sources cited above conclude that, both in absolute terms and by comparison with other African countries, Tanzania has made significant progress in combating corruption. But what does corruption mean in this context? Is it the *petty corruption* practised by low level civil servants, the *grand corruption* practised by senior civil servants and politicians, or the *political corruption* practised by the political class? The answer seems to be the first type: petty corruption. Both the WBI and Transparency International aggregate the results of a number of international surveys. Respondents are often managers of businesses, both national and international, investment risk analysts and others who are deemed to be well informed on the business and investment climates in particular countries. 'Corruption' for this group means corruption in government-business relations, including corruption in setting up businesses, obtaining work permits and land titles, trading licences, paying taxes, and so on.[33]

We may conclude that Tanzania's good recent performance in 'corruption control' reflects local and foreign *perceptions* that petty corruption in government-business relations is less serious a constraint than it was previously.[34] Whatever the case, nearly two-thirds of countries in the WBI data base have better scores than Tanzania even after the reduction in corruption identified by WBI and TI, and Tanzania still scores less than 3/10 in TI's global rankings. The glass is still 70 percent empty.

Of course, this leaves unanswered questions concerning the nature of and trends in grand and political corruption, which are discussed below.

---

[33] Grand and political corruption are also found in government-business relations, of course.

[34] The CPI has been challenged on the grounds that it is based on external perceptions of corruption. This is not entirely true, and comparisons show strong correlations between external and internal perceptions.

Petty corruption

Numerous reforms are underway to improve governance and reduce corruption in government. Yet considerable evidence presented in my report suggests that the government has not been successful in addressing petty corruption in service delivery. Most household and service delivery surveys find larger proportions of respondents who believe that corruption is increasing rather than going down.[35] Significant numbers indicate personal experience of corruption, particularly in relations with the police. One rough estimate suggests that the average civil servant obtains *around half* his or her income from corruption. The argument that petty corruption can be addressed by raising salaries does not seem a very powerful one.

Grand corruption

None of the available data on the incidence of corruption captures trends in grand or political corruption. However, there is broad agreement that the government of President Mkapa has marked up major successes in reining in some of the excesses of the Mwinyi years (1985-95). Reversing the abuse of aid money and poor revenue collection are cases in point. Yet a relative improvement does not solve the problem of grand corruption in procurement and contracting, waste in public investment practices and the large-scale misuse of public monies from local and external sources that are described in the recent literature, and summarised in *Appendix 1*. These continue to constitute a tremendous drain on public resources.[36] Equally sobering are the waste and inefficiency inherent in central and local government procedures and practices.

Political corruption

Tanzania benefits tremendously from relatively low levels of conflict and violence in the political process, and, related to this, a governance system that manages to rise above the country's ethnic, religious, regional and cultural divisions. These frequently mentioned attributes limit the extent to which *public resources are diverted for purposes of political corruption,* or to quell popular unrest. The move to competitive politics has not fundamentally undermined these attributes, though they are by no means unassailable in the medium- to longer-term.

---

[35] See Cooksey 2005b, Table 4 for a geographical breakdown. The better-off/urban respondents are more likely to perceive an increase in the incidence of corruption than the poor.

[36] A corrupt deal costing the Tanzanian people and donors (say) $40m would be the equivalent of $1.8 billion in Sweden in terms of its impact on the economy (Sweden's GNI is 45 times Tanzania's).

Disputes over Tanzania's rich and varied natural resources have not led to the systematic political violence and social disruption that are common in other countries. Yet some would argue that the unsustainable plunder of natural resources[37] has reached epidemic proportions.[38] Without politics, natural resource plunder would be less feasible, though there are also elements of both grand and petty corruption in natural resource 'exploitation'.[39]

In sum, there seems to have been a substantial reduction in the level of petty corruption affecting foreign and local business and investment, but the degree of corruption in service delivery does not seem to have fallen significantly, and on balance the public perceives such corruption to be increasing. Grand corruption trends are impossible to quantify accurately, but there is little to suggest that grand corruption in construction, tendering, procurement, the misuse of central government funds, foreign aid and natural resources is in any way under control. Political corruption has not reached typical SSA levels, meaning that public resources are not dissipated on maintaining public order and keeping rulers in power to the same extent as elsewhere. Maintaining 'peace and unity' may become more costly in future, however, for reasons outlined below.

Voice and accountability

The WBI data base indicates no significant progress in voice and accountability over the 1998-2004 period. The other side of the 'peace and unity' coin described above is an extremely unaccountable executive, and a state bureaucracy that provides mediocre social and economic services, protection of property and citizens' rights. Increasingly, *the executive appears to be frustrating the necessary improvements in governance and anti-corruption that are the fundamental preconditions for poverty reduction and broad-based growth.*[40] According to some critics, political competition has resulted in less, not more, freedom of public debate, with the executive systematically preventing parliamentary discussion of overly 'sensitive' matters and oversight of public expenditure, and greater public access to information.[41]

---

[37] Timber, fisheries, wildlife, gold and gemstones *outside* the main gold mines.

[38] According to one estimate, if current trends continue, most Tanzanian forests will have disappeared by 2020 with immeasurable knock-on effects on water catchment, soil erosion, bio-diversity, climate change, and so on.

[39] The poor are also involved in unsustainable natural resource use (for example, charcoal production) but their motives are 'need' rather than 'greed'.

[40] I give examples from parliamentary oversight, judicial reform, anti-corruption legislation and other sectors in my report.

[41] Donor support for democratisation may well have had negative consequences in this respect.

Government effectiveness

The WBI data base indicates no significant progress in government effectiveness over the 1998-2004 period. If true, this is extremely disheartening given the enormous efforts and resources dedicated to institutional strengthening and capacity building by government and donors in recent years. Debt relief and budget support have triggered substantial increases in key sector spending, but there is little evidence that additional resources have brought about improved basic services.[42] Key constraints to service delivery have not been addressed. Improvements have been unevenly distributed across the country, have been largely quantitative, and in some cases have not been sustained. The poor see fewer benefits from additional spending than the wealthy. The perception revealed by national surveys is that corruption is on the increase in relation to service provision, but waste and inefficiency are also major constraints.

Rule of law

Despite reform efforts, the rule of law seems to have deteriorated in recent years. The judiciary is widely considered to be corrupt and inefficient, and justice is routinely delayed and denied. Legal reform has been slow to take off, despite substantial donor support.[43] The judiciary is bureaucratic, passive, and incapable of forcing decisions on the government. A recent review concluded that: 'The courts in … Tanzania tend to restrain their judicial authority to hold government accountable because the legal culture, the institutional structure, and the social legitimacy of the courts serve to minimize their willingness to challenge the executive.' Mismanagement and corruption leading to the loss of lives and property go unpunished.

The President's Office (PSM) found that 64 percent of respondents considered Primary Court officers to be corrupt. The author concludes: 'Most troubling is the low honesty ratings given to the institutions responsible for upholding ethical standards: in particular, the Industrial Court, Judiciary, and Ethics Secretariat.'

---

[42]   See for example REPOA (2003) and Cooksey and Mamdani (2003).

[43]   Donors have basket-funded the Legal Sector Reform Programme ($44m) the major component of which is construction and rehabilitation work on court buildings in Dar es Salaam and elsewhere. Commercial cases have been dealt with in a more expedite manner since the establishment of the Commercial Court.

Political stability

WBI figures (2005) indicate a sharp deterioration in political stability in recent years. This is in large part a reflection of the standoff between the ruling party and the opposition CUF in Zanzibar and Pemba, where elections have been aborted and lives lost in political violence. Though the situation has been contained on the mainland, there are worrying signs of potential political conflicts based on religion, and the time-bomb of mass poverty, rising inequality and unemployment bodes ill for the future.[44]

Regulatory quality

Economic regulation can be inefficient for reasons other than corruption, and this seems to have been picked up by recent surveys. This at least would be one explanation for the substantial deterioration in regulatory quality reported by WBI compared with the improvement in corruption control. Examples of poor regulation and complaints by the private sector abound. A recent important trend is the empowerment of boards regulating export crops.[45] The boards both regulate and act as commercial players in input and export markets. Most of the boards' revenues are from trade licenses and levies on farmers but most of their expenditure is on administration and the cost of the boards of directors.

Though the WBI report a deterioration in the quality of regulation, many observers have signalled substantial gains at the level of macro-economic management (balanced budget and inflation control), the tax regime (substantial and sustained increases in tax income as a proportion of GNP), and in the performance of the formal economy (successful privatisation of productive sectors, banking and services; increased inward investment flows). In these and other respects, Tanzania has made great strides away from a state owned and managed towards a market-driven economy. Some of these 'gains' are hotly contested, in particular foreign investment in the mining sector and the privatisation of public utilities.[46]

The role of donors

Many believe that 'good governance' and anti-corruption policies and programmes are largely donor-inspired and therefore lacking in local

---

[44] See Cooksey and Mamdani (2003) for a review of recent findings on poverty and inequality. There are high expectations among young people that the Phase 4 government will deliver on its campaign promise of 'maisha bora kwa kila Mtanzania'.

[45] See Cooksey (2005a).

[46] Privatisation and private-sector regulation create new opportunities for corruption, of course, and Tanzania's first example of private-public partnership--the IPTL power plant--has been an unmitigated disaster, that is taking on a permanent character.

'ownership' and commitment. They are seen as half-hearted reactions to donor pressures rather than determined attempts to deal with the routine abuses of power and authority that continue to plague the country. In a word, there are no *authentic, national, anti-corruption politics.* Naturally, other observers, and aid recipients, dispute this view.

The report presents both 'pro'- and 'anti'-aid arguments, but leaves open the question of whether, on balance, aid supports or undermines efforts to improve governance and accountability, and reduce corruption. Whatever the case - and evidence is sorely lacking - there is no cause to see aid as *essentially* or *inevitably* a force for good, if 'good' is taken to mean supporting the creation of viable, 'developmental' public institutions.

One critical view is that government policy and donor aid are overly focused on the 'supply side' of service delivery, ignoring the need for greater downward accountability and less asymmetric access to information. While there is merit in this argument, it is still a major objective of donor support to strengthen the internal accountability mechanisms within state institutions.

Aid agencies do themselves no credit by ignoring or – worse - condoning egregious examples of bad governance and corruption that undermine both national development efforts and the rationale for donor support.

Mkapa's heritage[47]

President Mkapa's own changing position on corruption can be gauged from the trend in the tone and content of his public statements since coming to power (**Box 1**).

President Mkapa's discourse has evolved from a crusading anti-corruption stance that is impatient with due process to an increasingly aggressive and truculent posture challenging the public to 'bring proof', and not take 'wealth' as evidence of corruption. The burden of 'proof' now lies with the public, not the accused official. Corruption is assumed to be largely petty (bribing to get soap, traffic offences) and the public is now defined as the corrupter (bribing police officers and magistrates *for offences actually committed*) not the victim of corruption.

Impact of anti-corruption and good governance policies

The global perspective on a decade of anti-corruption is gloomy.[48] The World Bank Institute finds no evidence of a significant improvement in

---

[47] This section is reproduced almost verbatim from Cooksey (2005b:8).
[48] WBI, 2005.

Box 1: Mkapa on corruption 1995-2003

1. Corruption 'is a serious disease in our society; it is an impediment to justice and fairness. It has reached the point where it is a serious impediment to development. ... Corruption now at the political level is perceived as the use of public office for self-enrichment. ' 'Even when there is no evidence, you must be able to call in someone and say "Look ... the perception is that you are a liability. ... So please step aside."' *Interview by Martin 1995*

2. 'We must stop mudslinging [at] one another, but we should not hide corruption when there is evidence.' The President 'called on CCM members and the public as a whole, who have proof that certain individuals are corrupt' to have the courage to name them, 'and support their claims with evidence.' However, he added, wealth was not evidence of corruption. *Addressing the ruling party National Executive Committee, January 2003*

3. 'President Mkapa criticised the media and politicians for accusing his government of corruption, saying instead that such media owners should explain to the public where they got their capital...'. '... there are people, supposedly learned and informed, who would say the situation of ... corruption in Tanzania is worse today than it was two decades ago. It is not true.' '... which is the worse corruption: when you have to bribe to get soap, toilet paper, food and beer; or when you bribe a traffic police officer because of a traffic offence you actually committed, or bribe a magistrate to get off the hook because of a crime you actually committed?' *Addressing the Development Forum, April 2003.*

4. 'Our war on corruption ... cannot succeed without political commitment at all levels of government. I ... hope that ... you will have no reason to doubt the political commitment of my government, up to the highest level...' *Addressing the Southern African Forum against Corruption,* 9 August, 2003

5. 'There is corruption in Tanzania, as there is corruption in practically all countries, but at different levels. [World Bank] research shows[s] that in the whole of the sub-Saharan region only Tanzania made significant improvements in all three governance indicators – accountability; government effectiveness and control of corruption.' Addressing Parliament in Dodoma, August 2005.[2]

Source: Cooksey 2005b

global governance indicators in general, though some countries have done significantly better than others. What about Tanzania? The government and its supporters claim that anti-corruption efforts have been successful and that it is 'winning the war against corruption'. This view is contested by the public, who see corruption as widespread, and constant or increasing rather than going down.

The record of the Mkapa presidency teaches us that there is no obvious solution to the corruption problem, and, perhaps, that the 'supply-side' strategy supported by donors has run its course. More broadly, this holds for the entire 'good governance'/democratisation project. Whether aid agencies can support real changes in the balance between executive power and public accountability, rather than undermine such changes by continuing to provide massive financial support to the Tanzanian state, remains to be seen.

Van de Walle[49] defines 'stagnant low-income states'--Tanzania included--as combining 'poor economic performance with governance problems and corruption. Indeed, their poverty results in large part from their lack of virtue.' My review suggests that, despite progress in dismantling the commandist economy of the socialist era, as well as in eliminating some of the worst forms of short-sighted plunder that characterised the Mwinyi years, the underlying governance weaknesses that I have reviewed continue to overwhelm government-plus-donor attempts at reform.

Who wants to know?

Of course, research and reflection are not objective processes that create new knowledge in some pristine intellectual space.[3] The numerous ongoing international initiatives aimed at mobilising resources to reduce/eliminate poverty--particularly in Africa--have generally ignored the literature on aid (in)effectiveness and the moral hazards inherent in aid dependency. In an environment where the pro-aid lobbies are in the ascendant, voices urging caution are not particularly welcome.

My investigations lead me to conclude that, under present and foreseeable future circumstances, there is no empirical basis to suggest that further increases in aid to Tanzania will improve the country's chances of achieving significant poverty reduction or sustainable economic growth. The basic problem seems to be that GOT/donor policies to promote poverty reduction and growth are systematically frustrated at the implementation phase by the bad governance (=waste and inefficiency) and corruption that continue to characterise central and local government. Bad governance

---

[49] van de Walle (2005).

means systemic and unpunished corruption throughout the state bureau-cracy, lack of public accountability, ineffective and inequitable service delivery, a powerless judiciary and counterproductive economic regula-tion. That Tanzania still remains a relatively peaceful country owes more to the quiescence of its long-suffering populace than to the wisdom or statecraft of its rulers.

Tanzania's star has risen in the donor firmament in recent years as a result of President Mkapa's implementation of externally-driven economic reforms. Recent above average growth in GNI is largely driven by gold mining and tourism, not agriculture or other poverty-reducing sectors. President Mkapa's record on governance and corruption is much less impressive than the hype surrounding the end of his presidency would suggest. All indica-tors suggest that the Phase 4 government will continue, for better or worse, where Phase 3 left off. Donor agencies' lack of vision or preparedness to address the underlying issues does not encourage optimism that enhanced aid transfers can be mobilised to leverage virtuous change.

References

Chabal, Patrick and Jean-Pascal Daloz 1999, *Africa works: Disorder as a political instrument*. Oxford: James Currey.

Cooksey, Brian and Masuma Mamdani 2003, "Summary of conclusions from recent research and synthesis of key issues on poverty in Tanza-nia". Dar es Salaam: REPOA.

Cooksey, Brian 2005a, "Marketing reform? The rise and fall of agricultural liberalisation in Tanzania", in Frank Ellis and H. Ade Freeman (eds), *Rural Livelihoods and Poverty Reduction Policies*. London: Routledge, Chapter 10.

—, 2005b, "Corruption and Governance In Tanzania: What does the liter-ature say?" Report for the Royal Norwegian Embassy and the Gover-nance Working Group, Dar es Salaam, Revised Draft, September.

Kaufmann, Daniel 2004, "Corruption Matters: Evidence-Based Chal-lenge to Orthodoxy", *Journal of Development Policy and Practice*, Vol 1, No. 1. Canadian International Development Agency, December.

Oxfam 2002, *Rigged Rules and Double Standards: Trade, globalisation, and the fight against poverty*. Oxfam International: www.maketradefair.com.

Rabinow, Paul (ed) 1991, *The Foucault Reader*. Penguin Books.

Research on Poverty Alleviation 2003, "Policy and Service Satisfaction Survey: Main Survey Results", Dar es Salaam, October.

Rodney, Walter 1972, *How Europe Underdeveloped Africa*. Dar es Salaam: Tanzania Publishing House.

Sachs, Jeffrey D. 2005, *The End of Poverty: Economic Possibilities for Our Time*. New York: Penguin.

Sundet, Geir 2004, "How African countries have performed on the Transparency International Corruption Perception Index", mimeo, Dar es Salaam, October.

van de Walle, Nicolas 2005, *Overcoming Stagnation in Aid-Dependent Countries*, Centre for Global Development.

World Bank Institute 2005, "Governance and Anti-Corruption", World Bank, Washington: http://info.worldbank.org/governance.

Appendix 1

The following figures summarise the main findings from this literature review on trends in corruption and governance. **Figure 1** reviews corruption trends and issues, **Figure 2** trends in governance.

Figure 1 Trends in corruption & anti-corruption

THE GOOD NEWS	THE BAD NEWS
Perceptions and experience of corruption	
Tanzania's performance on Transparency International's *Corruption Perception Index* has improved significantly in both absolute and relative terms (1998-2004). World Bank estimates confirm the trend.	Half the respondents in a recent survey thought corruption was increasing, while a third thought it was going down.
	Recent research in six LGA found that 39% of respondents thought corruption was a worse problem than two years previously, and 27% that it was less of a problem.
	In another survey, 81% of respondents thought corruption was very or quite common among the police, and 62% among civil servants. In a summary of 36 service delivery surveys, a third of respondents said they were asked to pay a bribe and 13 percent actually paid; the average bribe was TShs 22,000 ($20). There is no serious deterrence to corruption in terms of employment sanction.
Official anti-corruption initiatives	
The *Report of the Presidential Commission of Enquiry Against Corruption (1996)* was compiled and published within a year of President Mkapa coming to power. After the publication of the 'Warioba Report' there were some attempts at 'house-cleaning' at the top and lower levels of central government and parastatal sectors.	Despite 'house-cleaning' initiatives, during 1995-2005, no senior official has been jailed for corruption.

The *National Anti-Corruption Strategy and Action Plan* addresses corruption in central ministries, and contains components for civil society and media involvement in anti-corruption activities.	President Mkapa and other government leaders urge the people to 'provide evidence' of corruption, even though officials do not take kindly to being exposed.
Since 1995, the *Prevention of Corruption Bureau* has enjoyed increased funding from central government and donors, allowing it to hire more staff and expand its regional activities. The number of complaints reported has risen sharply.	PCB lacks independence from the government, which prevents high-profile investigations from being taken to court. Very few complaints end up in court, and the majority of those that do are either dismissed or lost. Even the 'small fish' appear to get away with acts of petty corruption more often than not. A derisory sum of money has been returned to the state.
An *Ethics Secretariat* was established in 1995 under the Public Leadership Code of Ethics Act.	There is no attempt to verify whether declarations of assets are authentic. The Secretariat does not publish an annual report and there is no information on the number of complaints, the nature of the complaints, or the decision of the Commissioner on how they were handled.
On coming to power, President Mkapa declared his assets, and obliged his cabinet to do the same.	There were no public declarations of assets after the 2000 elections.
The *Good Governance Coordination Unit* implements the *National Anti-Corruption Strategy and Action Plans* (NACSAP). Since October 2000, government ministries, departments and agencies (MDAs) have developed their own action plans designed to promote transparency, simplify rules and procedures and make information accessible to the public.	NACSAP is heavily donor-driven rather than emerging from the internal (national) political process and is unlikely to have much impact on the incidence of official corruption. *NACSAP* relies heavily on the willingness of ministries and departments to regulate themselves.

In 2003, the *Commission for Human Rights and Good Governance* replaced the Permanent Commission of Inquiry.	The government is not bound by the decisions of the Commission, and has refused to abide by key Commission findings.
Under donor pressure, the government 'is preparing a new anti-corruption law to provide … a comprehensive framework for the effective prosecution of … corruption'.	The multitude of organisations created by the GoT to deal with ethics and corruption are administratively expensive and their effectiveness potentially hampered by inadequate resources, inappropriate powers and overlapping roles and responsibilities.
Political corruption	
Afrobarometer found that Tanzanians trust their president more that any other citizens in East and Southern Africa.	A 2003 survey found 41% of respondents agreeing that the government was doing its best to fight corruption and 50% disagreeing.
By regional standards, Tanzania exhibits an extremely *low level of political corruption*.	Sixty-two percent of Tanzanians believe that the best way to get ahead is to have contacts with people in high places.
Elections under the multi-party system are relatively peaceful (except in Zanzibar) and there have been no attempts to extend presidential terms beyond the current ten years.	The 2000 Presidential Elections were characterised by the following types of corruption: 1. Corruption in nominations. CCM's preferential voting system is alleged to be corrupted by vote buying at all levels; 2. Corruption in registration. Registering under-age voters (Zanzibar), selecting electoral officials through patronage, double registration; 3. Corruption in campaigns. Abuse of *takrima*, dubious door-to-door canvassing, donations from businessmen individually and in groups; 4. Abuse of political office: President, Vice-President, Prime Minister use public resources for party political ends, promising benefits to communities if they vote for them, threatening punishment if they do not, provision of T-shirts, khangas and caps. Conclusion: The 2000 elections were 'free but not fair'.

In the ruling party, an Ethics Committee screens parliamentary candidates, and giving gifts to potential supporters over and above traditional hospitality ('takrima') is formally banned.	During the short-listing process for the ruling party's presidential candidate, CCM's chief executive Philip Magula singled out Jakaya Kikwete and former Prime Minister John Malecela 'for excessive use of money in their campaigns' [for the presidential candidature].
Central and local government income and expenditure	
There was a significant *downward trend* in levels of questioned central government revenue and expenditure during the period 1998-2002.	There was a substantial *increase* in questionable expenditure in local government authorities during 1997-2003.
Government budgetary processes have improved in quality; expenditures are reported with more timeliness and accuracy.	The misuse of funds by agencies and individuals is not adequately reported or punished.
In recent years, budget allocations to 'pro-poor' sectors have risen significantly and been maintained.	A 1999 tracking study in three districts found that 57 percent of education non-salary spending was diverted to other uses and 88 percent in the case of health. Councils used other charges for health and education for staff allowances, supplies for the district office and fuel and maintenance for district vehicles. In primary education, the opacity of the financial flows makes reporting difficult and increases the chances of abuse. Leakages in the 'book component' of PEDP were more than 60 percent, compared with less than 20 percent for the 'cash component'.
	Based on some broad assumptions, a very tentative estimate is that on average public servants receive the equivalent of 45 percent of their salary through corruption.
A Public Procurement Bill was approved in November 2004 and received Presidential Assent in February 2005.	An estimated 20 percent of the government expenditure on procurement is lost through corruption, mainly through kick-backs and bogus investments. The loss is equivalent to about *USD 300 million* per year. Procurement capacity in LGAs is 'pathetic' and huge losses are being occasioned through poor procurement practices.

Natural resource management	
Investments in mining and tourism have stimulated Tanzania's growth rate in recent years.	Fishing, hunting and logging licensing and regulation, and building and agricultural land allocation, are all vulnerable to corruption, both petty and grand.
Disputes over the control of Tanzania's natural resources have not led to the systematic corruption, plunder, violence and social disruption that is common in other countries.	If current trends continue, most Tanzanian forests will have disappeared by 2020 with unmeasurable knock-on effects on water catchment, bio-diversity, climate regulation, cultural practices, ...
Capital investments	
The Warioba report identified roads, infrastructure and construction as foci of grand corruption. Senior officials, including a Minister, arraigned over corruption in aid to road construction.	Minister freed after successful appeal.
	Public investments contested on the grounds of alleged corruption, overpricing, and low investment priority include: $40m BAe radar system; $60m Bank of Tanzania Twin Towers; $63m Mafuta House; other parastatal-financed office buildings; $47m presidential jet.
	Merimeta, a joint venture between the Ministry of Defence and South African investors to purchase and export gold, collapsed with a loss to the government of at least $130 million.
Privatisation	
Since 1995, 219 parastatals have been privatised.	Privatisation of state corporations provides new opportunities for official corruption. Regulation of 'natural' monopolies like power and urban domestic water supply is easily corrupted. Senior officials are given shares in private companies and positions on their boards of directors (mining, telecommunications, cigarettes, banks).

Successful privatisations include Tanzania Breweries Ltd, Tanzania Cigarette Company, Kilombero Sugar Company, and the three cement factories. The end of the Tanzania Telecommunications Company telephone monopoly has introduced competition, with connections to the three private mobile phone companies far outnumbering TTCL's land lines.	Private power generation by Independent Power Tanzania Limited (IPTL) involved grand corruption leading to a derailing of power policy and huge additional costs to the Treasury, donor agencies and electricity consumers. Multi-million dollar rents will continue for 16 years if the project is not closed down.
	The sale of government housing to civil servants (and politicians) may have involved large losses to the Treasury.

Figure 2 **TRENDS IN GOOD AND BAD GOVERNANCE**

THE GOOD NEWS	**THE BAD NEWS**
Trends in governance indicators, 1998-2004 (World Bank 2005)	
Corruption control: +314 % Voice and accountability: +6 % Government effectiveness: +4 %	Political stability: -44% Regulatory quality: -44 % Rule of law: -18 %
Institutional reform	
A lot of progress has been made in recent years in improving the quality of public finance management......	... but there is still a long way to go. Issues of non- compliance, limited execution, inadequate monitoring, insufficient capacity and lack of enforcement need to be resolved.
The civil service has been 'downsized' from 355,000 in 1992 to about 270,600 in 1997. In June 2004, there were 282,000 public servants on the government payroll, less than half the sub-Saharan African average as a proportion of the total population. The wage bill-to-GDP ratio was a modest 4.3 percent in FY2002/03.	Productivity of government employees continues to be undermined by underfunding, low salaries, institutional norms undermining efficiency, waste and corruption.

From 1993-1998 average - real - civil service salaries increased by three-quarters in real terms...	... although the average hides the fact that many grades have lost out. Theory that higher salaries increase productivity and reduce corruption challenged.
In 1999, salaries rose by over half, largely as a result of increases for technical staff and higher cadres	Average salaries are still considered inadequate to meet basic needs, leading to widespread 'petty' corruption, undermining service delivery.
	During FY01/02-03/04, allowances increased by 135 percent, or 22.5 percent of the total wage bill. Sitting allowances and payments for aid-funded, consultancies and assignments constitute other salary supplements. The wrong incentive structure is again gaining prevalence within the public service.
Service delivery	
Since the first Poverty Reduction Strategy, resources committed to pro-poor sectors - in particular education, healthcare, and roads – have risen rapidly.	There is little evidence that additional resources have brought about improved basic services. Key constraints to service delivery have not been addressed. Improvements have been unevenly distributed across the country, have been largely quantitative, and in some cases have not been sustained. The poor see fewer benefits from additional spending than the wealthy. Basic services are under-funded in relation to demand, but corruption, waste and mismanagement make the availability and quality of services much worse.
Basic education has received a positive assessment from the public as a result of the abolition of school fees, new classroom construction and the expansion of enrolments under PEDP.	But quality issues have not been addressed, and system leakages have undermined attempts to increase per capita spending on textbooks and other teaching materials

Healthcare spending has increased significantly under the Poverty Reduction Strategy, with mixed results. REPOA (2003) found that: (1) half the respondents thought that facilities were cleaner than previously; (2) time to reach the health facility had improved in a quarter of cases, and worsened in only five percent; (3) availability of drugs had improved for nearly a third of the sample, it deteriorated for nearly a quarter (23 percent); (4) waiting time had improved in a quarter of cases, but deteriorated in almost a fifth..	(5) a fifth of respondents declared that the cost of treatment had declined; two-fifths said the cost of treatment had risen.
	The availability of domestic water improved during the 2000-03 period for less than a third of survey respondents (23 percent) nationwide and deteriorated for a similar proportion. The cost of water had gone down for 14 percent of respondents nationwide, and increased for 13 and 38 percent of rural and Dar es Salaam residents respectively.
Spending has increased significantly on road repair and maintenance as a result of the Road Fund. More than two-fifths of respondents (43 percent) saw no change in the quality of local road maintenance and repair, a third (35 percent) had seen an improvement, and a quarter (23 percent) noted deterioration.	Major urban roads are not routinely repaired or maintained despite the availability of funds from the Road Fund.
Aid effectiveness	
After the nadir in GOT-donor relations under the Phase II government, the last 10 years have seen major improvements in 'donor confidence' and the level of local ownership of development policies.	In a globalised aid world, local ownership of development policies can only be partial. Policies that are really locally 'owned' are often directly challenging the official (ie donor-driven) policies.

Budget support has boosted discretionary recurrent expenditure in priority 'pro-poor' sectors.	Spending in non-priority sectors has increased pro rata.
Aid has contributed to macroeconomic stability through policy advice and financial support.	Anti-corruption, good governance, and institutional reforms, are also donor-driven, uncoordinated, create parallel structures that serve to emasculate an already weak state in terms of service delivery, and lack local ownership.
Aid has contributed to the democratisation process through policy advice, financial support and support for NGOs.	Aid strengthens the executive at the expense of parliament, civil society and the private sector.
Major efforts have been expended on improving aid coordination and harmonisation.	The low level of aid coordination by recipient governments or by aid agencies themselves adds to transaction costs for senior government officials and increases opportunities for corruption.
Accountability: Role of parliament & the judiciary	
Parliamentarians sometimes embarrass the government by raising the issue of corruption, for example, members of the African Parliamentary Network Against Corruption have raised the IPTL issue.	The ten years of President Mkapa's presidency has not seen a significant improvement in parliament's oversight role, despite the transition to multi-party politics.
Parliament has not debated the Controller and Auditor-General's annual report for the past five years. Other important Public Accounts Committee (PAC) reports have not been debated by parliament.	
	Little evidence of parliament's scrutiny of the budget improving significantly since the expansion of discretionary spending in the budget.

Donors have basket-funded the Legal Sector Reform Programme ($44m) the major component of which is construction and rehabilitation work on court buildings in Dar es Salaam and elsewhere.	The judiciary is widely considered to be corrupt and inefficient, and justice is routinely delayed and denied. The judiciary is bureaucratic, passive, and incapable of forcing decisions on the government.
Official mismanagement and corruption leading to massive loss of lives and property go unpunished.	
Commercial cases have been dealt with in a more expedite manner since the establishment of the Commercial Court.	In a recent survey, two-thirds (64 percent) of respondents considered Primary Court officers to be corrupt.
Accountability: Government audit	
The Controller and Auditor-General (CAG) audits central and local government accounts. Donor aid has improved the promptness of reporting and extended coverage (LGAs and some donor projects are covered).	The annual reports are incomplete records of the misuse of funds and are still widely ignored by the executive and top government officials. Permanent secretaries are not held responsible for the misuse of government funds.
Accountability: Access to information	
REPOA found that 87% of respondents in a national survey had seen AIDS prevention posters,	but only 16% knew how to report corruption or make a complaint, and only 4% had seen a copy of a LGA budget.
Accountability: Civil society and the media	
There has been a significant increase in the level of collective engagement by civil society, both in service provision and in a number of government processes, including the Public Expenditure Review and the PRS.	Some officials see NGOs as self-appointed whereas the government is elected, they are foreign-funded and therefore probably following foreign agendas, for instance on issues of democracy, and are not well placed to criticise the 'governance' of others.

According to the International Press Institute's May 2005 report on the Status of World Press Freedom, Tanzania is among 50 countries in the world with partial press freedom. (Only seven African countries are considered to have a free press).	Journalists are frequently criticised for lacking professionalism, and for practising various forms of corruption. Despite numerous donor-financed training workshops, there is a widely recognised lack of investigative journalism dealing with issues of grand corruption and governance, as the table demonstrates.
Taxation	
Tanzania currently collects about 13 percent of GDP in taxes, up from 11.3 percent in 1999.	
After the Tanzania Revenue Authority was established government revenue collection improved very significantly between the early and mid-1990s and has continued to improve to date.	Clear indications that corruption is on the increase again.
In the 2004-05 Budget a large number of 'nuisance taxes' were abolished and LG cesses limited to 5% of crop value.	LGA tax administration lacks predictability, fairness, and efficiency of collection. Tax revenues are largely consumed by councillors and council officials rather than being used for providing services. Many taxes collected never reach the local council's coffers.
Regulation	
Tanzania has made great strides away from a planned/command economy towards a market-driven economy.	Rent-seeking and bureaucracy continue to frustrate attempts to translate policy into practice. The failure of reforms in sector after sector is evidence of a major 'disconnect' between formal policy-making and policy implementation.
Tanzania liberalised export agriculture in the late 1990s...	... but reversed the policy thereafter. Legislation gave virtually unlimited powers to a new set of crop boards to both regulate and to act as commercial players in export markets.

	Most of the boards' revenue is from levies on farmers. In addition, farmers pay a cess to local governments equivalent to 5 percent of farm-gate prices and a number of other deductions. Most of the boards' revenue is spent on administration and the cost of the boards of directors.
The Executive Agencies (EAs) concept has been widely applied in Tanzania, and things as diverse as statistical services, road maintenance and bore-hole drilling are now handled by EAs under government regulation.	
	In practice the parent ministry often retains key controls over crucial activities, including the award of contracts. Regulating requires capacity and probity, the widespread absence of which justified setting up in the first place. There is little evidence of improvement in service quality, or that competition improves performance.
Investment promotion	
The GOT has put in place policies and incentives to encourage private, including foreign, investment.	A control mentality among government officials, lack of empathy for business needs, deficiencies in the legal system and pervasive corruption continue to undermine investment.
Investments in mining and tourism have led to increased economic activity and export earnings.	In general, investors are frustrated by high local manufacturing costs, a relatively hostile tax regime, excessive bureaucracy and corruption in public offices.
	Many perceive foreign mining companies as making super-profits and paying little or no tax, a charge which the industry denies.

Appendix 2 Analytical Framework: Sources And Uses Of Rents From Official Corruption

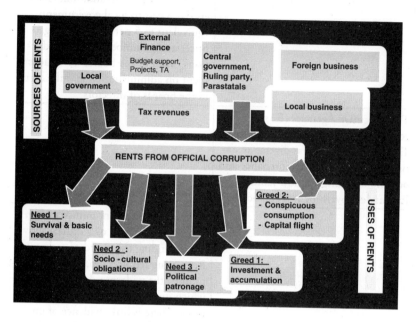

Appendix 3: Tanzania in Comparative Perspective
Table 17: Tanzania in comparative perspective – CPI 1998-2004

	2004	2003	2002	2001	2000	1999	1998
1	Botswana	Botswana	Botswana	Botswana	Botswana	Botswana	Botswana
2	Tunisia	Tunisia	Namibia	Namibia	Namibia	Namibia	Namibia
3	S Africa	Namibia	Tunisia	Tunisia	Tunisia	Tunisia	S Africa
4	Mauritius	S Africa	S Africa	S Africa	S Africa	S Africa	Mauritius
5	Namibia	Mauritius	Mauritius	Mauritius	Mauritius	Mauritius	Tunisia
6	Ghana	Ghana	Ghana	Egypt	Malawi	Malawi	Malawi
7	Egypt	Egypt	Egypt	Ghana	Ghana	Zambia	Zambia
8	Senegal	Senegal	Senegal	Malawi	Senegal	Senegal	Zimbabwe
9	Malawi	Malawi	Malawi	Senegal	Zambia	Zimbabwe	Senegal
10	**Tanzania**	Zambia	Zimbabwe	Zimbabwe	Egypt	Ghana	Ghana
11	Uganda	**Tanzania**	Ivory C	Zambia	Zimbabwe	Egypt	Ivory C
12	Zambia	Zimbabwe	**Tanzania**	Ivory C	Ivory C	Ivory C	Egypt
13	Zimbabwe	Uganda	Zambia	**Tanzania**	**Tanzania**	Uganda	Uganda
14	Cameroon	Ivory C	Cameroon	Uganda	Uganda	Kenya	Kenya

15	Kenya	Kenya	Uganda	Kenya	Kenya	*Tanzania*	Nigeria
16	Ivory C	Cameroon	Kenya	Cameroon	Cameroon	Cameroon	*Tanzania*
17	Nigeria	Nigeria	Nigeria	Nigeria	Nigeria	Nigeria	Cameroon
Av	**3.2**	**3.1**	**3.4**	**3.3**	**3.5**	**3.5**	**3.6**
Tz	**2.8**	**2.5**	**2.7**	**2.2**	**2.5**	**1.9**	**1.9**
Tz/av	**.88**	**.81**	**.79**	**.67**	**.71**	**.54**	**.53**

Source: Adapted from Sundet (2004). The 'top five' countries listed have scores of 4 and above on a scale of 10=no corruption to 0=totally corrupt. Countries in italics have the same score/rank as Tanzania in a given year.

The 17 African countries listed are those that figure in the CPI throughout 1998-2004. The average CPI score for these countries is at the bottom of the table, along with Tanzania's score and this score as a proportion of the sample average. Tanzania's performance on the CPI has improved significantly in both absolute and relative terms. In absolute terms, Tanzania's score has improved by 47 percent over the last seven years. Whereas in 1998, Tanzania scored only just over half the average CPI score for the sample, in 2004 it was almost 90 percent. In relative terms, Tanzania has moved away from the bottom of the sample to just below the middle.[26]

---

[26] A word of caution on the reliability of the data. Some observers have shown, including Lambsdorff, that the differences between most African country scores are not significant at the 90 percent level and above. Tanzania's score in 2000 is only significantly different from the scores of Botswana, Namibia, South Africa, Mauritius and Malawi. Comparisons between Tanzania and the rest of the sample countries are therefore probably not significant. Most surveys are based on small sample sizes.

Endnotes

i 'Governance is defined as the exercise of authority through formal and informal traditions and institutions for the common good, thus encompassing the process of selecting, monitoring and replacing governments, the capacity to formulate and implement sound policies and deliver public services; and the respect of citizens and the state for the institutions that govern economic and social interactions among them' (Kaufmann, 2004:16). 'Good' governance is not reducible to democratic institutions.

ii See above for the exact figures: in fact, neither accountability nor government effectiveness have improved significantly, and rule of law, government effectiveness and regulatory quality have all deteriorated significantly.

iii According to Foucault: 'Truth … is produced only by virtue of multiple forms of constraint. … Each society has its regime of truth, its "general politics" of truth: that is, the types of discourses which it accepts and makes function as true; the mechanisms and instances which enable one to distinguish true and false statements, the means by which each is sanctioned; the techniques and procedures accorded value in the acquisition of truth, the status of those who are charged with saying what counts as true' (Rabinow, 1991:72-3).

CHAPTER NINE

CHANGING AID MODALITIES AND TANZANIAN DEVELOPMENT ASSISTANCE PARTNERSHIPS

Samuel Wangwe

Introduction

Background and context

Tanzania is one of the most aid dependent countries in Africa. Historically, however, Tanzania has been associated with a high degree of independence in policy making including its foreign policy.

Development cooperation in Tanzania goes back to the early 1960s and since then its relationship with the donors and the development effectiveness of aid have been evolving over time.

Following the economic crisis of the late 1970s and early 1980s, Tanzania adopted a structural adjustment programme in 1986 under the supervision of the international financial institutions. The first phase of reforms, as elaborated in the Economic Recovery Programme (1986-89), was essentially aimed at getting the prices right and consisted of price decontrol, devaluation, freeing the interest rates and liberalizing markets. The implementation of the programme was facilitated by resumption of aid flows. The period 1989-92 started to address the social dimensions of adjustment and institutional reforms. The reforms became more difficult as they were entering the terrain of institutional reforms which require a higher degree of political commitment than the earlier phase of getting prices right. This political commitment fell short and donors expressed concern in the early 1990s. Donors felt that Tanzania was falling short in implementing the reform programme with commitment and in mobilizing domestic resources. The Tanzania government was feeling that donors were interfering too much and eroding ownership of the development agenda. This situation led to a deterioration of the aid relationships between the Government of Tanzania (GoT) and donors.

Since 1995, the year Benjamin Mkapa started his first presidential term, a substantial history of aid relationships has been recorded in numerous reviews. These reviews have examined the relationships between the GoT and aid donors and have been conducted by observers independent of both sides. This in itself is a notable innovation of the government of Tanzania.

Relations between the two sides (Tanzania government and donors) deteriorated to a low level in the early 1990s. In order to address this situation an independent group of experts led by Professor Gerald K. Helleiner was appointed to study the situation and make recommendations. The study was completed in 1995 and subsequent discussions between the government and donors were based on that report. Based on the Helleiner report the third phase government accorded high priority to dialogue between the government and donors starting with the dialogue of September 1996. This was followed by a workshop that was held between the government and donors in which an agreement was reached in January 1997 between the GoT and its development partners to jointly set out a programme to redefine the terms of their development co-operation. The result was a set of 'agreed notes' (in the form of 18 points) stating, among other things, that there was a need to ensure enhanced Government leadership in development programming, increased transparency, accountability and efficiency in aid delivery. The elaboration of a framework for co-operation culminated in the preparation of the Tanzania Assistance Strategy (TAS) from 1998/99 which was finally published in 2002 following many sessions of dialogue and refinements. The TAS was meant to be a framework for partnership which would also define the role of external resources for development in Tanzania.

In 1997 the Government of Tanzania (GoT) and the development partners (DPs) agreed to adopt the recommendations of the Helleiner Report. Thus they agreed on taking medium term action to redefine GoT-DP relationships in conceptualizing and managing development and in the broader definition of local ownership of the development agenda as well as in enhancing transparency and accountability in the delivery and utilization of aid. The redefinition of aid relationships meant that the GoT would take the necessary steps to provide leadership in designing and managing the development process and in enhancing effectiveness of aid and other public resources. For the new aid relationships to be realized, it was recognized that the GoT and DPs had a role to play and these matters were defined in the agreed points and refined in the Tanzania Assistance Strategy.

The Tanzanian Assistance Strategy provides the framework for strengthening donor coordination, harmonization, partnerships and national ownership in the development process. It provides a three-year strategic national framework covering aspects of the national development agenda and related policies, best practices in development cooperation, and a frame for monitoring its implementation and priority areas and interventions. The TAS Action Plan was developed with a view to setting out practical steps for GoT and development partners to follow in implementing TAS.

The GoT and development partners agreed to institute monitoring and evaluation mechanisms in which progress in the aid relationships would be reviewed and review reports submitted to GoT and development partners for discussion and agreement on the next steps. Initially Prof. Helleiner made the reviews in December 1997, March 1999 and May 2000. Subsequently, the task of monitoring had two strands: joint evaluations and through an independent review mechanism. Undertaking independent reviews was entrusted to an independent group known as the Independent Monitoring Group (IMG) appointed jointly by GoT and DPs. The first IMG Report was presented to the Consultative Group Meeting in December 2002. The second IMG was presented in April 2005 which provided a review of the status of the development partnership (aid/donor) relationship in Tanzania and made an assessment of the progress made since late 2002 towards principles and objectives set out in the Tanzania Assistance Strategy document.

The preparation of this paper has relied largely on independent evaluations that Professor Helleiner and the Independent Monitoring Group have been carrying out since 1995. These reports have been collecting data from both primary and secondary sources. Data was gathered from various documents in the Government of Tanzania and donor agencies as well as from recent OECD-DAC sources.

By 2005, the GoT has become more assertive, better organised and makes better preparations in dialogue with the development partners. Progress has been made in terms of leadership and ownership in developing a clearer view of its role in the development agenda as has been defined in the second generation of Poverty Reduction Strategy (MKUKUTA) which has been more consultative and more national in character. Nonetheless, the level of ownership is still rather narrow in GoT with many sector ministries showing rather low level of ownership. In conclusion, my assessment is that GoT leadership and ownership of the development agenda, its content and implementation, has indeed been strengthened during the first half of the 2000 decade.

Ownership, Leadership and Partnership: Clarification of the concepts

The ownership principle adopted in this chapter is that Tanzania and not donors should be in charge of its development, should be able to identify its development goals and formulate its development strategy. Then the donors should be invited to support the national development goals and priorities. The concept of ownership and country leadership that is adopted in this report is consistent with the one used in OECD (2003)[1] and World Bank (2003)[2]. Taking ownership and country leadership seriously implies, among other things, determination of aid modality and form of dialogue that would be in Tanzania's interest and best meets the country's requirements. Strong national ownership, however, cannot be confined to government circles alone. National ownership of development policies must mean systematic, broad-based stakeholder participation, under government leadership, including civil society, the private sector and local governments, with involvement of the Parliament. This implies that the process and strategies developed are to enjoy wide public support from the top political leadership be backed by intellectual conviction on the part of key policy makers and have strong links to institutions.

Donors are not to be passive in this context, but they are expected to change their policies and practices to give more space for domestic initiatives and facilitate progress towards national ownership by encouraging and supporting processes of analysis and discussion that lead to more informed and balanced domestic decision making.

Consistent with national ownership, country-led partnership represents a paradigm shift towards putting Tanzania in the driver's seat. Key instruments for fostering effective country-led partnerships include country-led coordination mechanisms, alignment of donor support to country strategy and priorities, more effective modes of aid delivery and harmonisation of donor practices and procedures.

The front-line initiatives in ownership, alignment and harmonisation of aid in Tanzania are now getting international backing as evidenced in the Paris Declaration on Aid Effectiveness of the Paris High-level Forum of 2nd March 2005 in which partner countries and developed countries made specific commitments with target dates for achievement in favour of these objectives. The derived tasks and goals for Tanzania's implementation should be reflected in the Joint Assistance Strategy (JAS) (The process related to Paris Declaration on Aid Effectiveness was followed up by the Accra Declaration in 2008).

Tanzania assistance strategy

The GoT launched TAS as a coherent national development framework for managing external resources to achieve the stated development objec-

---

[1]   OECD: Harmonising Donor Practices for Effective Aid Delivery. A DAC Reference Document. DAC Guidelines and Reference Series. OECD, Paris, 2003.
[2]   World Bank: Toward Country-led Development: A Multi-Partner Evaluation of the Comprehensive Development Framework: Synthesis Report. Washington DC, 2003.

tives and strategies. TAS represents the national initiative to restore local ownership and leadership in promoting partnership in the design and execution of development programmes. TAS has been followed by an action plan from 2002/03 which has set out more practical steps for implementation in four areas: promoting GoT leadership, improving predictability of external resources, increasing capture of aid flows in the government budget and improving domestic capacity for aid coordination and management of external resources.

The Tanzania Assistance Strategy process has continued to be institutionalized at all levels of GoT and Development Partner Groups (DPGs). The implementation of TAS is now supervised by the Joint TAS/Harmonisation Group and Joint TAS Technical Secretariat, both draw membership from sector ministries, the President's Office, the Vice President's Office, the Ministry of Finance and Development Partners and are chaired by the Ministry of Finance.

Progress made in achieving leadership and ownership

It has been acknowledged that GoT leadership has been strengthening in many respects. Evidence is also seen in the higher level of assertiveness, better organization and better preparation of policy documents. GoT leadership of the reform process, development agenda as well as the aid relationships has improved. The Ministry of Finance (MoF) in particular has become more direct and more assertive in asking development partners to be committed to the national development priorities. Government leadership is evidenced by an enhanced level of understanding of issues, especially by the MoF. This has led to greater clarity and coherence in the guidance to sector ministries. The level of ownership is high in respect of the MoF but for most sector ministries the level of ownership is still low. Leadership in dealing with local governments is still not good enough as it is not well defined in practice. The role of the Parliament in its involvement in policy processes and result evaluations is still unclear: the Parliament seems to be consigned to just approving the budget and the legal instruments for policies, if their legalisation is required.

The most notable progress in the reform process is in the arena of macro-economic management, where leadership and improving relations with IMF and the World Bank have been observed. For instance, the IMF has been supporting the reform agenda through PRGF. The decline of the Poverty Reduction and Growth Facility (PRGF) from $60-70 million per annum during 2000-2003 to $15 million per annum in 2005 is one indicator of success whereby Tanzania is graduating from special balance of payments support towards a more sustainable situation. The core of reforms in during the years 2002 to 2005 has been fiscal management reform, which has been characterized by improved domestic revenue mobilization and hardly any domestic borrowing. The PRGF was in 2005 preoccupied with domestic resource mobilization, enhanced financial sector reform and improvement of the business environment. Support is likely to shift more into institutional support and technical assistance.

Ownership has improved as evidenced by the fact that for the past 3 years the GoT has been drafting the letter of intent on its own. Transparency has also improved as evidenced by putting the letter of intent on the web. The emerging challenge is that of managing so many processes to avoid being overloaded, as dialogue moves towards GoT leadership.

Progress has been made in terms of leadership and ownership in developing a Poverty Reduction Strategy Paper in 2000 and making further improvements on it to produce a clearer view of its role in the development agenda as has been defined in the second generation of the Poverty Reduction Strategy (PRS). Compared to the first generation of PRS, the formulation of the second generation poverty reduction strategy, MKUKUTA, has been more clear, more consultative and participative with greater demonstration of GoT leadership. However, this participation is still not broad-based across the various relevant ministries. The preparation of MKUKUTA has demonstrated a greater level of ownership in its formulation with development partners given the opportunity to make comments. These comments have been coordinated better than before. Result orientation has been endorsed in accordance with the approach of MKUKUTA. The challenge is to show evidence that implementation is in progress from input based towards output based results.

The GoT leadership and ownership should continue to be consolidated. GoT should clearly decide on the kinds of signals that should be sent out to development partners. Challenges of trust must be addressed and dialogue mechanisms at the political level need to be strengthened and their links to technical level dialogue be better articulated. Donors need to see that their gradual withdrawal from the policy space is an integral part of building stronger leadership and ownership by GoT.

While leadership by GoT is improving, there are four concerns that need to be addressed: First, the number of active change agents within government is still quite small making the process rather fragile. Second, the spread of GoT leadership within GoT and across ministries is still narrow. Some ministries have rather a low level of awareness and capacity to play their role as leaders in policy dialogue. Third, the question of incentive structure should be addressed to underpin efforts at enhancing harmonization and ownership. The incentive structure considerations should address pay reform, the place and role of workshops and the power and resources that are often associated with projects and parallel programmes. Fourth, there is the issue of policy coordination between two parts of the Union where the policy coordination system has not been functioning in unison. Development strategies have been formulated at different times without adequate coordination. For instance, the Poverty Reduction Strategy process has not been fully coordinated at the government level. The formulation of national priorities and processes in Tanzania Mainland and Zanzibar have not been harmonised.

Progress Made in Harmonisation and Alignment

Progress has been made in rationalisation and harmonisation of processes with a view to reducing transaction costs.

Alignment of development partners' calendars to the national calendar has improved through the Public Expenditure Review (PER) and the Medium Term Expenditure Framework (MTEF) processes and by drawing up a calendar of a rationalised cycle of policy mechanisms and consultative processes. The calendar is increasingly being adapted. Progress in this matter is bringing the timing and output of all processes in line with the Poverty Reduction Strategy and budget cycle. More specifically, "quiet times" have been identified with the aim of providing GoT with adequate time to concentrate on preparing the budget and participation in the Parliament budget sessions.

Progress has been made in the use of common review frameworks such as the Performance Assistance Framework (PAF), which has increasingly been drawing from policy reforms and national priorities and policies contained in the Poverty Reduction Strategy. The move away from rigid and one-sided (donor-driven) conditionality towards the adoption of jointly agreed prior actions that are an integral part of the government's reform programme has been consistent with promoting GoT ownership and leadership as well as reducing uncertainty in external resource inflow.

Moving from the Tanzania Assistance Strategy to the Joint Assisstance Strategy

The Joint Assistance Strategy (JAS) is planned to move TAS to a higher stage of attaining national ownership and leadership in the development process, reduce transaction costs by enhancing harmonisation and alignment to national priorities and national systems. The Joint Assistance Strategy is intended to be a broad framework for all partners (domestic and external) to operate at a higher level of commitment to the principles of best practices in development cooperation as stated in Tanzania Assistance Strategy and hopefully to be more concretised in the Joint Assistance Strategy. It is envisaged that the JAS will replace individual donor country assistance strategies as one way of reducing the multiplicity of donor processes and enhancing aid coordination and promote collective support to Tanzania consistent with its national development goals and priorities. The JAS is expected to contribute to consolidating and institutionalising current efforts towards harmonisation, alignment and managing for results.

Ownership, Policy Dialogue and Harmonisation with Sectors and Local Governments

Aid relationships in sectors and local governments have taken on a dimension which warrants separate consideration. The relationships bring together the role of central ministries, line ministries and Local Government Authorities (LGAs).

Local Development Management

Progress in decentralisation

The decentralisation policy of 1998 was meant to transfer more power and facilitate greater participation on the part of Local Government Authorities and communities. At district level some progress has been made in district restructuring and planning. First, the setting up of the managerial organisation, allocation and training of local LGA staff and tax streamlining are being carried out. Second, district planning has become better institutionalized with the adoption of the O and OD methodology. Planning processes have been installed in the districts and the LGR process using zonal training teams is reaching to lower levels of local government. LGAs face the challenge of unharmonised transfer and reporting modalities for the various basket funds, Tanzania Assistance Strategy Aid Facility (TASAF) and emerging sector development grants (PORALG, 2004). A coordinated approach is needed to address this challenge. Sector Wide Approaches (SWAPs) and baskets are unlikely to work smoothly for decentralization by devolution unless they are aligned to the district planning and budgeting processes.

Development Partners and Dialogue Processes

The Development Partner Group (DPG)

From the development assistance commmittee to the development partner group: towards formalisation

The development partner group (DPG) has organised itself more formally partly in response to the launching of the Tanazania Assistance Strategy at national level and the publication of the Rome Declaration at international level. The rationale for the DPG, which replaced the local Development Assistance Committee, is to complement the GoT's own coordination efforts by promoting internal coherence among the DPs in the context of the Tanzania Assistance Strategy and the Rome Declaration. The Development Partner Group addresses harmonisation with a view to reducing transaction costs.

The main objective of DPG is to increase the effectiveness of development assistance in support of GoT's national goals and systems. It seeks to move beyond information sharing towards actively seeking best practice in harmonisation. Consistent with the main objective DPG operates according to principles of recognition of the Poverty Reduction Strategy and Tanzania Assistance Strategy and facilitating the realisation of their outcomes, inclusivity amidst relative diversity and early acknowledgement of constraints to harmonisation so that solutions may be found.

Streamlining the dialogue process

A plethora of policy processes has been put in place as a sign of improving participation in the policy process. However, there are concerns that have arisen in the course of time. GoT officials have expressed the wish to see effective but less complicated and less interfering dialogue with the donors.

Participation of Broader Constituencies: Deepening and institutionalising

Participation in policy dialogue has been broadened and is becoming more institutionalized. The policy-making processes have been broadened in terms of participation e.g. in the Poverty Reduction Strategey and the Public Expenditure Review processes. The PER, the PRS and Poverty Policy Week (PPW) processes have been broadened and deepened. The number and quality of exchanges have been much higher. The sectors have been involved more explicitly. The regions have been involved more widely than in the past. The Poverty Policy Week for example has involved national as well as regional dialogue. Tensions have been reduced as trust has increased. The participation process has been better institutionalized. For instance, parliamentarians have participated through the Parliamentary (Bunge) Foundation as well as through a general workshop for the whole Parliament and through chairpersons of various Parliamentary Committees. The opposition in parliament has been involved more explicitly. While the role of Parliament has been enhanced, the discussions could be deepened further.

Overall, is has been found that the level of participation in policy dialogue has grown considerably. However, there are concerns that the level of participation is still relatively weak on the part of the mass media and Parliament. The role of Parliament needs to go beyond the annual budget and influence medium term and long term planning and policy making. This may call for capacity building of Parliament and revisiting the structure and processes employed. There is need to establish capacity needs in the area of research and technical support for Parliament. The legitimate and positive role of Parliament will be facilitated by participation in appropriately early stages of policy and plan formulation. There are wrong beliefs that Parliamentarians would politicise technical issues in the policy or plan formulation processes, forgetting that many Parliamentarians have technical backgrounds and are well placed to present the views and experiences of grassroot communities.

Budget Process and Public Financial Management and Accounting Systems

A major development that has been identified is the adoption of a more strategic approach to public spending through the Medium Term Expenditure Framework and the Public Expenditure Review with focus on priorities as articulated in the Poverty Reduction Strategy. The link between the Public Expenditure Review and the Poverty Reduction Process and the budget in general has been strengthened. Sectors engage in prioritization of their activities more than they did in the past. Budget guidelines have been rewritten to reflect new developments. Mechanisms for continuous monitoring of progress are being created and impacts of development initiatives and actions have been put in place on the heels of progress after the first round of the public financial management. Further challenges of financial control as well as those of allocation of resources according to priority are being tackled. Public resource management have improved considerably. Transparency and accountability of public financial resources has improved. All regions have been computerized. In the last two years the priority has been given to strengthening the infrastructure needed to make computerized sub-Treasuries work more effectively. Investment in capacity building in local government authorities is getting some attention. Tanzania has been acknowledged as a leading country in implementing the IFMS and many African countries are keen to learn from Tanzania's experience and to emulate it. These improvements have contributed to giving comfort to the DPs.

Public resource management has improved considerably. Transparency and accountability of public financial resources has improved. The IFMS has been rolled out to all regions. Progress has been made in strengthening the predictability of resources. However the weakest link is in the *quality of the budget process*. The budget does not yet function as the strategic policy and resource allocation tool it is supposed to be. In the policy-budget-service delivery chain, the budget formulation is seen as the weak link.

In the last two years, progress has been made in strengthening the predictability of resources especially through budget support. Projections of scheduled expenditures on projects and programmes were submitted by the development partners to the Ministry of Finance through the Public Expenditure Review process. The fact that disbursements started to be made under the harmonized PRBS and the Poverty Reduction Stategy Credit (PRSC) mechanisms has contributed to improving predictability of budget support inflows.

There is evidence of increased predictability of resource flows and improved data on commitments and projections of resources. For instance, during 2003 about 70% of development partners indicated to the Government their planned aid releases for the next 3 years. Similarly, 75% of the DPs reported comprehensive and regular data in aid disbursement. The GoT has established a mechanism of collecting full projections as part of the routine activities of the annual Public Expenditure Review. The tracking and recording of resource commitments and actual disbursements has improved. General Budget Support (GBS) disbursements have improved considerably compared to commitments.

From 2002/03 to 2004/05 GBS disbursements were 100% with 80% of the total amount committed being disbursed in the first half of the financial year (FY). Disbursements within the first quarter of the FY increased from 8% in FY 2002/03 to 50% in 2003/04 and further to 80% in 2004/05. This development facilitated smooth release of government funds during the year. Predictability especially as the aid delivery modalities shift towards GBS is likely to be influenced by the manner in which

PAF is redefined. Conditionality incorporated in the Performance Assessment Framework (PAF) should take into account the need to enhance predictability of resource flows.

Aid Delivery: Efficiency and Effectiveness

Recent developments in aid fatigue, actual or perceived corruption and modest achievements in reducing poverty combine to raise a question for an exit strategy and to press for improving the effectiveness of aid. *Concerns have been expressed about the dangers of deepening aid dependence.* Yet this has not been an explicit point of policy dialogue. In our opinion, the foundations for a smooth exit from aid dependence should be laid down. It is in this context that we argue that an exit strategy should be part of the dialogue between development partners and government. This should lead to a common understanding of exit, leading to a common target for phasing out aid to the public sector budgets. This would create a mutual understanding of macroeconomic targets and a direction for the discussion on sustainability.

However, recent global level reports have expressed concern that the Millennium Development Goals (MDGs) may not be achieved largely due to inadequate donor resources to developing countries (Millennium Project Report, 2005 and Report of the Commission for Africa, 2005). Both reports have recommended a doubling of aid to Africa if the MDGs are to be achieved. In our opinion, even in cases where more aid is needed to achieve MDGs, the foundations for a smooth exit from aid dependence should be laid down. It is in this context that we argue that an exit strategy should form part of the dialogue between development partners and governments.

The Government of Tanzania has expressed preference for GBS as an aid modality. In practice the GoT has not been sufficiently emphatic on this preference. In my opinion, the general budget support (GSB) should continue to be the preferred aid modality because it is more consistent with greater levels of ownership and greater degree of budget management, contestability of resources and strengthened government systems for expenditure management initiatives. However, the Joint Assistance Strategy should be more assertive on this preference, by laying out the transitional plan in which the right mix of GBS, basket funds and project aid modalities coexist.

Technical Assistance and Challenges of Capacity Building

The Technical Assistance (TA) modality of aid has continued to be the most challenging because it continues to be supply driven, involves tied procurement and has little built in capacity building. The matter is worsened by the absence of government policy on the Tanzania Assistance Strategy. The GoT should prepare a clear technical assistance policy specifying that technical assistance should primarily play the role of capacity building and that its recruitment procedures for technical assistance should be more open and competitive and untied to the source of funds.

Several sector development partners have indicated that they are shifting away from making use of long-term expatriate specialists and of technical assistance tied to project implementation and that they are engaging in capacity building which is needed if the government is to take leadership in the reform process. The importance of capacity building is acknowledged in recent OECD/DAC guidelines on harmonization around procurement practices (2005). The centrality of capacity building is emphasised in this context.

Technical assistance in Tanzania is usually engaged to augment the capacity of Tanzania as a temporary gap filler to enable specific tasks to be carried out in the absence of adequate local capacity or to facilitate local capacity building in the process. The first type of technical capacity is TA that is supposed to augment the capacity of Tanzania and is expected to give priority to domestic capacity building. Technical assistance has been one of the most problematic aid delivery modalities. TA has been tied to finance, packaged into projects, not necessarily demand driven and sometimes has resulted in erosion or replacement of local capacities rather than building those capacities. Sometimes expediency and speed of delivery have prevailed over needs of sustainability and capacity building.

In spite of the problems faced in this aid modality, three positive approaches to providing TA have been observed in the way TA is being managed. First, there are cases of pooling technical assistance. TA pooling has worked well in the PER process.

Second, there are cases of untying TA and subjecting its procurement to more open, transparent and competitive recruitment procedures. Untying of TA is challenging for most donors. Good progress has been made in some MDAs regarding TA procurement using this open and competitive procurement of TA. Third, there is one instance of providing TA on the basis of pooling of resources at regional level, thereby facilitating institutional capacity building in the process. This case is represented by the IMF's African Technical Assistance Committee (AFRITAC) which was established in 2002 at the request of the Heads of State.

Government should come up with a clear policy towards technical assistance. The policy should consider delinking TA from financing and from projects to permit the use of TA for capacity building and to make it more demand driven based on identification of TA needs.

Conclusions and Recommendations

Strategic aid management and a quality budget process

The GoT has demonstrated greater realism and assertiveness about national objectives and priorities. The expression of these priorities in MKUKUTA has shown encouraging progress. What is needed in the future is to elaborate these priorities in terms of sector level strategic development.

Conditionality must shift from the one-sided approach to the collaborative approach. It is recommended that the move away from rigid and one-sided (donor driven) conditionality be replaced by the adoption of jointly agreed prior actions that are based on and are an integral part of the government's national development programme.

Deepening participation

Participation in policy dialogue has been broadened and is becoming more institutionalized. However, participation by the mass media and Parliament should be enhanced. The role of Parliament needs to go beyond the annual budget and influence medium - and long term planning and policy making.

Technical Assistance and Capacity Development

There is need to develop a national technical assistance (TA) policy. The policy should consider lessons from TA pooling and transparent recruitment procedures with a view to delinking TA from financing and from projects to permit the use of TA for capacity building and to make it more demand driven based on identification of TA needs.

Good Practices in Relationships among Development Partners

The Development Partner Group should develop and agree on a working definition of what it means by harmonisation and alignment to facilitate common interpretation at the operational level, work out a time-bound action plan in accordance with the 2005 Paris Declaration targets. GoT could coordinate the latter exercise.

Good Practice between Government and Development Partners

The challenge is to invest the time to come to a genuine understanding. This is a serious challenge against the current imbalance of power in donor/recipient relationships. There must be an acknowledgement of and work to address the capacity gaps which exist on both sides. More can be done by insisting that development partners do more to understand country specific issues and challenges.

Exit Strategy: Towards smooth transition from aid dependence

In the dialogue between development partn ers and governments there should be a common target for phasing out aid to the public sector budgets. This would create a mutual understanding of macroeconomic targets and a direction for the discussion on sustainability. This objective should be mentioned in the Joint Assistance Strategy.

CHAPTER TEN

CHALLENGES TO THE DEMOCRATISATION PROCESS IN TANZANIA

Jonas Ewald

Introduction

Tanzania has managed to develop a reasonable degree of political stability and nationhood, in a context where most neighbours are or have been ravaged by conflicts. Thus Tanzania provides an interesting possibility to create a future beyond crises and conflicts on the African continent. The economic development has improved, with a growth of around 5% per capita since 2002. A state with a degree of legitimacy has been developed, despite the harsh economic conditions. The role of Tanzania's first president Julius Nyerere was important for that (Legum and Mmari, 1995; Mbelle, Mjema et al., 2002). The issue is, whether Tanzania can maintain her political stability and nationhood at a time with rapid integration in the global economy and an increasing rift between those included or excluded in the growth/modernisation process.

Tanzania's third multi-party election was held in 2005, judged by African and international election observers as reasonably fair and free, even if the playing field was uneven. Three shifts of president have thus been made peacefully.[1] The process of political liberalisation began in 1992 and a relatively free and fair multi-party election on a national level was held in 1995. There were, however, a number of limitations (Ewald, 1996; Mushi and Mukandala, 1997; TEMCO, 1997). In December 1999 elections were held at "grass root" level and in October 2000, to the local and national assemblies and the presidency. In October and December 2005 elections to local government, parliament and the presidency took place. Both rounds of elections were regarded as free, but not fully fair (TEMCO, 2001; EISA Election Observer Mission Report, 2005; The Guardian, March 16 2006). The election in Zanzibar was more problematic both in 2000 and 2005

---

[1] Julius Nyerere was president of Tanzania from 1961 to 1985; Ali Hassan Mwinyi, 1985-1995; Benjamin Mkapa was elected twice, since multi-party politics was introduced, in 1995 and 2000. He was succeeded by Jakaya Kikwete in December 2005.

(Maliyamkono, 2000; Bakari, 2001; Commonwealth Observer Group, 2001; 2005). The liberal international organisation Freedom House defines Tanzania's democracy as "partly free" (Freedom House 2006). A number of challenges remain, however, to be handled by the democratisation process, not the least the reforms and development within the economic and administrative sectors. This chapter aims to highlight and discuss some of these challenges.

The *economic reforms* have created expectations, but so far delivered little in terms of reduced poverty. However, Tanzania is now among the fastest growing economies in Africa, with a real per capita GDP growth rate of 5% in 2005 (World Bank 2005; International Monetary Fund 2006). Average real per capita GDP growth rate for the five years 2001-2005, was 4.8%, putting Tanzania as number eight of the 48 countries in Sub-Saharan Africa, and far ahead of its neighbours in East Africa (World Bank, 2000-2006). A middle class is emerging as well as different elites that explore new opportunities that have been opened within tourism, mining and construction. The *political reforms* have created expectations on deepened democratic governance, more effective governance and less corrupt practices. The elections in 2000 and 2005, however, displayed how shallow and fragile the democratisation process is, as the situation on Zanzibar and Pemba clearly has shown (see Bakari, 2001). The tensions that off and on have existed around some of the mosques in Dar es Salaam and the Zanzibar crisis clearly indicate the strong tensions that exist in some parts of Tanzania today.

This inquiry will not take a theoretical point of departure or assess the relevant literature. However, the context of the arguments is the literature discussing the prerequisite for democratic and economic development in Africa. From a more liberal standpoint some authors (Bratton and van de Walle, 1997; Chabal, 1999; van de Walle, 2001), argue that neo-patrimonialism is one of the most important institutional characteristics that can help explain the lack of economic development and continued authoritarian governance in multi-party structures in Africa. The problem thus is localised within the state itself. The structural adjustment programmes of the 1980's and 90's strengthened the status quo rather than promoted reforms. In order to establish a liberal market democracy, further liberal reforms of the state and the societies are necessary. A large body of literature studies elections, their driving force and debate their relative short comings and democratising effects, like for instance (Cowen and Laakso, 2002). A study covering all elections in Africa 1989-2003 (Lindberg, 2006) concludes that elections go beyond formal procedures because elections foster expansion and deepening of democratic values and thus tend to expand and solidify civil liberties in societies.

Others take a broader approach. (Abrahamsen, 2000) discusses democracy and good governance as a western (neo-liberal) discourse aimed to maintain western hegemony in African societies. The democratic institutions that are promoted aim to strengthen SAPs and external actors, rather than domestic constituencies and the poor, hence resulting in fragile democracies unable to respond to the needs of the poor.

Some analyse the democratisation process from a more "African" perspective. (Ake 2000) for example, argues that democratisation has the potential to promote a "second independence" from indigenous post-colonial leadership but that the minimalist western liberal model, with its focus on multi-party elections, is at odds with a deeper social democracy that can fulfil the needs for material betterment, equality and concrete rights. Gyimah-Boadi (2004) assesses the democratic reforms in Africa with a focus on the internal structures and institutions that promote or undermine a democratic development, pointing at the need for institutional reforms. A recent critical assessment of the neo-liberal reform agenda (Lumumba-Kasongo, 2006) emphasises that the form and substance of democracy are two fundamentally different aspects. Western-derived institutional forms are not necessarily the most appropriate or the most practical in the current African context. Consequently, the need emerges for rooting democratic norms in African political cultures.

In an assessment based on about ten years of research on continent-wide opinion polls, (Bratton, Mattes et al., 2005), on the other hand, conclude that the popular support for democracy is widespread but shallow.

Most of these analyses attempt to bring together economic and political factors, which is also the approach of this chapter.

In this chapter I will discuss the interface between the economic reforms and the democratisation process in Tanzania. In particular the focus will be on the conditions for a continued democratic development, in a broader sense. By doing this, some of the challenges facing Tanzania four decades after independence are highlighted. The chapter first makes a brief analysis of the economic and political spheres, to provide the basis for analysing the linkages between economic and democratic reforms. The second section analyses the interaction between economic and political reforms. The third addresses the elections and how the economic/political linkages strengthened the ruling party's election result in 2000 and 2005. The chapter is derived from a major study on the interface between economic reforms and the democratisation processes in Tanzania. [2]

The economic structure

Limited structural change took place in Tanzania from independence until the early 2000s. The World Bank estimates that per capita income increased by only 30% from 1961 to 1999 and that there was a negative per capita growth between 1978 and 1997 (World Bank, 2001). In East Africa only war-torn Burundi has a lower GDP per capita income (World Bank, 2000-2006).

The structural change that started in the late sixties was reversed in the eighties and nineties (Gibbon, 1995; Msambichaka, Kilindo et al., 1995) and apart from Burundi, Tanzania today is the most agriculture depen-dent country in East Africa. Rapid change has unfolded since the late 1990s. Mining, tourism, construction as well as new industries generated a comparatively rapid real GDP growth of 6,7% in 2004 (IMF, 2006), and 6,8% in 2005, by far the highest in the region (Bank of Tanzania (BOT) 2002-2006) and among the higher growth rates in Sub-Saharan Africa (SSA) (World Bank, 2000-2006). In 2006 the economic growth dropped marginally to 6.7% whereas in 2007 it increased to 7.1% in (EIU, 2009). The EIU estimates for Tanzanian economic growth in 2008 is 7.1% followed by a drop in 2009 to 5.0% due to the effects of the international financial crisis (ibid.)

A reasonable macroeconomic stability has been achieved (URT, 2005b). Tanzania was among the first countries to qualify for a reduction of its debts via the HIPC framework from the year 2000. Tanzania's political stability, management of the economy and relatively effective implementa-tion of reforms have been acknowledged by the international society. Aid per capita has increased from USD 29.1 in 1999 to 46.4 in 2004. Aid as percentage of Gross National Income (GNI) has increased from 11.6% in 1999 to 15.4% in 2004; still considerably lower than the all time high of 30.3% of GNI in 1993 (World Bank, 2000-2006).

The challenge is that these positive macro economic developments do not (yet?) trickle down to the vast majority of the population (Chaligha,

---

[2] If no references are made in the text, the information is based on informant interviews and conclu-sions from the field material. The study is built on three case studies: one in a poor rural district – Pangani District, Tanga region – one in the most urbanised area in Tanzania — Kinondoni District (one out of three districts in the economic capital Dar es Salaam) — the third case study was made at the national level. Field studies have been conducted several times in all three areas in connec-tion with village elections in 1999, the local government and national elections in 2000, 2004 and 2005. The last follow up study was done in May 2006.

Mattes et al., 2002; Chaligha and Davids, 2004; URT and REPOA, 2005; Afrobarometer/REPOA, 2006b; Afrobarometer/REPOA, 2006c). Partly this is due to the fact that the sectors that are growing, mining, tourism and construction, create few employment opportunities and have limited linkages to the rest of the economy (Chachage and Gibbon, 1995; Njau, 2001; Phillips, Semboja et al., 2001b; Campenhout, 2002; Kulindwa, 2003; Wangwe, Semboja et al., 2004; Kikula, 2005).

Poverty remains widespread and deep with more than 50% of the population below the poverty line, according to the most recent household budget survey and poverty reports (TAKWIMU, 2002; URT and REPOA, 2005).[3] Under-five mortality decreased between 1960 and 1985 - but *increased* from 160 to 165 deaths per 1000 live births between 1985 and 1999. Gross enrolment to the first grade *dropped* from 93% in 1980, to 63% in 1996 (UNICEF, 2002). Even if per capita growth has increased slightly in the late nineties, social indicators deteriorated for the majority until the end of the nineties, and the social situation still remains difficult. This illuminates that the majority of the population are deprived of their rights to increase their capabilities to improve their living conditions. Thus they are also dis-empowered to participate in the political processes, according to Amartya Sen's theoretical framework (Sen, 1999).

Gradually improvements have been emerging since 1999, not the least in the education sector where gross enrolment increased to 106% in 2005.[4] On the other hand the large increase of primary school enrolment since 2002 has also affected the quality of the education provided. The student-teacher ratio increased from 38 pupils per teacher in 1999 to 56 in 2005. Net enrolment to tertiary education, which is an important indicator for the capacity to build human capital, was only 0.6% in 1998. It increased to 1.2% in 2005, but is still the lowest in East Africa. Although under-five mortality rates have decreased to 126 deaths per 1000 live births in 2004 a large number of the children continue to face a very difficult situation (World Bank, 2000-2006). For example, 22% of the children were underweight in 2004 (TAKWIMU, 2005).

A number of policies have been launched to promote economic growth and reduce poverty. The main guiding policy document is *Vision 2025*, adopted in 1999 after country-wide, but shallow, consultations. It outlines Tanzania's long-term development visions. *The National Poverty*

---

[3]   A new household budget survey was conducted in 2007 and preliminary results were released by the Bureau of Statistics during 2008 and 2009, showing only marginal reductions in the poverty context in Tanzania during the period 2001 – 2007.

[4]   The reason for gross enrolment over 100% is that a large number of children above the age of seven have enrolled in primary schools after cost sharing was abolished.

Eradication Strategy (NPES) was developed as a guiding frame-work for the implementation of *Vision 2025*. The objectives of the *Vision 2025* and NPES have continued to inform policy formulation under the new "Fourth Phase" government elected in December 2005. The most influential policy process is, however, related to the Public Expenditure Review (PER) and work around the budget and the development of the Poverty Reduction Strategy (PRS). The first PRS was developed in connection with the HIPC Initiative and covered the period up to 2002/03. The second PRS was developed 2003-2005 through a series of consulations at different levels and approved in February 2005. The shift from the priority sector approach, to outcome based orientation and emphasis on growth is reflected in the name, *The National Strategy for Growth and Reduction of Poverty* (NSGRP) or in Kiswahili *Mkakati wa Kukuza Uchumi na Kupunguza Umaskini Tanzania* (MKUKUTA) (URT, 2005a). Even if the process was comparatively inclusive and innovative and a step forward, observers outside governmental circles have pointed to that the process was still shallow and had the character of "guided participation" (Gould and Ojanen, 2003). Among the tools used for consultation were seminars and workshop with stake holders at different levels, including political parties and CSO, TV/radio programme and newspaper articles (URT, 2004).

The political structure[5]

Tanzania is still in transition from a one-party to a fully-fledged multi-party system. The formal and informal institutions of democracy are still weak, even if efforts have been made to strengthen them. This section analyses some features related to different political institutions in order to identify major challenges for the democratisation process – and how it interacts with reforms in the economic sector.

Characteristics of the ruling party and the opposition

The ruling party CCM has a well-developed organisation with elaborated procedures and structures for (democratic) decision-making. But it also contains strong central authority and personal networks, with close links to the administration at different levels (Hyden, 1999; Hyden, 2005).

---

[5] This section is based on a review of documents provided by the Government of Tanzania, Sida and secondary literature, consisting of reviews, research reports, and books – with both empirical and theoretical approaches. Interviews/discussions with staff at Sida Stockholm and the Embassy in Dar es Salaam have been triangulated with interviews with different actors in Tanzania, independent researchers in Tanzania and Sweden, ten members of parliament, and donor agency staff.

The one-party culture to a large extent still defines parts of the party, the administration and the political culture — not least on a local level.

In 2000 CCM was divided in three major factions. The basis for the factions was not strongly related to different political visions, policy or ideology but rather to the power struggle involving three charismatic leaders and their factions. All three had been among the major presidential candidates since the election of 1995. The first was, Benjamin Mkapa the ruling President, chairman of the party and Nyerere's candidate in the 1995 election; the second was Jakaya Kikwete, the Minister of Foreign Affairs, representing a new generation and pragmatic policies, considered by Nyerere to be too young (45 years at the time) and inexperienced in the 1995 election; the third challenger was John Malecela (Vice-Chairman of CCM, former Prime Minister and not favoured by Nyerere in 1995 and regarded to represent the "old hardliners" and elders in the party). Some political differences were ascribed to the candidates, related to their views on the reforms, where the Malecela fraction criticised the neo-liberal aspects of the reform policies implemented by the Mkapa government and claimed to represent a more socialistic tradition. But in practice the competition between the factions within the party turned out to be limited, as could be expected in an election in between the first and the second of the two presidential periods allowed by the constitution. In CCM's internal nomination to the presidential election 2000, Mkapa in the end was the only candidate presented to the party's national congress for election.

The nomination of a new presidential candidate and MPs in 2005 was a much more open, unpredictable and competitive process. The internal nomination process within CCM is well elaborated, institutionalised and fairly democratic. Nominations start from the party branches. CCM's Central Committee selects five candidates. The National Executive Committee (NEC) recommends three of these to the CCM's National Congress, which elects the party's presidential candidate. Mkapa at an early stage announced that he would follow the constitutional rules and not attempt to change the constitution to obtain a third term, unlike the situation in several other African countries, such as Museveni in neighbouring Uganda. But there were widespread allegations that the internal nomination process was more corrupt than the election process itself, in particular as regards MP candidates. This happened even though the party set up teams to monitor the process both at national and local levels. This issue was raised in almost all the interviews we conducted with political contestants both from CCM and from the opposition, as well as from outside observers and media. After Kikwete won the presidential election in December 2005, he has strengthened his position in the party. Mkapa announced he would resign prematurely from the post of party chairman and in June 2006, Kikwete was elected the new chairman of CCM.

Although CCM is formally detached from the governmental structures, the old ties between the party and the administration still exist, both formally and informally (Mukandala, Mushi et al., 2005 and interviews). An example of the formal ties is that all key government functions down to District Commissioners and judges are directly appointed by – and thus dependent upon – the Presidency. As most "political opportunities" arise within the government administration – rather than the political structures or the private sector – incentive exists even for strong leaders from the opposition parties to join CCM. This could be observed during the preparation and campaigns for presidential and parliamentary elections both in 2000 and 2005.

With a high degree of fungibility of funds, support to the government may be indirectly or directly diverted to the ruling party. The opposition is therefore weakened by CCM's control of the government, administration and media, not least at the local level. The strong donor interests in the managerial issues of the public sector may undermine the efforts to build a strong political community and opposition, due to the informal interlinkages of the ruling party with central and local government administration.

Tanzania has 18 registered political parties, of which five are represented in the arliament. No real challenges exist to CCM, in particular in rural areas, as the opposition parties neither have the organisation nor the resources to develop structures at the district/local level. No strong nationwide opposition has emerged – as in most other African countries (Olukoshi, 1998). Most parties lack a comprehensive and realistic political programme. All are based on individuals, have a narrow social base, and are urban biased (Mmuya, 1998). After the election in 1995 the opposition parties disintegrated and were even weaker in 2000 than during the previous election. After the election of 2000 the situation changed slightly for the majority of the parties. The CUF, CHADEMA, NCCR-Mageuzi and to a lesser extent TLP and UDP, might be considered more fully developed parties. The remaining 12 parties are very small.

A large part of the parties' energies is devoted to internal power struggles. In particular who should be chairman and/or presidential candidate as demonstrated by the Tanzania Labour Party (TLP). The struggles often relate to which faction has the right to the government subsidies to the parties. The strongest and most prominent opposition party during 1994-1999 was the National Convention for Construction and Reform (NCCR-Mageuzi). It was splintered in 1999, however, when Augustine Mrema, a strong and popular former minister, who joined the party in 1995 to run for the presidency, left with the majority of the followers to join TLP. As a result both NCCR and TLP were immersed in internal power struggles. In the new situation, the Civic United Front (CUF) emerged as the strongest opposition party during the 2000 election. It continued to improve its organisation and policies in the period up to the 2005 election. The CUF is often accused of being mainly an Islamist party, with its strong base being in Pemba/Zanzibar and along the Coast. This is strongly denied by the party[6]. Several of its leading cadres are Christian and the party also had one of the most developed programmes among the opposition parties. The struggle within TLP, however, continued after the election. CHADEMA developed its organisation and changed leadership prior to the elections in 2005. Its presidential candidate, the young and dynamic businessman Freeman Mbowe, attracted young and aspiring businessmen and women during the election campaigns with a message of modernity, technological and market based development. He was the first politician in Tanzania to use a helicopter in his election campaigns, which drew enormous attention in the rural areas.

The media

The media developed strongly from the mid-nineties, printed as well as broadcasted and Internet based media. In 2006 there existed more than 100 newspapers, even if most have very limited distribution. The media played an important role as a catalyst for political reforms, in the absence of a strong civil and political society. The media now plays a major role as the opposition and helps keep the government in check, providing a voice for the opposition, citizens, and different interest groups. Even if limited to urban areas, the press also plays an important role in public education with regard to issues related to democracy and human rights. Dar es Salaam based newspapers are available in most district headquarters and other urban centres the day after they are published. Regional and local newspapers are also emerging. The outreach of newspapers in rural areas is, however, very limited.

The Internet and e-mail have also started to provide access to global information. Internet cafes are found in most regional centres and district headquarters. In a survey conducted in the year 2000, it was estimated that Dar es Salaam had over 1000 Internet cafés, indicating that Tanzania is among the most computerised countries in Africa. The government has developed an ICT strategy as well.

In the mainland, approximately 20 television stations (including those owned by District Councils which are largely receiving stations) and 30 radio stations are in operation. The government-owned radio was trans-

---

6   Personal interviews with CUF national party secretary and information secretary, mainland October 2000, June 2001, May 2002, and District Party Secretary, and District Chairman Pangani October 2000, August 2002, December 2005 and May 2006.

formed into an executive agency in 1997 and today formally provides broadcast time for views for all political parties. In addition opposition parties, NGOs, or private enterprises can buy time to air their programmes. In practice however, there is limited broadcasting of competing views, according to the opposition in the interviews we carried out. The opposition lack economic resources to buy airtime and have limited capacity to make radio programs. A number of competing radio stations and community-based radio activities have been established. Mostly, however, they are owned by either religious associations or commercial enterprises and provide little space for political debate. Television reception and coverage are limited to the major cities and the richer strata of the population that can afford to buy TV-sets. A major problem for the media producers is the limited purchasing power of the population and the high production and distribution costs of TV programmes.

Most newspapers tend to be dominated by "yellow" journalism. But a number of more serious newspapers have emerged, particularly those printed in English and targeting external and internal elites. Among them are the authoritative weekly *Business Times* and its competitor *Financial Times* and the dailies *The Guardian* (IPP), *This Day* (IPP) and the *Citizen* (Mwananchi) with their Kiswahili sister papers *Nipashe* and *Mwananchi*. *Mtanzania* from Habari Corporation is also among the more serious papers. Overall journalist salaries are very low, which makes them susceptible to go for extra income, which might interfere with their capacity to give objective reports. The level of education of most journalists is comparatively low. This gives journalists a low social status. Together these aspects affect their ability and capability for quality journalism (Interviews with journalists, MISA, Tanzania Media Council, political parties and Kilimwiko, 2002).

The legal framework circumscribes the freedom of the media. However, the freedom of the press is relatively high on Tanzania mainland. There have been a number of cases, however, where the government has tampered with the press, on the mainland and in Zanzibar. The 1976 Newspaper Act with its limitation of press freedom is still in place, but in the process of being reviewed. Other acts that infringe on media are the National Security Act, 1970 and the Broadcasting Services Act, 1993. In April 2003, the National Assembly enacted the Tanzania Communications Regulatory Authority Act, which was followed by a new policy regarding information and broadcasting. These actions were regarded as positive for media independence and freedom of expression, but the government still maintains controls and influence over the media through the legislation mentioned above. For example, the Kiswahili newspaper *Daima* was suspended by the Ministry of Information for two days in December 2005 for printing an unflattering photo of President Mkapa. This was imposed under the Newspaper Act, which allows the minister for information and culture to prohibit any publication of any newspaper "in the public interest" or "in the interest of peace and good order". Journalists – not to mention the public – do not have the right of access to public information. It is illegal to receive information from an official who is not authorised to pass on that information (*HakiElimu*, 2005). Even if existing legal restrictions are not frequently used, they tend to instil self-sensor ship among the media (Interviews with journalist and media organisations). Currently, there is an ongoing debate on a bill regarding freedom of access to information that is being prepared for tabling to parliament. The media owners association has charged that it is too restrictive and retrogressive on freedom of the press.

Three private media groups control a substantial part of the media: the IPP group, the Maarifa group, which includes the Habari corporation and the Business Times group. The IPP and the Maarifa groups are regarded as being close to CCM, even if they are private. A change was brought about in 2003 when the Nairobi based Nation Media group, the biggest and most professional media company in East Africa, bought *Mwananchi* with the aim of publishing two high quality newspapers (*The Citizen* and *Mwananchi*). The improved salaries, management, editing, equipment enhanced working conditions for journalists and improved the quality of their work. This development has challenged the media sector in Tanzania and has led to improvement of most papers inducing better researched stories and more investigative journalism. IPP media started a new paper, *This Day*, in order to meet the challenge from the Citizen (Interviews with journalists and TMC).

Corruption in the media is an issue that has continuously been discussed, not the least in connection with the elections in 2000 and 2005. It ranges from "petty" corruption in terms of political candidates having to pay for transport and food for journalists in order to get election rallies or press conferences covered to more large-scale corruption (see also chapter 8).

Legal system/constitution

The judiciary is relatively independent of the executive (Widner, 2001), but the legal system is characterised by a patchwork of different amendments to the 1977 one-party constitution. Tanzania has a pluralist legal system based on (English) common law, colonial laws, customary law and religious law. A challenge has been to merge different legal systems to a shared set of norms, without creating injustice. Conflicts between customary law and common law have been most evident in cases related to inheritance and land issues, where often customary law suppress women's rights.

Lack of resources reduces the capacity of the judiciary and the legal system to enforce the laws. Lack of educated staff with reasonable salaries opens up as well for arbitrariness and corruption in the court system (Interviews and Peter and Juma, 1998). Legal processes become unpredictable and slow – which creates abuse of human rights in terms of long periods of remand prisons and constraints for commercial activities. Poor people's rights and access to justice are limited as they have little knowledge of their rights and cannot afford legal assistance.

Legal reforms are underway, with a Legal Sector Reform Programme in place since 1999. The implementation process has however been very slow. One of the most debated issues is the constitutional status and structure of the union. A white paper on a new constitution was worked out and a number of amendments approved by the parliament in February 2000 after several years of consultative work with the community. This process strengthened the authority of the president and confirmed the structure of the union. Nonetheless, the new amendments are contested both by the civil society and the opposition that argues for the need for a new constitution.

Corruption and Nepotism/clientele networks

The government's white paper of 1996, based on the "Warioba Report", concluded that corruption, petty as well as grand pervades all levels of society. The detailed investigation of the Warioba Report revealed the extent of corruption sector by sector, including names, institutions and the embezzled amount clearly stated. Expectations were created that the Mkapa government would take a firm anti-corruption stand. The government stated it has a policy of zero tolerance of corruption, but little happened in practice. In 1999, the government adopted a National Anti-Corruption Strategy and Action Plan, aimed at improving competence and attitudes in the public service, and strengthening the legislative framework. A Public Corruption Bureau (PCB) was established in the President's Office, in order to be close to the executive. The PCB makes investigations, works to prevent corrupt practices and is open for the public to report suspected corruption. Campaigns are also undertaken to make the public more aware about corrupt practices. The second Mkapa government re-confirmed the commitment to fight corruption.

The critique against the PCB is massive from various sources, both within the opposition and among intellectuals in the wider civil society. Three types of critique are put forward: 1) the PCB should be an independent body with its own statuary power. Its location in the President's Office makes it difficult for PCB to investigate grand corruption 2) the PCB does not have enough resources (both in terms of staff and competence) to make effective investigations, and work preventively 3) the legal system is in itself corrupt. When the PCB manages to bring cases all the way to court, the process is often delayed or sabotaged in court. So far the only cases that have been brought to court and concluded are related to petty corruption.

The *"State of Corruption in Tanzania. Annual Report 2002"* (Economic and Social Research Foundation (ESRF) and Front Against Corruption 2002) made a detailed investigation of corruption for the period 1996-2001 and concluded that legal and institutional prerequisites for effective anti-corruption work were at hand. According to the report, a slight improvement of the situation as regards corruption occurred in the early 2000s but with variations between sectors. The most corrupt sectors, according to the report, are the health sector, the police, business licensing, the judiciary, the tax authorities, education and public utilities. (Afrobarometer/REPOA, 2006a) claim that corruption is increasing, while Transparency International (TI) contends that it is decreasing, according to the *State of the Public Service Report 2004*. According to the same report the key areas of accountability remained weak. However, Tanzania's ranking on TI's corruption perception index (CPI) has improved from 2.2 (out of a full score of 10) in 2001 to 2.9 in 2005, placing Tanzania as number 91 out of 163 ranked countries (Transparency International, 2000-2006). In the CPI, Tanzania is ahead of its neighbours Mozambique ranked as 99, Uganda as 105, Rwanda 121 and Kenya 142 (out of 163 countries).

Corrupt practices have involved different societal elites. The "thin" elite stretches across different sectors and influential families often have relatives or followers in both the public and the private sectors. Different elites are joined in complex networks of mutual dependence and favours. The liberalisation of the economy has strengthened Asian commercial groups and enabled new investors to establish in Tanzania, often perceived with distrust or dismay by factions of the "internal elite". In this context the issues of the need for "indigenisation" of economic activities have been reintroduced.

Civil society and participation

The civil society in Tanzania is a complex web of traditional institutions, CBOs, professional organisations and semi-state NGOs, political parties, and NGOs. The proliferation of NGOs (from 187 in 1986 to more than 9,000 in 1999) is a result of a combination of democratisation, weakened state capacity to deliver social service, and a deliberate government policy of allowing larger involvement of NGOs in the provision of different services. The vast majority of the NGOs are based in Dar es Salaam, often with limited membership and they do not necessarily have democratic structures or culture. Very few CSOs have the skills needed to undertake comprehensive policy analysis and formulation, research, advocacy or outreach activities. Few have a clear vision. Many are to be regarded more as consultancy firms or small enterprises providing social or consultative services of different kinds. Not least the NGOs hiving off from the public administration or the universities are among these.

The NGOs are heavily dependent on donors and closely connected to professional interest groups, very few are to be regarded as social movements. Four major NGO umbrella organisations exist; TAMWA, TACOSODE, TANGO, and TGNP. A new NGO policy was decided on in 1999, after long debates. One of the main constraints for the emergence of a more democratic society was and still is the lack of arenas for participation and voicing opinion (Gibbon, 2001; African Forum and Network on Debt and Development, 2002 and Kiondo, 2002). Global networks and better communications have increased the capacity of NGOs, even though most have limited capacity both in terms of human, institutional and economic resources.

The more participatory processes around the budget process and the formulation of policies have gradually provided the NGOs with new arenas. A few developed NGOs have managed to use the new space to forward their views and participate in the policy formulation process. This does not always concur with the government's interest or perceptions of what an NGO should or should not do. This was clearly illustrated in September 2005 when *HakiElimu*, the strongest educational NGO in Tanzania, disseminated a critical report on the first phase of the primary education programme. The report was based on the government's own reports and findings and highlighted a number of challenges in the education sector. *HakiElimu* was banned from undertaking any studies or publishing any reports on the education sector, because it was relaying misleading information on education in Tanzania and gave the ministry of education a bad image. President Mkapa stated that *HakiElimu* should not set foot in Tanzanian schools again until it apologized for what was described as "ridiculing government efforts in development of the education sector in the country" HakiElimu refused to apologize as the report was based on the government's own findings or well-founded research (Interview with *HakiElimu, The Guardian,* October 19 2005, April 7 2006 and February 2 2007).

Democratic culture

One of the major constraints for a deepening of democracy is the elitist attitude of administrators and political leaders on different levels in the society – as well as in the NGOs and political parties (REDET, 1997). A culture of dominance and patronage characterizes the society, from the top down to the household level and the relationship between different strata in society, man/woman and children/parents, a situation that is not unique to Tanzania. The secret service, *Usalama wa Taifa*, is still perceived to have a widespread network and reporting system. People in general express their views freely, but are careful about saying too critical things about the government or leaders if a suspected secret service agent or government official is present. The government, in particular at local level, is regularly accused of using its powers in order to suppress criticism. A businessman may not get his license renewed or is afraid that it might happen.[7]

Gradually, however, a change is being brought about. After the 2000 election, the President pushed democratic reforms firmly ahead, including establishing a more democratic culture. Some of the measures included mechanisms to facilitate better communication between the public and the government. President Mkapa introduced monthly radio speeches were he elaborated on different policies. A feedback mechanism was created where citizens could respond to the speeches. A communication unit was established in the President's Office in order to create better communication between ministries and the public. Reforms are also being undertaken within all government sectors in order to facilitate a change of attitudes as part of the PSR. However, people's satisfaction with services provided is still low. In particular at the local government level, where as many as 50-75% of the respondents are dissatisfied with the services, compared to 25-50% of the central government services (URT, 2005d; State of the Public Sector Report, 2004).

The human rights situation

In Zanzibar, violations of both human and civil rights occur frequently. On the mainland, civil rights are relatively respected, apart from the slowness of legal processes and prisoner conditions. There are, however, a few cases where civil rights are threatened even on the mainland. Freedom of the press and association has been violated, for example, the right to organise demonstrations and public meetings. Police use the pretext that order is being disturbed to intervene, and

---

[7]   This was stated in several interviews in Pangani, Tanga and Kinondoni districts during the election campaigns in 2000.

in some cases with brutality. Ibrahim Lipumba, CUF National Chairman and presidential candidate was beaten up in public and arrested at a demonstration in Dar es Salaam in 2001 against perceived irregularities in the 2000 election.

The situation deteriorated during 2000 and 2001 due to the irregularities in connection with the 2000 election in Zanzibar. The work of political parties in the opposition were constrained, for example, the office of the registrar of political parties forced two of the bigger parties to dissolve because they had not observed the constitutional obligation to elect the party leadership. The brutal killings, assaults, mass arrests, and other human rights abuses carried out by the security forces on 27 January 2001 in Zanzibar highlight the need for a careful analysis of the impact of economic reforms on the democratisation process. The human rights situation on the mainland has improved since 2001, but still the conditions in prisons are of great concern as well as the long waiting time for trials (TLHRC, 2002-2005).

The interface between economic, political, and administrative reforms in Tanzania – is a democratic pro-poor growth development regime established?

Economic reforms – undermining the democratisation process?

Since 1994, Tanzania has managed to accomplish a successful structural adjustment programme, according to the IMF and the World Bank the "basics are right". The macro economy is in balance and inflation is below 5 percent. In November 2001 Tanzania reached the completion point in the HIPC program and got a substantial reduction of its debt. Between 2000 and 2006, the GDP growth rate has been around 5% per annum. In 2005 the GDP growth was 6,8% (URT, 2005c; URT, 2006). This makes Tanzania one of the better achievers among reforming African countries. The government has been rewarded with increased aid flows from major donors.

These achievements on the macro level are, so far, not reflected in the everyday life of the majority of Tanzanian citizens. Or at least not in a way so that the majority perceive that their situation has improved up to 2003. Quite the opposite, the number of poor is perceived to have increased (Ewald, 2007). This macro-micro paradox was also mirrored in a number of social indicators until around 2002/3; food production per capita was sinking, the number of underweight children increasing and the hospitals were not fully utilised because of the perceived high cost for medical treatment.[8] Since 2004 this situation might have changed. The massive inflow of resources to the primary and lately secondary schools as a result of the HIPC and the following years increased budget for the social sectors, have brought about a change in every primary school. After the abolishment of school fees in 2002 enrolment rates have increased dramatically.

The economic reforms have, on the other hand, created new opportunities for entrepreneurs, both small scale on the village and large scale on the national level. Economic liberalisation has attracted a few transnational corporations to invest, mainly in mining and tourism. Goods are now available almost everywhere – but at a high price for most consumers. Social stratification is on the increase. Local communities are under severe stress and the fabric of rural and urban societies is changing. Popular culture from different corners of the world is trickling all the way down to the villages, creating expectations that is difficult to realise. The traditional extended families' security networks are getting thinner. Almost all households responded that the extended family networks have been drastically reduced (Ewald, Mellander et al., 2004). The level of trust in local communities of district and national administration was gradually undermined during the crisis years from the early eighties to the early 2000s. It is unclear if the last few years' development has been able to change that.

Hence, the economic reforms have to a large extent undermined people's trust in the nation building process and the state. On the other hand, increased donor support has strengthened the ruling party's resource base – in monetary and prestige terms. For example, in April 2000 among others Sweden and Japan decided to disburse budget support for 1999 and 2000 that had been frozen in 1999, just when the internal nominations for the presidential candidates started. This gave the incumbent president a strong position in internal as well as external campaigns. When donors three weeks before the election in October 2000, gave a new injection in the form of rescheduled debt within the HIPC framework, the ruling party received another boost in the election campaigns. These two incidents of increased donor support were used in almost every election campaign, we observed, as an argument that the ruling party was able to manage the economy and had the support of the donors. The decision to increase donor support followed all rules and procedures, but there appeared to have been limited analysis of the political consequences of the support to the economic reforms and how it would affect the political balance in the country. Another challenge for the opposition is that the room for

---

[8]   Conclusions in this and following paragraphs are based on a study done in Pangani, Rombo and Geita Districts 1999-2003 for the project "A Matter of Choice" (Ewald et al., 2004/2007).

economic decision-making is circumscribed by the conditions contained in the SAP/PRS. This leaves little room for competition among the parties on economic policy or ideology.

Administrative reforms – good management rather than democracy

The reforms of the public sector at different levels are strongly influenced by the New Public Management Approach aimed at establishing a small, accountable, transparent, efficient, and less corrupt public sector (Bangura, 2000; Therkildsen, 2001). This is an important step towards a more efficient state apparatus that can facilitate economic growth, and democratisation. An efficient, transparent civil service is a corner stone in the building of a democratic society. However, in the context of the elitist attitudes of public servants, the hierarchic and centralistic structure of the public administration, and focus on managerial reforms rather than accountability, the administrative reforms might also undermine the democratising aspect.

The weak resource base of the parliament, opposition and CSO hinders them from developing their capacity at the same rate as the public administration. The public sector reform might in that way even maintain undemocratic forms of governance, if reforms do not include making the parliament, opposition and CSO strong enough to monitor the work of the civil servants and the presidency, including access to information and openness (Abrahamsen, 2000; Kelsall, 2003; Kelsall and Mercer, 2003; Kelsall, Lange et al., 2005). There is also a need for changing the mindset of public servants to be accommodative to the public's demands (Mwapachu, 2005).

One of my major hypotheses is that the Presidency, the Ministry of Finance, and the donors form an "iron triangle" around the budget work. The Tanzanian Assistance Strategy process strengthened the Ministry of Finance at the cost of other ministries. The parliament, however, has little control over the administration and major decisions are not always anchored in the parliament (Ewald, 2001). The executive and managerial functions of the government are asymmetrically strengthened compared with the representative ones. This observation is also supported by an evaluation of the budget support 1999-2004 (Daima Associates Ltd, 2005) a study on the patterns of accountability in Tanzania (Mmari, Sundeet et al. 2005) and a study on the PRSP process (Gould and Ojanen, 2003).

This is also true for the extensive local government reform process. The better educated "technocrats" in the local administration are empowered through the local government reforms, at the expense of the democratically elected district councils. Most of the councillors are peasants with at best seven years of primary education, and feel that they have little opportunity to monitor the administration, according to our interviews.

After the election of 2000 efforts have been made to strengthen the parliament and the councillors in the local government. MPs and councillors have been educated, and the institutions strengthened. The parliament has a working homepage with information on procedures and bills. A new parliament building was inaugurated in 2006, with better facilities for the MPs. But the imbalances between the executive and the representative functions and between the ruling party and the opposition still exist.

Political reforms and the 2000 and 2005 elections – the consolidation of electionalism?

The first multi-party elections were held during the colonial time in 1958/59, supplemented with elections for a transitional government in 1960. After independence in 1961, a republican, multiparty-based constitution was adopted. The first post-colonial elections were held in 1962, with several parties contesting. TANU won and 99.2% voted for Julius Nyerere for President. A one party system was gradually introduced from 1963. The main argument behind this was to strengthen democratic practices and avoid the "trickery and dishonesty" and conflicts usually connected with (multi-party) politics (Nyerere in Mazrui, 1967). In 1965 the first competitive elections within a single-party system were held. A number of new leaders challenged – and defeated "old guards" from the nationalist movement on the ground that they had neither worked for their constituencies nor the country, showing an emerging democratic culture in Tanzania. Several ministers lost their seats (Cliffe, 1967). Subsequent elections to parliament and to the presidency were held every five years up to 1992, when the multi-party system was (re)introduced. Three "multi-party elections" were held in Zanzibar before the revolution in 1964, but could barely be called democratic as the political processes were limited by the British colonial rule, and its favouring of the economic elites of Arab and Indian decent. It was first in 1980 that Zanzibar resumed the conducting of its elections. Elections have been held in Tanzania in 1992 (Local Government), 1994 (Village Government), 1995 (Local Government, Parliament and President), 1999 (Village Government) and 2000 (Local Government, Parliament and President), and again in 2004 to Village Government, and 2005 to the Local Government, the Parliament and the Presidency.

The old one-party legislation has not been replaced, but amended to accommodate a multi-party system. The Nyalali commission[9] recommended in 1992 the writing of a new constitution and the removal of forty laws considered to be anti-democratic and anti-human rights, for multi-partyism to unfold. Those laws have not been repealed and still restrict activities of the opposition parties, as well as administrative procedures and the media. (Interview with Prof. C.P. Maina and LHRC May 2006). The opposition has demanded the writing of a new constitution since the inception of multi-partyism. In February 2007 the opposition threatened to boycott the 2010 election if comprehensive constitutional reforms had not been undertaken to broaden the democratic space and level the political playing field (The East African Standard, February 10 2007).

The weak resource base of the opposition parties is a severe constraint for the creation of an opposition that could match the ruling party. *Chama Cha Mapinduzi* command assets and income generating activities built up during the mono-party era and, until recently, also had access to state resources. The party has well-established structures down to the 10-cell system at household level.

Donors provided some funds for the campaigns in the 1995 election. During the period 1995-2000, the government provided a party subsidy, distributed according to the parties' representation in the parliament. As CCM was the most well organised party, and could use some of the state funds for its campaigns, CCM gained the vast majority of the parliamentary seats in the 1995 election, and thus also received the lion's share of the party subsidies, further adding to its advantage vis-à-vis the opposition.

In the 2000 election, the state and the donors gave very limited support to parties for election campaigns. The bulk of the support was divided between the electoral commission, which organises the election, and voter education conducted by NEC and different NGOs.

The uneven distribution of resources between the parties was sharpened during the 2000 election campaign. To quote just one example, the largest opposition party, Civic United Front, claimed that it only had funds to print 1,500 copies of its election manifesto, in a country with 32 million inhabitants, while CCM was well supplied with election manifestos and other materials. The unevenness was further sharpened when outgoing MPs were paid their entire pension immediately after leaving parliament.

---

[9] A Presidential Commission set up in 1991 under the leadership of Chief Justice Francis Nyalali to collect the views of citizens and make recommendations on whether the country should continue with the single party system or adopt a multi-party system. The commission recommended amending both the Union and Zanzibar Constitutions, to make Tanzania a multi-party state. Up to 2006 15 constitutional amendments have been made.

Outgoing MPs received 24 million Ths each – a substantial sum in a country where a well-educated teacher gets 1 million a year –when the election campaigns started. This provided them with a superior economic base for the re-election campaigns. In addition, the CCM candidates had strong backing from the party.

Another constraint for free and fair elections and a strong opposition is that publicly employed staff at any level or in any branch are not allowed to stand in any election. If a public servant wants to contest, he/she has to resign. If he/she loses, he/she then has to reapply for his/her job. In a context where economic activities and job opportunities outside the state apparatus are limited, one either needs to be sure of victory or very committed in order to take such a risk. Several of the interviewees stated that it was not certain that one would be re-employed in a state or local government or teaching institutions if one had contested for the opposition. In addition, most donor funds are channelled through the CCM-controlled state apparatuses. As a consequence, the opposition has huge difficulties recruiting qualified candidates. This situation was already highlighted in the 1992 election, in 1995 and again in 2000 and 2005. The government had both few resources and limited interest to build up a strong opposition. It might not be the role of the government to do that either, but there should be a levelling of the playing field in order to create the pre-conditions for healthy opposition.

Despite the debate/critique against the donors for their bias in supporting elections rather than democratic processes, the same bias prevailed in 2005. The difficulty for an aid administration to handle democracy support could be one explanation. The capacity of Tanzanian organisations is low as well. It is also politically difficult for an external government to support opposition parties in another country. This was highlighted in May 2001 when the Netherlands government proposed channeling resources through an NGO to the political parties in Tanzania.

The opposition parties themselves are weak, in terms of both organisational and policy making capacity (Maliyamkono and Kanyongolo, 2003). Only two parties, the NCCR and the CUF, had more elaborated political programmes in 2000. The situation improved in the 2005 election, but apart from CUF and CHADEMA and to a certain extent TLP and NCCR-Mageuzi, other opposition parties' programmes were not elaborated. The lack of comprehensive policy alternatives to CCM, was also one of CCM's critiques against the opposition in the 1995, 2000 and 2005 election, a critique shared by media, CSO, key informants and voters interviewed. A personal account of the creation and development of one of the Tanzanian opposition parties, CHADEMA, was presented recently by Edwin Mtei, one of its founders (Mtei, 2009).

The 2000 election

The election on the mainland was reasonably well conducted by the National Election Commission (NEC), but severely mismanaged by the Zanzibar Election Commission (ZEC) (TEMCO, 2001). The 2000 (and 2005) election in Zanzibar was a highly sensitive issue, since the 1995 election was charged with mismanagement and rigging. It is still not known whether the 2000 elections in Zanzibar were mismanaged or – as the opposition claims – rigged. Due to lack of voting materials and severe irregularities, the counting was stopped in all constituencies in Zanzibar. In 16 (out of 50) constituencies, the irregularities were so severe that the election had to be repeated a week later. In the meantime, the ballot boxes from the other constituencies were moved to ZEC administrative head-quarters, without the proper presence of the monitors of the opposition parties. This led to strong distrust in the process, from election monitors and the opposition. The opposition demanded that ZEC should be restructured and that the whole Zanzibar election should be repeated. When this was not done, the opposition boycotted the election in the 16 constituencies. The elected Zanzibar opposition MPs boycotted the union parliament and the House of Representatives (the Zanzibar parliament). As a consequence, the elected CCM government and president in Zanzibar had a limited legitimacy, from the opposition point of view.

The opposition continued to press for a rerun of the election in Zanzibar and organised a series of peaceful demonstrations. The newly elected CCM President, Amani Karume, took a more reconciliatory tone than the former distrusted hardliner, Salim Amour. Almost all senior officials were changed and only a few ministers remained in the government. It appeared to be a move towards a settlement of the conflict. However, the brutal police attack on a peaceful demonstration for a new election on 27 January 2001 severely undermined that process and created hatred and further distrust for the government. At least 23 people were killed, hundreds were detained, tortured, and raped, the wounded were denied hospital treatment, and at least 2,000 people felt forced to take refugee in Kenya and the mainland.

The mainland election results (see table 1) showed that the opposition was severely undermined as a political force in 2000. Mkapa strengthened his edge from 62% of the votes in 1995 to 72% in 2000. The main rival Augustine Mrema was far behind with a mere 8%, a drastic reduction from 1995, when Mrema got 27% of the votes. The main opposition competitor in 2000 was the CUF and CHADEMA joint candidate, Professor Ibrahim Lipumba, a respected economist. He, however, received only 16% of the votes, mainly from Zanzibar, along the mainland coast and in the Lake Zone.

Table 1: The Union Presidential elections 1995, 2000 and 2005
(% of total votes, mainland Tanzania and Zanzibar)

	1995	2000	2005
CCM (Benjamin Mkapa 1995 and 2000, Jakaya Kikwete 2005)	61.8	71.7	80.3
CUF (Ibrahim Lipumba (¹))	6.4	16.3	11.7
TLP (Augustine Mrema (²))	27.8	7.8	0.75
UDP (John Cheyo)	4.0	4.2	-
CHADEMA (Freeman Mbowe)		- (1)	5.9
NCCR-Mageuzi (Mvungi Sengondo (²))			0.5

Source: NEC 2001, 2006
[1] I. Lipumba was a joint candidate for CUF and CHADEMA in 2000
[2] A. Mrema was the presidential candidate for NCCR-Mageuzi 1995 but crossed over to TLP from 2000

In the election of 2005, CCM increased its domination even further to 80.3% of the presidential votes for its candidate Jakaya Kikwete. The 2000 election alliance between CUF and CHADEMA behind CUF's presidential candidate Ibrahim Lipumba ceased after the election of 2000. Lipumba got 11.7 percent of the votes in 2005. CHADEMA elected Freeman Mbowe as national chairman and later presidential candidate, a "young" (born 1961) and dynamic businessman. He attracted 5.9 percent of the votes after a spectacular election campaign. The CUF and CHADEMA votes taken together were roughly the same as the alliance result in 2000. Apart from these three candidates, the remaining candidates got less then 1% each of the votes.

The parliamentary election results of 2000 show an even more crushing defeat for the opposition (Table 2). On the mainland, the opposition only managed to win 14 constituencies (6.1% of the 181) while the CCM won in 164. In the union as whole, the opposition won 29 seats (12.5% of the 232 constituencies) and the CCM 198 seats. In 2005 the loss of the opposition on the mainland continued. The opposition only managed to get seven seats on the mainland (3.8% of the 182 constituencies on the mainland) and 26 in total (11-2% of the 232 in the union). 19 of the opposition seats derive from Zanzibar, and moreover 16 of these from the small island of Pemba. From the 46 directly elected seats the opposition got in 1995 it remained with only 26 in 2005. In percent that equals a fall from around 20% of

Table 2   *Results of the Union Parliamentary elections in Tanzania. Comparison between 1995, 2000 and 2005[10]*

	1995			2000			Difference 1995-2000	2005			Difference 2000-2005
	% of votes	No. of seats	% of seats	% of votes	No. of seats	% of seats	No. of seats	% of votes	No. of seats	% of seats	No. of seats
CCM	59,2	186	80	65.2	202	87.4	30	70	206	89	4
CUF	5	24	10	12.5	17	7.4	-13	14.3	19	8.2	2
CHADEMA	6.2	3	1.3	4.2	4	1.7	0	8.2	5	2.2	1
UDP	3.3	3	1.3	4.4	3	1.3	-2	1.4	1	0.4	-2
NCCR-Mageuzi	21.8	16	6.9	3.6	1	0.4	-17	3.6	0	0.0	-1
TLP	-	-		9.2	4	1.7	5	2.7	1		-3
Total	95,5	232	100	99.1	231	100	3	100	232	100	1
Total for opposition	36.3	46	19.8	33,.9	29	12.5	-17	30.2	26	11.2	-8

Sources: TEMCO 2001, NEC 2000, 2006, EIU 2000 and 2006

the directly elected seats in 1995 to around 11% in 2005. In addition to the directly elected MPs, there are special seats for women distributed according to the election results. The number of special seats for women was increased from 20 to 30% of the directly elected MPs in 2005.

However, even if CCM has increased its share of the votes in elections to the parliament from around 60% in 1995 to 70% in 2005, the opposition still gets 30% of the votes. That is 3.25 million voters, a substantial number of people. And even if the opposition only managed to get a majority in seven constituencies on the mainland it still has a substantial share of the votes in a number of regions.

---

[10] In 2000 the Parliament was made up of 231 members elected by popular vote in single member constituencies (50 from Zanzibar and 181 from the mainland); 48 seats allocated for the representation of women (20% of the seats); five seats elected by the House of Representatives of Zanzibar; 10 members nominated by the president; and the Attorney General, in total 295 MPs. In 2005 the parliament was increased to 323 members: 232 members elected by popular vote in single member constituencies (50 from Zanzibar and 187 from the mainland); the seats allocated for the representation of women were increased to 75, or 30%; five seats elected by the House of Representatives of Zanzibar; 10 members nominated by the President; and the Attorney General (TEMCO 2001, NEC 2000 and 2006, Parliament of Tanzania home page January 15 2007).

Electoral system – strong government, underrepresented opposition

The electoral system, where the MPs are elected via single-member constituencies with winner-takes-all, or first-past-the-post principle, has been hotly debated. The merit of the system is that it creates strong governments, is an easy mechanism for appointing MPs and a straightforward link between the constituencies and their representatives. The draw-back is that it reduces the number of parliamentary seats the already weak oppositions get. This is a source of concern not only among opposition party members but also in civil society. The system was debated in connection with the election in 1995, but remained due to lack of administrative capacity and financial resources to build a new system in 2000. As emerges from table 3 below, CCM got 59% of the votes in the 1995 Union Parliament Election, and received 80% of the seats. In 2005 CCM obtained 70% of the votes and 89% of the seats, virtually reintroducing the single party system. If a proportional system had been applied in 1995, the opposition would have received a substantially greater representation in the parliament of about 50 seats. In the 2000 election, the balance between the CCM and the opposition should have changed with roughly 40 more seats to the opposition — corresponding to about 17% of the seats in the parliament. In addition a number of women's seats would also have been distributed to the opposition.

A proportional system would have made it more difficult for the ruling party to get the necessary two-thirds of the votes for constitutional changes. To get the 181 votes needed, the ruling party must negotiate with the opposition. It might not have been possible to pass the amendments to the constitution made in the prelude to the election campaign during spring and summer of 2000 that strengthened the incumbent president and the CCM party candidates in such a case.

In 56 constituencies the opposition got more then 40% of the votes that are in 30% of the 186 constituencies on the mainland, including the

Table 3: Balance opposition-CCM with different electoral systems, example from election in 2000, number of seats in the parliament

	Winner-takes-it-all,	Proportional
CCM	202	151
Opposition	29	80
Total number of seats	231	231

Source: Own calculations built on NEC 2000

14 where the opposition candidate won. In four of these the opposition would have received the majority of the votes, if they had presented a joint candidate. In a further six constituencies the margin was very narrow, for instance in Tarime both candidates got 48.7% of the votes, but with 29 votes more to the CCM candidate. In Mwanza region the opposition was close to getting a mandate in two further constituencies, with a margin of less than 2%.

In 2000 the opposition won in only 14 constituencies on the mainland, compared to 23 in 1995 (NCCR 16, CHADEMA 3, UDP 4). In a great number of constituencies the opposition were either unable to raise a candidate or were barred from doing so. Seven government ministers were for example running unopposed. In Arusha region CCM was unopposed in eight of the 14 constituencies. A dramatic shift compared with 1995 when the opposition had candidates in most of the constituencies.

The 2000 election can consequently hardly be regarded as a step towards consolidation of democracy. It was at best a consolidation of "electionalism" and rather a step backwards for democracy, in wider terms. This development might threaten long-term stability in the country, in particular if the economy does not expand and more inclusive forms of governance on all levels are not developed.

Developments 2000-2005

During first quarter of 2001 political tension continued. The promising peace talks on Zanzibar between CCM and CUF did not yield results. CUF continued to boycott the parliament as a protest against what they considered an illegitimate election and Government. As a consequence, all 19 CUF MPs lost their seats in the parliament for being absent for three consecutive sessions without permission from the speaker. As a result, the parliament nearly became a single party parliament, with the opposition remaining with only 19 seats, including the special seats for women. A by-election was organised in May 2003. With 15 new CUF members voted into the parliament, an official opposition could be organised in the parliament from June 2003 onwards.

The opposition was weakened outside the parliament due to internal power struggles. For example, the second biggest opposition party, Tanzania Labour Party, was ravaged by a conflict between the founder and the charismatic Augustine Mrema who crossed over from NCCR-Mageuzi with followers in order to become TLP's presidential candidate in 1999. The conflict was mainly related to who had the right to the party, including its finances.

In September 2001, a second and more far-reaching Peace Agreement (*Mwafaka*) was reached between CCM and CUF in Zanzibar. Despite these gains, tensions continued due to the slow implementation of the agreement. The agreement, and the issue how to handle the situation on Zanzibar, was not only a source of conflict *between* CCM and CUF, but also one of the most hotly contested issues *within* CCM and CUF. With a number of irregularities in connection with the voters registration in 2004, allegations that CCM encouraged CCM members on the main-land to return to Zanzibar and controversies related to re-demarcations of constituencies there was a fear that the election 2005 might spark off pockets of violence.

A number of important reforms were made after the 2000 election on the mainland. A permanent voters register was established. A human rights commission has been initiated. The public sector and local govern-ment reforms have changed the structures and contributed to emerging changes of the attitudes prevailing in the administration (URT 2005d). The work is done in a more transparent manner. It is expected that the reforms of the education sector will create more educated citizens who have the capability to participate in the political process. The laws regu-lating the media are being reviewed. There are, however, a number of debates. The law(s) regulating media and NGOs is still criticised for giving room for the government to control and infringe on the freedom of press and assembly. Corruption is still deep. Even if more infor-mation is available on the workings of the public sector, the question is still access to information, which is circumscribed by laws, practice and attitudes.

The 2005 election

Political party activity increased from late 2003. Parties prepared for the creation of the permanent voter's register and the 2005 election. CCM's nomination process ended at the party congress in May 2005, when the presidential candidate was elected among the 11 aspiring candidates. In the process the "old guard" fraction representative, the Vice Chair-man John Malecela (71 years old) was out- manoeuvred. The National Executive Committee had nominated Mark Mwandosya (transport and communication minister), Salim Ahmed Salim (former general secretary of OAU and chairman of the Nyerere foundation and originating from Zanzibar) and Jakaya Kikwete, the Minister for Foreign Affairs. Kikwete was a popular candidate. He was comparatively young (54 years) and symbolised a new generation of political leaders and was supported by the youth wing; he had a long party history and had served in several senior governmental positions, which made him appeal to the older CCM cadres. He was perceived to be a reflecting but pragmatic politician. As a Muslim he also appealed to the marginalised Muslim community, not the least the poor Muslims in urban areas and to those in the party that had argued that it was time for a president from Zanzibar.

The relations between the CCM and CUF in Zanzibar deteriorated and formal channels of communication were suspended. A formal dialogue between the Secretaries-General of CCM and CUF in Zanzibar resumed after facilitation by the international community. A wider Inter-Party Consultative Committee was created, chaired by the Secretary-General of CCM, Mr Philip Mangula, involving the leadership of all political parties.

One important political issue in the run up to the 2005 election was the debate on the nature of the Union, particularly in Zanzibar. CCM argued for the established policy of two governments, while CUF advocated three. CCM alleged the CUF proposition would lead to the break-up of the Union. CUF denied this, and argued that the CCM wanted to end Zanzibar's autonomy. A second major political issue revolved around proposals for the formation of a Government of National Unity in Zanzibar after the election. The CUF pledged to implement this if it won the election, while CCM only agreed to consider it, as the issue was highly controversial within CCM. The idea was later ruled out as against the constitution by the attorney general.

In their manifestos, the major parties also attempted to engage in debate on other concrete issues such as economic development, health, education and jobs. There were differences regarding public policy priorities and the pace and scope of political and economic reform, but there was at same time consensus that the reform process should be continued. The alternatives to government policies in the opposition parties' election manifestos were in general weakly developed. Two of the opposition parties had more developed programmes, CUF and CHADEMA. In the CUF the presidential candidate former Professor in Economics Ibrahim Lipumba, contributed to strengthened policy formulation capacity, together with a number of well educated or political experienced party members in the comparatively large and well organised opposition party. The revitalised business oriented CHADEMA attracted a number of dynamic people, from the university and the private sector. The election manifestos of the other 15 opposition parties were in general more developed in 2005 than in connection with the election of 2000, but still far from matching CCM's.

In Zanzibar, presidential candidate Amani Karume narrowly defeated CUF's Hamad on October 30, 2005, in an election surrounded by accusations of fraud, intimidation, unfair electoral laws, a biased electoral commission, a dishonest tabulation of the ballots, and limited implementation of the amendment to the Election Act. CUF claimed that the party was repeatedly denied the right to organize campaign rallies (Civic United Front, CUF, 2005). In addition the large number of security personnel from the mainland intimidated opposition members on the CUF-dominated island of Pemba and on Unguja, where pockets of CUF supporters were outnumbered by CCM's. The Civic United Front (CUF) did not have fair and equal access to the media during the campaign period, despite assurances by the government. The CCM campaign dominated government radio, television, and print outlets, limiting coverage of opposition campaign events. Long before the formal campaign began, it was clear that the elections would be keenly contested (Commonwealth Observer Group, 2005).

On the mainland, the election campaigns went relatively smoothly. The reformed NEC pursued its work reasonably well, including the management of the new permanent voters registers. But the playing field between CCM and the opposition parties was not level. The election was postponed to December, after the death of CHADEMAs vice-presidential candidate.[10] This prolonged election campaign period was difficult for the already weak opposition parties to manage. The election result was a landslide victory for CCM (table 3). CCM got 80% of the presidential votes, and increased its constituency seats from 202 to 206 of the 232 seats in the parliament, that is, almost 90% of the MPs belong to CCM. CUF lost its two mainland seats and received 18 seats from Pemba and one from Zanzibar Stone Town. *CCM won in all but seven constituencies on the mainland.* CHADEMA increased its number of seats, from four to five. TLP lost its three seats but received one. UDP lost two seats, but John Cheyo, the UDP chairman, retained his seat. Only three of 14 opposition MPs elected on the mainland in 2000 were re-elected in 2005. CCM argued that this reflected that the opposition MPs were less able than CCM's to deliver. The opposition argued that CCM focused its attention on constituencies where they had lost in the previous election.

Local and foreign election monitors declared the 14 December 2005 general elections largely free and fair. Foreign monitors included groups from the AU, SADC, EU, and EAC. The Tanzania Election Monitoring Committee (TEMCO) coordinated the local monitors. In its preliminary

---

[10] The 2005 election was scheduled to take place on 30 October 2005. Four days before the elections, the CHADEMA vice-presidential candidate, Jumbe Rajab Jumbe, died. According to the electoral law, elections should be postponed if one of the presidential candidates or their running mates passes away. The NEC decided to postpone mainland elections to 14 December. Elections on Zanzibar for the presidency and parliament were allowed to proceed on schedule as the death of Jumbe was considered to be of less relevance here. CHADEMA itself proposed that it would have been enough to postpone the election one week.

statement on the elections it observed that in spite of a few irregularities, 'the 2005 general elections in Tanzania should be accepted as being broadly free and fair'(TEMCO, 2005).

The situation on Zanzibar was criticised by foreign observers and the opposition. CUF was convinced it would have won, if the election had been free and fair (CUF, 2005). The opposition parties argued that even on the mainland, wide spread irregularities occurred, most of all in the local government elections (Interviews with representatives of TLP, CUF and CHADEMA on various occasions). A number of court cases were investigated. This also shows that there are structures and mechanisms for managing challenges arising from the election processes, and that aspects of a culture of democracy are getting established. The media was reported to have covered the election reasonably well, even if the ruling party, received more comprehensive coverage (Media Institute of Southern Africa, MISA, 2005).

Opposition parties acknowledge that the defeat was not only linked to suppression from the ruling party and the government, but also on internal weaknesses. In a study in May 2006, we observed the systematic work that parties like CUF, CHADEMA and NCCR-Mageuzi had started to develop the organisational structures, education of party members in policy issues and organisational skills and strategies for increasing membership and development of policies and positions.

The new president and his government started by pushing the CCM election manifesto slogans into practice. The struggle against corruption was said to being intensified. Improved efficiency in central and local government is another area where the new government has made an impact. The parliament and in particular the opposition, appear to find it challenging to keep up with President Kikwete's election slogan *Ari Mpya, Nguvu Mpya, Kasi Mpya*, "new vigour, new zeal and new speed." A vision that one year after the inauguration seems to a large extent to have been realised, even if it is too early to see the long term results, particularly on the local level in rural areas.

Although progress has been made, the challenges to build credible parties based on competing visions will still remain for a long time. Issa Shivji puts it like this:

> Today we have some 18 or so parties with perhaps two or three credible ones. But there is hardly any great difference in their vision, outlook or major policies. All are donor-dependent; all are driven by the neo-liberal policies of liberalisation, privatisation and the enrichment of the minority; the so-called "Washington consensus"; and none has a credible vision of constructing

a national, democratic economy and polity in the interest of the large majority. (Shivji, 2005)

Does the overwhelming victory for CCM imply that democracy is undermined in Tanzania? We conclude with a quote from Nyang'oro, a long term observer of the democratisation process in Africa (and Tanzania).

> We have to examine why the electorate in Tanzania chose CCM over the competition. Numerous newspaper reports and political commentaries before and after the elections indicate that the majority of people in Tanzania do not think that the political opposition is mature enough to govern the country. All opposition presidential candidates are heard from only during election campaigns. It is therefore difficult for the electorate to say with any confidence that they know the candidates well. Further, all opposition parties have done a poor job of organising their parties across the country and none has an elaborate, countrywide party structure. One or two have pockets of support in a particular district or constituency, but that is more a reflection of an individual candidate's qualities or a localised issue such as an unpopular CCM candidate. In the circumstances, it is fair to say that CCM's dominance is a result of the electorate's will, and therefore fundamentally democratic. (Nyang'oro, 2006)

Concluding discussion

Tanzania has after independence developed an interesting political culture that has facilitated peaceful development, despite large parts of the population suffering from continuing economic hardships. Tanzania is one of the better reformers in Africa, with respect to democratic governance, the economy and public administration. The question is, how long can the majority of the people endure a situation of little economic progress and poverty? For many youths the situation is worse than it was for their parents. Even for those who might have gained in absolute terms, the gap between aspirations and what it is possible to realise, the relative deprivation, has most likely increased. This context creates a large potential for instability, unless new opportunities emerge.

The interplay between the economic reforms and the democratisation process was to a large extent neglected when the reforms were designed. The negative spill- over from some of the economic reforms and the reforms within the public sector has undermined important aspects of the democratisation process. Some of this neglect has been overcome during the last few years, but it still needs to be addressed.

The economic reforms have generated processes of exclusion and marginalisation. In combination with rising expectations, such real or relative deprivation can create a platform for widespread discontent. The capabilities for resource weak strata to participate in the democratisation process were hollowed out up to the early 21st century, including reduced literacy. The expansion of primary and secondary schools since 2001, might have changed the situation by the 2010 elections, when a new generation will reach voting age. Few income opportunities still exist outside the public or public controlled sector. Combined with the weak social and economic base of the opposition, this makes it difficult for the opposition to recruit qualified leaders and mobilise public support.

At the same time, the administrative reform strengthens the central and local governments' technocratic capabilities, while other reforms have not strengthened the capacity of the parliament and other accountability mechanisms to have an influence over the executive, at the same pace. At the local level the technocrats dominate the elected councillors. The asymmetrical strengthening of the executive and managerial functions of the government compared with the representative ones have contributed to policy making to a large extent being confined to the Presidency, the Ministry of Finance, and the donors who form an "iron triangle" around the budget work. The Tanzanian Assistant Strategy process strengthened the Ministry of Finance at the cost of other departments. It is very difficult for opposition parties or the civil society to get into that "iron triangle".

Taken together these processes led to the 2000 election ending up with almost a 90% dominance of the ruling party *Chama Cha Mapinduzi* (CCM) in the parliament. Rather than being a step forward for democracy, the reforms have become a step forward for "electionalism", the capacity to arrange and carry out formal multi-party elections. A number of reforms were undertaken and implemented and new policies developed after the election, not the least those aiming to restructure the central and the local government, the education sector and the new National Strategy for Growth and Reduction of Poverty. But again in 2005, the ruling party strengthened its dominance even further, raising a number of issues concerning how democratic processes could be strengthened. The challenge now is to deepen democratic processes before the 2010 election.

As economic reforms have a direct bearing on the democratisation process, there is a need for greater coherence between different sets of policy interventions and development cooperation. Support to the economic and administrative reforms must be designed so that they *do not undermine* the room to manoeuvre for the opposition, the parliament, the civil society or other political institutions, that can support the development of a healthy democracy.

In order to deepen democracy, ways must be found to go beyond the electoral procedures. Participative structures and citizens' capabilities to participate must be strengthened and a culture of democracy developed *on all levels* of the society.

There is a need to strengthen the opposition as a political institution. With the extremely uneven distribution of resources it was difficult for the opposition to create a healthy challenge to CCM in the 2000 and 2005 elections. As a result the parliament became even more dominated by CCM with almost 90% of the MPs. If there is to be a change at the 2010 election, that process must start early to have any effect. Preparation of donor support to the 2000 election started in 1998, two years before the election, which was too late. The critique was acknowledged, but the support to the 2005 election came late. Building capacity and knowledge for democratic process takes time, particularly on the local level.

The parliament at national and the councils at the local level need to be further strengthened in order to enhance their capacity to match the executive branch of the government at different levels.

The participatory elements in the ongoing public service and local government reforms need to be further strengthened. The electoral system and the size of constituencies need to be considered, as part of the process to create a more inclusive political culture.

Substantial economic improvement for the majority of the population is required to maintain a stable political development. Since 2003 it appears that Tanzania has entered a new phase of economic growth. A number of institutional reforms have been concluded and the institutional framework for democracy is gradually being established, in public administration, local government, media, education systems and reforms of the law. The challenge is to fill these frameworks with participating well-informed citizens that could use their participation to influence decision-making and accountability. For this to be effective, a well functioning party system is required.

Tanzania is at a stage of promising development both within the economic and political sector, managing a number of challenges it has wrestled with since independence, both from the global, local and national level, including scarce economic, human and institutional resources. It surely deserves to be supported to overcome the challenges that are facing the emerging democratisation processes and economic gains being achieved.

References

Abrahamsen, R. 2000, *Disciplining Democracy: Development Discourse and Good Governance in Africa*. London and New York: Zed Books.

African Forum & Network on Debt and Development 2002, *Civil Society Participation in the Prsp Process: a Case for [Name of Country]*. [Harare], AFRODAD.

Afrobarometer/REPOA 2006a, *Combating Corruption in Tanzania: Perception and Experience*. Briefing Paper 33. Dar es Salaam/Pretoria/ Kampala, REPOA/IDASA/Wilsken Agencies, Ltd. Michigan State University.

—, 2006b, *Despite Economic Growth, Tanzanians Still Dissatisfied*. Briefing Paper 36. Dar es Salaam/Pretoria/Kampala, REPOA/IDASA/ Wilsken Agencies, Ltd. Michigan State University.

—, 2006c, *Delivery of Social Services on Mainland Tanzania: Are People Satisfied?* Briefing Paper 34. Dar es Salaam/Pretoria/Kampala, REPOA/IDASA/Wilsken Agencies, Ltd. Michigan State University.

Ake, C. 2000, *The Feasibility of Democracy in Africa*. Dakar, Senegal, Council for the Development of Social Science Research in Africa.

Bakari, M.A. 2001, *The Democratisation Process in Zanzibar: A Retarded Transition*. Hamburg, Institut fur Afrika-Kunde.

Bangura, Y. 2000, *Public Sector Restructuring: The Institutional and Social Effects of Fiscal, Managerial and Capacity-Building Reforms*. Occasional Paper 68. Geneva, United Nations Research Institute for Social Development.

Bank of Tanzania (BOT) 2002-2006, *Quarterly Economic Report (S)*. Dar es Salaam, Bank of Tanzania.

Bratton, M., R.B. Mattes, et al. 2005, *Public Opinion, Democracy and Market Reforms in Africa*. Cambridge, Cambridge University Press.

Bratton, M. and N. van de Walle 1997, *Democratic Experiments in Africa: Regime Transitions in Comparative Perspective*. Cambridge and New York: Cambridge University Press.

Campenhout, B. v. 2002, "The Impact of the Mining Industry on the Future Development of Tanzania". Dar es Salaam, Economic and Social Research Foundation: 15.

Chabal, P. 1999, *Africa Works*. London: Zed Books.

Chachage, C.S.L. 1999, "Land Issues and Tanzania's Political Economy." In P.G. Forster and S. Maghimbi (eds), *Agrarian Economy, State and Society in Contemporary Tanzania.* Aldershot: Ashgate.

—, 1993, "Forms of Accumulation, Agriculture and Structural Adjustment in Tanzania." In P. Gibbon (ed.), *Social Change and Economic Reform in Africa.* Uppsala: Nordiska Afrikainstitutet.

—, 1995, "The Meek Shall Inherit the Earth but Not the Mining Rights: The Mining Industry and Accumulation in Tanzania." In P. Gibbon (ed.), *Liberalised Development in Tanzania.* Uppsala: Nordiska Afrikainstitutet.

Chaligha, A. and Y.D. Davids 2004, *Public Perceptions on Democracy and Governance in Tanzania.* A Report Based on the 2003 Afrobarometer Survey. Dar es Salaam.

Chaligha, A., R. Mattes, et al. 2002, *Uncritical Citizens or Patient Trustees? Tanzanians' Views of Political and Economic Reform.* Dar es Salaam/ Cape Town/Accra, Afrobarometer.

Chambers, R. 1983, *Rural Development: Putting the Last First.* London: Longman Press.

—, 1997, *Whose Reality Counts? Putting the First Last.* London: London Intermediate Technology.

Civic United Front (CUF) 2005, *Report on the General Election in Zanzibar of 30 October 2005.* Zanzibar, Office of the Secretary General, 2005, p. 3.

Cliffe, L., ed. 1967, *One-Party Democracy.* Nairobi: East African Publishing House.

Commonwealth Observer Group 2001, *The Elections in Zanzibar, United Republic of Tanzania, 29 October 2000: The Report of the Commonwealth Observer Group.* London: Commonwealth Secretariat.

—, 2005, *The Elections in Zanzibar, United Republic of Tanzania 30 October 2005. The Report of the Commonwealth Observer Group.* London: Commonwealth Secretariat.

Cowen, M. and L. Laakso (eds) 2002, *Multi-party Elections in Africa.* Oxford: James Currey.

Daima Associates Ltd 2005, *Joint Evaluation of General Budget Support Tanzania 1995-2004. Report to the Government of Tanzania and to the Poverty Reduction Budget Support (Prbs) Development Partners.* Revised Final Report, Dar es Salaam, Daima Associates Ltd.; ODI.

Economic and Social Research Foundation (ESRF) and Front Against Corruption 2002, *State of Corruption in Tanzania.* Annual Report. Dar es Salaam, ESRF.

EISA Election Observer Mission Report 2005, *Tanzania Presidential National Assembly and Local Government Elections 14 December 2005.* Eisa Election Observer Mission Report No 20. Johannesburg, EISA.

EIU 2000, *Country Profile Tanzania and the Comoros 2000.* London: The Economist Intelligence Unit.

—, 2006, *Country Report Tanzania February 2006.* London: The Economist Intelligence Unit.

—, 2009, *Country Report Tanzania October 2009.* London: The Economist Intelligence Unit.

Ewald, J. 1996, "Tanzania Och Sydafrika. Demokratisering På Vems Villkor?"In B. Kaufman, *Demokratins Utmaningar.* Göteborg: Peace and Development Studies, Göteborg University.

—, 1997, *The Political Economy of Structural Adjustment. The Case of Cotton, Coffee and Maize Production in Arumeru and Geita District, Tanzania.* Göteborg: Peace and Development Studies, Göteborg University.

—, 2001, "The Interface between Democracy and Economic Change. The Case of Structural Adjustment and Democracy in Tanzania". In A. Närman and J. Ewald, *Göteborg University in Africa. Africa at Göteborg University.* Göteborg: Centre for Africa Studies, Göteborg University.

Ewald, J., L. Mellander, et al. 2004, "A Matter of Cho ice? Cost Sharing in Health and Education from a Rights of the Child Perspective". Göteborg: Centre for Africa Studies, Göteborg University.

Ewald, J., L. Mellander, R. Mhamba and I. F. Shao 2007, "A Matter of Choice? Cost sharing in health and education from a rights of the child perspective in Pangani, Rombo and Geita Disticts in Tanzania". Final report. Göteborg: Centre for Africa Studies, Göteborg University.

Freedom House 2006, *Countries at the Crossroads 2006. Country Report - Tanzania.* Washington DC: Freedom House.

Gibbon, P. 2001, "Civil Society, Locality and Globalization in Rural Tanzania: A Forty-Year Perspective." *Development and Change* 32(5).

—, (ed.) 1995, *Liberalised Development in Tanzania: Studies on Accumulation Processes and Local Institutions.* Uppsala: Nordiska Afrikainstitutet.

Gould, J. and J. Ojanen 2003, *Merging in the Circle. The Politics of Tanzania's Poverty Reduction Strategy.* Helsinki: Institute of Development Studies, University of Helsinki.

The Guardian 22 January 2002, "Kikwete Upbeat About Tanzania's Economic Resilience". Dar es Salaam.

The Guardian 16 March 2006, "Temco: Elections Were Free and Fair in Both Mainland and the Isles". Dar es Salaam.

Gyimah-Boadi, E., ed. 2004, *Democratic Reform in Africa. The Quality of Progress.* Boulder and London: Lynne Rienner Publishers.

HakiElimu 2005, *Access to Information in Tanzania: Still a Challenge. A Research Report.* Dar es Salaam: HakiElimu/REPOA.

Hyden, G. 1999, "Top-Down Democratization in Tanzania." *Journal of Democracy* 10(4):142-155.

—, 2005, "Why Do Things Happen the Way They Do? A Power Analysis of Tanzania". Unpublished consultancy report. Dar es Salaam, Embassy of Sweden.

IDEA 2002, *Voter Turnout since 1945.* Stockholm International Institute for Democracy and Electoral Assistance.

IMF 2006, United Republic of Tanzania: Fifth Review under the Three-Year Arrangement under the Poverty Reduction and Growth Facility. Staff Report; Staff Statement; Press Release on the Executive Board Discussion; and Statement by the Executive Director for the United Republic of Tanzania. Imf Country Report No. 06/138 Washington DC: IMF.

Kelsall, T. 2003, "Governance, Democracy and Recent Political Struggles in Mainland Tanzania." *Commonwealth and Comparative Politics* 41(2).

Kelsall, T., S. Lange, et al. 2005, *Understanding Patterns of Accountability in Tanzania. Component 2: Bottom-up Perspective.* Oxford/Bergen: Oxford Policy Management, Chr. Michelsen Institute.

Kelsall, T. and C. Mercer 2003, "Empowering People? World Vision & 'Transformatory Development' in Tanzania." *Review of African Political Economy* 30 96:293-304.

Kikula, I., Kipokola, J., Shivji. I., Semboja, J. and Tarimo, B. (eds) 2005, *Researching Poverty in Tanzania. Problems, Policies and Perspectives.* Dar es Salaam: REPOA.

Kilimwiko, L.I.M. 2002, *The Fourth Estate in Tanzania.* Dar es Salaam: Color Print.

Kiondo, A. (2002), "Civil Society in Tanzania". *Democratisation and Conflict Management in Eastern Africa.* Göteborg: Center for Africa Studies, Göteborg University.

Kulindwa, K., Mashindano O., Shechambo F., Sosovele H. 2003, *Mining for Sustainable Development in Tanzania.* Dar es Salaam: Dar es Salaam University Press.

Legum, C. and G. Mmari, (eds) 1995, *Mwalimu. The Influence of Nyerere.* London: James Currey.

Lindberg, S. 2006, *Democracy and Elections in Africa.* Baltimore: The John Hopkins University Press.

Lumumba-Kasongo, T. (ed.) 2006, *Liberal Democracy and Its Critics in Africa. Political Dysfunction and the Struggle for Social Progress.* London: Zed Books.

Maliyamkono, T.L.(ed.) 2000, *The Political Plight of Zanzibar.* Dar es Salaam: Tema Publisher.

Maliyamkono, T.L. and F.E. Kanyongolo 2003, *When Political Parties Clash.* Dar es Salaam: Tema Publishers.

Mazrui, A.A. 1967, "Tanzaphilia. A Diagnosis". *Transition* 31.

Mbelle, A.V.Y., G.D. Mjema, et al., (eds) 2002, *The Nyerere Legacy and Economic Policy Making in Tanzania.* Dar es Salaam: Dar es Salaam University Press.

Media Institute of Southern Africa (MISA) 2005, Election Monitor (Various Issues). Tanzania Media Election Monitoring Project. Dar es Salaam.

Mmari, O., G. Sundet, et al. 2005, Understanding Patterns of Account-ability in Tanzania. Component Iii: Analysis of Values, Incentives and Power Relations in the Budget Allocation Process. Oxford Policy Management, Oxford; Chr. Michelsen Institute, Bergen; Research on Poverty Alleviation, Dar es Salaam.

Mmuya, M. 1998, *Tanzania Political Reform in Eclipse. Crises and Cleavages in Political Parties.* Dar es Salaam: Friedrich Ebert Stiftung.

Msambichaka, L.A., A.A.L. Kilindo, et al. (eds) 1995, *Beyond Structural Adjustment Programmes in Tanzania. Successes, Failures and New Perspectives.* Dar es Salaam: Economic Research Bureau, University of Dar es Salaam.

Mtei, Edwin 2009, *From Goatherd to Governor. The autobiography of Edwin Mtei.* Dar es Salaam Mkuki na Nyota Publishers.

Mukandala, R., S.S. Mushi, et al. (2005), *The Political Economy of Tanzania.* Consultancy report commissioned by the World Bank, Dar es Salaam.

Mushi, S.S. and R. Mukandala, (eds) (1997), *Multiparty Democracy in Transition. Tanzania's 1995 General Elections.* Dar es Salaam: Tanzania Election Monitoring Committee.

Mwapachu, J. 2005, *Confronting New Realities. Reflections on Tanzania's Radical Transformation.* New Dehli: Sona Printers.

Narayan, D. 1997, *Voices of the Poor: Poverty and Social Capital in Tanzania.* ESD Monograph No.17. Washington DC: World. Bank.

NEC 1997, *The Report of the National Electoral Commission on the 1995 Presidential and Parliamentary Elections.* Dar es Salaam: National Electoral Commission, United Republic of Tanzania.

—, 2000, *General Election 2000 Parliamentary Election Results and Statistical Data.* Dar es Salaam: National Electoral Commission, United Republic of Tanzania.

—, 2006, *General Election 2005 Presidential Election Results, Mainland and Zanzibar.* Dar es Salaam: National Electoral Commission, United Republic of Tanzania.

Njau, A. 2001, "Tanzania Gets Raw Deal in Its Mining Sector". *Business Times.* Dar es Salaam.

Nyang'oro, J. 2006, *The 2005 General Elections in Tanzania: Implications for Peace and Security in Southern Africa.* Occasional Paper. Johannesburg: Institute for Strategic Studies.

Olukoshi, A. O. 1998, *The Politics of Opposition in Contemporary Africa.* Uppsala: Nordiska Afrikainstitutet.

Peter, C. M. and I.H. Juma (eds) 1998, *Fundamental Rights and Freedoms in Tanzania.* Dar es Salaam: Mkuki na Nyota Publishers.

Phillips, L.C., H. Semboja, et al. 2001, *Tanzania's Precious Minerals Boom: Issues in Mining and Marketing.* Dar es Salaam: Equity and Growth through Economic Research (EAGER): 48.

REDET 1997, *Political Culture and Popular Participation in Tanzania*. Dar es Salaam: REDET.

Sen, A. 1999, *Development as Freedom*. Oxford: Oxford University Press.

Seppälä, P. 1998, *Diversification and Accumulation in Rural Tanzania: Anthropological Perspectives on Village Economics*. Uppsala: Nordiska Afrikainstitutet.

Shivji, I.G. 2005, "Elections in Tanzania: In Search of a Principled Vote". *Pambazuka News*.

TAKWIMU 2002, *Household Budget Survey 2000/01. Final Report*. Dar es Salaam: Tanzania National Bureau of Statistics ((TAKWIMU).

TAKWIMU 2003, *2002 Population and Housing Census: General Report*. Dar es Salaam: Central Census Office, National Bureau of Statistics, President's Office, Planning and Privatization.

—, 2005, *The 2004-05 Tanzania Demographic and Health Survey (2004-05)*. Dar es Salaam:National Bureau of Statistics (TAKWIMU).

TEMCO 1997, *The 1995 General Election in Tanzania. Report of the Tanzania Election Monitoring Committee*. Dar es Salaam: Tanzania Election Monitoring Committee (TEMCO).

—, 2001, *The 2001 General Election in Tanzania. Report of the Tanzania Election Monitoring Committee*. Dar es Salaam: Tanzania Election Monitoring Committee (TEMCO).

—, 2005, *Temco Interim Statement on the 2005 General Elections in Tanzania*. Dar es Salaam: Tanzania Election Monitoring Committee (TEMCO).

Therkildsen, O. 2001, *Efficiency, Accountability and Implementation: Public Sector Reform in East and Southern Africa*. Geneva: United Nations Research Institute for Social Development.

TLHRC 2002-2005, *Human Rights Annual Reports*. Dar es Salaam: Tanzania Legal and Human Rights Centre (TLHRC).

Transparency International 2000-2006, *Corruption Perception Index*. Retrieved 11 November 2006.

UNICEF 2002, *The Situation for the Children in Tanzania*. Dar es Salaam.

URT 2004, *An Analysis of Respondents' Views as Expressed in Questionnaires for Prsp Review*. Dar es Salaam, United Republic of Tanzania,Vice President's Office.

—, 2005a, *National Strategy for Growth and Reduction of Poverty (Nsgrp)/ Mkukuta (Mkakati Wa Kukuza Uchumi Na Kupunguza Umaskini Tanzania)*. Dar es Salaam, United Republic of Tanzania, Vice President's Office.

—, 2005b, "Speech by the Minister for Finance Hon Basil Mramba Introducing the National Assembly to the Estimate of Government Revenue and Expenditures Financial Year 2005/06". Dar es Salaam, United Republic of Tanzania.

—, 2005c, "Speech by the Minister of State, President's Office, Planning and Privatization, Hon. Dr. Abdallah Omari Kigoda (MP), Introducing the National Assembly to the Economic Survey 2004 and Proposal for Medium Term Plan and Expenditure Framework for 2005/06-2007/08". Dar es Salaam, United Republic of Tanzania.

—, 2005d, *State of the Public Service Report 2004*. P.S.O. United Republic of Tanzania.

—, 2006, *The Economic Survey 2005*. Dar es Salaam, United Republic of Tanzania, The President's Office, Planning and Privatization.

URT and REPOA 2005, *Poverty and Human Development Report 2005*. United Republic of Tanzania and Research and Analysis Working Group of the Poverty Monitoring System on behalf of the Government of Tanzania/REPOA. Dar es Salaam: Mkuki na Nyota Publishers.

van de Walle, N. 2001, *African Economies and the Politics of Permanent Crisis, 1979-1999*. Cambridge and New York: Cambridge University Press.

Wangwe, S.M. 1997, *Economic Reforms and Poverty Alleviation in Tanzania*. Dar es Salaam: Economic and Social Research Foundation.

Wangwe, S.M., H.H. Semboja and L.C. Phillips 2004, "Tanzania: Policy Research and the Mining Boom". In L.C. Phillips and D. Seck (eds), *Fixing African Economies: Policy Research for Development*. Boulder: Lynne Rienner Publishers.

Widner, J. 2001, *Building the Rule of Law. Francis Nyalali and the Road to Judicial Independence in Africa*. New York and London: W.W. Norton and Company.

World Bank 2000-2006, *World Development Indicators (WDI)*. Washington DC:World Bank.

—, 2001, *Tanzania at the Turn of the Century. From Reforms to Sustained Growth and Poverty Reduction.* Washington DC: World Bank and The Government of Tanzania.

—, 2005, *The Poverty Reduction Strategy Initiative: Findings from Ten Country Case Studies of World Bank and IMF Support.* Washington DC: World Bank.

CHAPTER ELEVEN

POSTSCRIPT: TANZANIA IN TRANSITION – SUMMARY AND TRENDS 2005 – 2010[1]

Kjell Havnevik

This book describes and analyses transitions in Tanzania related to the agrarian sector (chapters 4, 5 and 6), forestry (chapter 7), development cooperation (chapter 9) and governance and democratization (chapters 8 and 10) with emphasis on the Mkapa era. All the areas analysed in the book are critical for Tanzanian development. The majority of the population in rural areas, development assistance is dominant for the country's development activities and democratization aims at promoting agency so that people can influence their own lives and livelihoods, i.e. exercise their freedoms. The attempts to promote transitions both during the Mkapa era and beyond, however, rest on a legacy of colonialism and more than three decades of one-party state rule. The understanding of this legacy is outlined in the historical parts of the book (chapters 2, 3 and partly chapter 4) and with particular attention to the role and influence of Julius Nyerere, president of Tanzania from 1961 to 1985, and later given the official title, "Father of the Nation". In addition, the context of transitions in Tanzania has, since the mid-1980s, been embedded in the process of economic liberalization (Shivji, 2006), pushed by International Financial Institutions and gradually embraced by the Tanzanian governments. Thus the outcomes of Tanzanian transitions are connected with both domestic and external strategies and processes of change.

Agrarian Transitions and Growth Performance

As to the agrarian transitions analysed, certain dynamics have been identified in the research presented in this book. In particular expanding urban-like rural settlements, wealth accumulation and class differentiation are emerging and capitalist investors are taking a stronger grip on land and use of wage labour (Katoro-Buseresere in the north) (chapter 4). However, findings from rural settings show that land policies aimed at agrarian transitions are unable to challenge the customary land ownership systems (Njombe and Maswa districts in the south-west and north/central). The customary system prevails with only a slow movement in the direction of

---

[1] I am grateful for constructive comments on this postscript by Jonas Ewald and Mats Hårsmar.

land markets until the mid-2000s (chapter 6). In all cases agrarian forms of livelihood are foundational to material and cultural security although economic diversification has been spread and intensified during recent decades.

The continued reliance on customary ownership systems may reflect a sense of insecurity or uncertainty as regards rural people's trust in formal institutions, including those related to individual land titling. Many rural informants stated that privatization of land would lead to landlessness and poverty. As well rural diversification can be seen as a way for small-holders to spread risk or to counter uncertainty and to withdraw from state controlled agricultural marketing systems. Economic diversification into extra-agricultural activities, including trading, handicrafts, forestry, fishing etc, emerged on a larger scale in Tanzania in connection with economic stagnation during the 1970s and has intensified since, including rural-urban migration (Ellis, 1983, Maliyankono and Bagachwa, 1990, Havnevik, 1993, Havnevik and Hårsmar, 1999 and Bryceson, 2000). The diminishing role of agriculture as an income earner in sub-Saharan Africa today, and a manifestation of rural dynamics, is reflected in that more than 50% of rural incomes are extra-agricultural (Havnevik et al, 2007).

More recent empirical studies have conceptualized rural dynamics in terms of vulnerability defined as the likelihood of experiencing future loss of welfare, weighted by the magnitude of expected welfare loss. The level of vulnerability is connected with the characteristics of the risk and the capacity of the household to respond to it through various risk management strategies. Household vulnerability could be conceptualized as existing of several components, including (i) uncertain events, (ii) the possibilities for managing risks or risk responses and (iii) the outcome in terms of welfare losses.

A recent study by Sarris and Karfakis (2007) focusing on Kilimanjaro (north) and Ruvuma (south-west) regions shows that vulnerability in the rural regions of Tanzania is quite high and considerably higher in poor (Ruvuma) as compared to more well off regions (Kilimanjaro). However, vulnerability as well appears to differ considerably among different areas within Kilimanjaro as well as in Ruvuma. Differences in vulnerability were found to be much higher in Kilimanjaro region in spite of this region being the better off region (Sarris and Karfakis, 2007).

Recent developments connected with the external or global context may have added to the vulnerability of smallholders in Tanzania and other sub-Saharan African countries. One trend is the increase in establishment of vertical agricultural value chains, connecting smallholders or contract farmer arrangements in Africa with consumers in the north, in which transnational agri-business and northern supermarkets are becoming increasingly dominant (Gibbon and Ponte, 2005). In addition, the leasing of land to large scale food production and agro-fuels has been accelerating during the last decade (IFPRI, 2009, Cotula et al, 2009 and Havnevik, 2009). Such large scale land accessions have been brought about by a quest for food security, energy security and in response to climate change by Northern, Arab and Asian countries. However, on the African side, the outcomes are already recorded in growing food insecurity and environmental problems in some of the affected areas (UN Special Rapporteur on the Right to Food, 2009). The above processes have often been pursued without due concern being given to the land rights of rural communities, smallholders and despite, as in the case of Tanzania, the fact that customary and village land rights are protected by the Tanzanian Land Acts of 1999. However, rural people are (as shown in chapter 6) to a large extent uninformed about the content of the Land Acts. Rural people also lack education, insights and organisation to struggle for their land rights. Agency for women has, however, widened through the land legislation and led as well to more active engagement in income earning activities.

Economic liberalization of agricultural production and trade has not triggered agricultural production and productivity when comparing the pre-liberalisation period, 1976-1986, and the post-liberalisation period, 1986-1996. On the contrary economic liberalization of the agricultural sector has, in combination with varying weather conditions, led to higher agricultural producer price variability in the latter period which made it more difficult for smallholders to plan financially (chapter 5). Historically and currently, in order to protect the incomes and price stability of farmers in e.g. Europe, agreements were made between governments and farmers' organizations. Moreover, the "infant industry" argument was strongly held up by most governments. A more thorough historical analysis has shown that experiences from agricultural and industrial developments in the north are actually overlooked when advice is given to Tanzania and Africa to develop (Chang, 2003).

Actual statistics show that agricultural growth in Tanzanian has continued to record a stable increase from 2000 onwards. From 2005 to 2007 the agricultural growth ranged from 3.9 % to 4.4 %. Estimates for 2008 (4.8 %) and 2009 (3.4 %) show an increasing variability in agricultural growth (EIU, October 2009). The figure for 2009 is, however, to some extent affected by the impact of the international financial and economic crisis.

The average annual national per capita real GDP growth (in constant 2000 USD) for the decade 1990-1999 was negative, - 0.2 %. During Mkapa's second presidential period, per capita average annual real GDP growth increased to 3.6 % (World Development Indicators). Mining, tourism and construction were the main drivers in this GDP growth that reached 6.7 % in 2004 (IMF, 2006) and 7.4 % in 2005 (EIU, 2009). The figures for real GDP growth during president Kikwete's first period were 6.7 % in 2006 and 7.1 % in 2007 (EIU, 2009). The EIU estimates for real GDP growth in 2008 are 7.1 % and 5 % for 2009. Industrial GDP growth is ranging between 10.4 % and 8.5 % during the period 2005 – 2007, whereas estimates for the subsequent years are lower. Inflation has increased rapidly during the last year, reaching 12.2% in October 2009 (BoT, 2009).

At the end of the 2000s, minerals, including gold and gemstones, not agriculture, emerged as the major export earning sector. Thus a change in the composition of export earnings within the natural resource sectors has emerged, but it is hardly transformational. What is of further importance is that the fast growing sectors, such as mining and tourism, are dominated by external owners, individuals and firms so that the Tanzanian government and society have less control over the incomes and profits generated in these sectors. Increased dependence on tourism and the mining sector for export incomes also made Tanzania more vulnerable to changes in global markets. Gold prices have soared as a result of the financial crisis, thus increasing Tanzanian export incomes. On the other hand the number of tourists has been reduced and foreign investment has been falling in the sector.

Trends in poverty over time

Fears about the significance of GDP as a measure for domestic and societal development also emerge when looking at the relationship between GDP growth and change of the incidence of poverty over time. Recent statistics from the Household Budget Survey 2007 show that the link between GDP growth and poverty has been negligible. According to the National Bureau of Statistics the percentage of the population below the food poverty line declined from 22 % in 1990/91 to 19 % in 2000/01 and to 17 % in 2007. The parallel decline in the percentage of the population below the basic needs poverty line was 39 % (1990/91), 36 % (2000/01) and 33 % (2007). The total reductions in the poverty indicators over a 16/17 year span, and encompassing Mkapa's two presidential periods, are thus only 5 % and 6 % respectively.

The situation in rural areas is bound to be worse since the incidence of rural poverty is higher than urban. Poverty reduction, both in terms of food and basic needs, may thus not have improved for large sections of the rural areas. As to hunger, statistics from 2005 show that for all categories measured, rural people were worse off than those of the urban popula-tion (Afrobarometer, 2005). The lack of change over time is also manifested by figures showing that the poorest 20 % segment of the population accounts for only 7 % of total consumption throughout the period 1990/91 to 2007 (National Bureau of Statistics, 2009). Average household size shows a decline from 5.7 in 1990/91 to 4.9 in 2000/01, but only a slight further reduction in 2007 (4.8). During the same period the mean percentage of dependants was quite stable, increased from 40 in 1991/92, to 42 in 2000/01 and 43 in 2007. The most important structural change at household level is the increase in female headed households from 18 % in 1990/01 to 25 % in 2007 (National Bureau of Statistics, 2009).

The outcomes of a decade of Tanzanian Poverty Reduction Strategies on rural poverty, economic and household structures can thus be taken to be limited. Tanzanian economic growth in the 2000s has in other words not been pro-poor. In spite of this, Tanzania is held up, as mentioned in the introduction to this book, as model reformer by the World Bank, IFIs and other donors to be followed by others. This however, cannot be for the dismal poverty reduction outcomes that Tanzania has achieved, but rather for the country's ability to instill more discipline in its macro-economic management. The question as to how long macro-economic stability can be maintained when people's expectations are not met, is discussed in chapter 10.

Institutional change and local agency in the forestry sector

As shown in this book, important institutional, policy and legal developments occurred in the forestry sector during the Mkapa era. Policies and laws have opened a space for rural agency where people can use existing institutions from below for the purpose of community and joint forest management (chapter 7 and Havnevik et al, 2006). Although the Tanzanian experience with participatory forest management shows some promise, there are also doubts that collaborative management can deliver according to rural and national expectations. It has in particular been difficult to design benefit sharing mechanisms between state agencies and the villages when it comes to reaping the material benefits from improved forest management. The development and sustainability of successful community forestry experiences in Babati (Duru-Haitemba), Singida (Migori) and Kiteto (Suledo) districts during the Mkapa era, supported by development assistance, are currently being threatened in various ways.

Corruption related to the forestry and natural resources sector have come into the open through various studies. In addition, withdrawal of development assistance, due to the new development assistance paradigm, to promising long term community forestry development projects and programmes, is threatening their sustainability. The withdrawal of project and programme assistance from 2005 onwards, in response to the new development assistance architecture connected with the Paris Declaration, has, however, left many communities and villages on their own when it comes to the crucial process of harvesting the gains of long term forest conservation efforts. Some of the community and participatory forestry projects can definitely be seen as test cases as to whether development from below is possible in rural Tanzania, and a case in point is the cooperation among nine villages in Kiteto district, Manyara region to reap the benefits from management of a huge forest, Suledo.

Trends in corruption

The overall findings related to corruption in Tanzania, as presented in chapter 8 in this book, show that it did not change significantly during the reign of Mkapa. Petty corruption linked to foreign business and investments appears to decline during his reign, while that linked with household service delivery did not. On the contrary, the public perceives that such corruption has increased (chapter 8).

President Mkapa for his part, started out with a crusading anti-corruption stand in 1995 and with the commissioning of the Warioba report in 1996, but ended his second presidential term by asking for proof of corruption from the public, not proof of their innocence from the accused government officials. Corruption related evidence from Mkapa's era, including evidence that has emerged since 2006, shows corruption to be on the increase during and after Mkapa's second presidential period. The number of corruption cases before the courts in 2005 was about 50 whereas information shows such corruption cases to have increased to 578 in 2009 (including 27 cases of grand corruption) (EIU, 2009). The increase in corruption cases before the courts from 2005 to 2009, however, partly relates to Mkapa's second presidential period, including some cases of grand corruption.

In connection with grave corruption claims, President Kikwete dissolved the cabinet in February 2008, and sacked the Prime Minister and prominent business man Edward Lowassa. Likewise the Governor of the Bank of Tanzania Daudi Ballali, was sacked for his involvement in dubious payments in the range of some US$200 to US$800 million (there is uncertainty about the figure) from the Bank's commercial external debt account. He was also charged with inflating the cost of the extension (Twin Towers) of the Bank of Tanzania's headquarters which was originally budgeted to cost $ 80 million, but later increased to US$340 million. Ballali later passed away. In spite of this development, however, no high profile people have so far been brought to trial. Speculations are that this will not occur before the elections in 2010. There is also doubt, in many quarters, whether the fight by the current president, Jakaya Kikwete, to curb corruption, is a first priority, since so many important ruling party members and high profile businessmen are implicated in the corruption cases that have become public.

A difficult consideration in the fight against corruption is anyway, when it is becoming entrenched at different levels, to draw the line between corruption and non-corruption. What has certainly emerged from the spread and exposure of corruption during the last decade is that decent and hard working people in urban and rural areas, including the young generation, are almost left without political leaders as examples to follow in creating a vision for the future of Tanzania that they can believe in. The landslide win by Kikwete in the presidential elections in 2005, showed him to be the preferred leader of the Tanzanian people. But he has yet to prove that his leadership can be sustainable, and an example to follow, over time.

The experiences from the last decade of corruption in Tanzania show that it does not necessarily prevent economic growth. However, lack of poverty reduction, high levels of development assistance and weak social security arrangements for professional groups can be seen as structural features fueling corruption. The combination of the spread of a culture of corruption, rapid privatization of state property, and weak monitoring institutions can make it difficult to uproot corruption. The fact that there have to be two or more partners involved for corruption to occur, may make it hard to pin it down and address, and particularly when some of the partners are based outside Tanzania. In the longer run corruption that most often benefits from conserving social power relations, is also likely to undermine transformational processes.

Democratisation

The process of multi-party democratization, however, aimed to make government and other institutions accountable and transparent and thus restore trust in and improve the country's governance structure. Starting from the first multi-party elections in 1995, the former single political party, CCM, remained dominant throughout Mkapa's presidential periods. The oppositional parties have been experiencing continuing and ever more crushing defeats which continued in the third multi-party election in 2005, when Jakaya Kikwete and CCM captured a landslide 80 % of the votes (chapter 10).

One reason for the continued dominance of CCM, is that the former one-party legislation has not been replaced with new legislation in support of the multi-party system, as recommended by the Nyalali Commission of 1992. Some changes and amendments have been made in the Constitution, but not sufficient to offer the opposition parties a level playing field. These parties have been weak both in resources and capacity since the initiation of multi-party democratic rule. The electoral system with single member constituencies where the "winner takes all" seriously undermines the possibilities for the opposition to win parliamentary seats, as discussed in chapter 10. The outcome is an election democracy rather that a genuine democracy that can provide space for agency and influence on a wider societal scale. The most likely possibility for creation of a substantial political opposition to CCM, that can dynamise the multi-party political system, is through the fracturing of CCM itself into different political factions and political parties. Rumours about such developments have occurred from time to time throughout the Tanzanian post-independence period. However, history has shown that CCM has always been able to mobilize to restore unity when its political hegemony has been threatened.

The outcomes of the multi-party elections also reflect the lack of transformational change in the Tanzanian economy. Limited societal differentiation has occurred that can be the basis for the emergence of broader interest groups that may constitute new political parties. Tanzania is still a country with an economic basis in natural resources and agriculture with a predominantly poor and politically unorganized rural population. The National Household Budget Survey 2007 found that 18.6 million of the Tanzanian population of 21 million that are above 15 years of age are economically active. 68 % of them were found in agriculture, hunting and forestry. In rural areas this figure reached nearly 82 %. Only 1.4 % of the economically active population was found to be employed in manufacturing (National Bureau of Statistics, 2009).

Development Assistance, International Financial Institutions and Macro Economic Management

Tanzanian development has been closely intertwined with development assistance. Increases in project based development assistance accelerated in response to the Arusha Declaration in February 1967. It is a paradox that Tanzania was overwhelmed with willing donors when the country declared its principle for development would be self-reliance. During the 1970s the country became heavily dependent upon development assistance to large scale industrial projects and for securing imports for expansion of parastal

companies that meant as well growth of the state and state-related bureaucracy. Heavy subsidies from the Tanzanian government to parastal companies
including the state controlled crop sector that performed poorly, if at all, led
to a gradual undermining of the Tanzanian economy which was exacerbated
by the forced ujamaa villagisation campaigns from 1973 to 1976, droughts
in 1973/74, and the oil price shocks of 1974 and 1979 (Havnevik, 1993).
The second phase of development assistance to Tanzania and sub-Saharan
Africa was linked to emergence of neo-liberal economic thinking or ideology
in the early 1980s that envisaged the market as the engine of development
(Wangwe, 1987, Gibbon, 1992, Gibbon et al 1993, Mtei, 2009).

The changes in development assistance during Mkapa's presidential periods
reflect the coming of a third phase of development assistance but now in
the context where political reforms were superimposed on the economic
reforms. The economic aspects of this development assistance phase
gradually shifted from the traditional structural adjustment programmes,
through debt reduction to broader poverty assessments and poverty reduction strategies (PRS). The new development assistance paradigm led to an
increase in the space for agency for the Tanzanian government as well as
for local communities (refer to chapters 7 and 9). But the outcomes were
not uniform across the national-local levels. The ownership was much
higher at the Ministry of Finance, compared to sectoral ministries and
local government levels.

However, the Mkapa reign clearly led to increased discipline in the state
finances that stabilized the economy through enhanced macro-economic
management. This restored trust, as well, among the IFIs and international donors to the country, leading to further increases in development
assistance (chapter 9). However, the continued aid dependence of the
Tanzanian government may also put into question the claim of increased
government agency and the proposal made in chapter 9 for Tanzania to
prepare a long-term plan to exit from development assistance. It remains
to be seen whether the Paris Declaration of 2005, and the subsequent
Accra Declaration in 2008, that aim to promote recipient ownership and
increased efficiency in development assistance, can meet the expectations.

The recent exposure of corruption and broader governance problems, has
again led to mistrust among the IFIs and international donors. The ground
gained under Mkapa in the perception of improved economic management and governance, in particular during his first presidential period,
seems to have been partly lost under president Kikwete. International
donors have threatened to withhold disbursement of government budget
support during the last few years and in 2009 the World Bank is planning
to reduce its concessional lending to Tanzania by 14 % over the next three
year period. Tanzania has also dropped seven places in the World Bank's

annual borrower assessment which may have an effect on reducing development assistance from other donors (EIU, 2009).

A major problem with this new development assistance paradigm seems to be its continued reliance on external and domestic experts, although with increased space for the latter group, rather than it being driven by the country's own democratic process. This, however, is also a reflection of the problems of spreading and deepening the democratic processes based on the multi-party political system. Statistics show that people trust the president more than the parliament/national assembly, which is again trusted more than the elected local government councils (Afrobarometer, 2008).

Transitions to what?

The research analyses and findings presented in this book thus show that transitions in major societal areas in Tanzania with emphasis on Mkapa's reign from 1995 to 2005 have hardly been supportive of transformational outcomes. Although a number of dynamic developments and transitions have been documented, structural changes that could promote broad based economic development and increased agency and participation among the population in governance and democratic processes in the country are lacking. Rural poverty remains high and has only been reduced marginally in the period 1991 to 2007 (National Bureau of Statistics, 2009). Although increases have been recorded in agricultural production during Mkapa's reign and beyond, this has happened primarily through expansion of the land area cultivated, and not through increased labour productivity. Dynamic developments since 2000 have mainly occurred in the mining and tourism sectors where the influence and capture of benefits to a large extent are found among external interests.

The challenges facing Tanzania will be to restore trust among broad sections of the population in the democratic process and in government institutions, including their guidance towards a process of broader transformational development. The Tanzanian transitions during the Mkapa reign, can only to a very limited degree be seen to constitute elements in the direction of broad based and sustainable development that can enhance agricultural and rural productivity, reduce poverty and take account of environmental and climate related issues.

The role of Julius Nyerere and the legacy of the Tanzanian post-independence development model

The death of the Father of the Nation, former president Julius Nyerere in 1999, seems to have left Tanzania without a firm guiding hand, which in spite of its faults and increasing authoritarianism, encompassed an ethos of morality and justice. Tanzania, as argued in chapters of this book, is an example of a country where the influence and impact of one person's ideas and philosophy, i.e. those of Nyerere, have marked the post-independence development path strongly. Nyerere's contribution to nation building and peace in Tanzania, as argued using an ethical interpretation (refer to chapter 2), has, however, been carried forward by both the former president Benjamin Mkapa and the current president Jakaya Kikwete. To protect the legacy of Julius Nyerere in these important areas is in itself a significant contribution which has to be acknowledged.

When it comes to the pre-conditions for transformational change it can be argued, alongside the Marxist oriented interpretation, that Nyerere, misread the situation. His emphasis on ujamaa and the rural policies promoted, including increasing dependence upon development assistance, led to stronger integration in the global economy without agricultural productivity increases. Lack of emphasis on industrial development, based on Tanzanian realities, in the Arusha Declaration in 1967, also undermined the possibility for broad based economic development. The industrial development that did emerge later, in the 1970s, and in a context of global economic stagnation, was basically donor driven and unsustainable and contributed little to Tanzanian broad based development. On the other hand it increased the country's external debt and donor dependence, which still persists. Former president Mkapa was not able to promote strategies, as documented in this book, that could generate transitions with transformational outcomes including the reduction of poverty in the country. The current president, Jakaya Kikwete, and his government have yet to prove that they will be able accomplish this.

References

Afrobarometer, 2005 and 2008.

BoT (Bank of Tanzania) 2009, *Monthly Economic Review October 2009.* Dar es Salaam, October 2009.

Bryceson, D.F. 2000, "Peasant Theories and Smallholder Policies: Past and Present", in Bryceson, D.F., C. Kay and J. Mooij (eds), *Disappearing Peasantries? Rural Labour in Africa, Asia and Latin America.* London: ITDG Publishing, pp. 1-16.

Chang, Ha-Joon 2003, *Kicking away the Ladder – Developoment Strategy in a Historical Perspective*. London: Anthem Press.

Cotula, L., S. Vermeulen, R. Leonard and J. Keeley 2009, "Land grab or development opportunity? Agricultural investment and international land deals in Africa". IIED, FAO and IFAD.

EIU (Economist Intelligence Unit) 2009, *Tanzania – country report*. London, October 2009.

Ellis, Frank 1983, "Agricultural Marketing and Peasant-State Transfers in Tanzania", *Journal of Peasant Studies*, Vol. 10, No. 4, pp. 214-242.

Gibbon, Peter 1992, "The World Bank and African Poverty 1973-91", *Journal of Modern African Studies*, Vol. 30, No. 2.

Gibbon, Peter, Kjell J. Havnevik and Kenneth Hermele 1993, *A Blighted Harvest. The World Bank and African Agriculture in the 1980s*. London and Trention NJ: James Currey and Africa World Press.

Gibbon, Peter and Stefano Ponte 2005, *Trading Down: Africa, Value Chains and the Global Economy.* Philadelphia. Temple University Press, USA.

Havnevik, Kjell 1993, *Tanzania – The Limits to Development from Above*. Uppsala and Dar es Salaam: The Nordic Africa Institute and Mkuki na Nyota Publishers.

—, 2009, "Outsourcing of African land for energy and food production – challenges to smallholders". Paper presented to a conference organized by the Africa Task Force, Pretoria, South Africa, July 10-12.

Havnevik, Kjell, Deborah Bryceson, Lars-Erik Birgegård, Prosper Matondi and Atakilte Beyene (eds) 2007, *African Agriculture and The World Bank. Development or Impoverishment?* Policy Dialogue No. 1. Uppsala: The Nordic Africa Institute.

Havnevik, Kjell, Tekeste Negash and Atakilte Beyene, 2006, *Of Global Concern. Rural Livelilhood Dynamics and Natural Resource Governance*. Sida Studies no. 16. Stockholm: Sida.

Havnevik, Kjell and Mats Hårsmar 1999, *The Diversified Future – An Institutional Approach to Rural Development in Tanzania*. Expert Group on Development Studies, EGDI, Swedish Foreign Ministry, Stockholm.

IFPRI, 2009 (Joachim von Braun and Ruth Meinzen-Dick), "'Land Grabbing' by Foreign Investors in Development Countries: Risks and Opportunities". IPFRI Policy Brief, 13 April, 2009. A comprehensive listing of overseas land investments is available on IFPRI's webside at www.ifpri.org/pubs/bp/bp013.asp.

IMF 2006, United Republic of Tanzania: Fifth Review under the Three-Year Arrangement under the Poverty Reduction and Growth Facility. Staff Report; Staff Statement; Press Release on the Executive Board Discussion; and Statement by the Executive Director for the United Republic of Tanzania. IMF Country Report No. 06/138 Washington DC, IMF.

Maliyankono, T.L. and Mboyo S.D. Bagachwa 1980, *Second Economy in Tanzania*. Ohio University and Swallow Press.

Mtei, Edward 2009, *From Goatherd to Governor. The autobiography of Edwin Mtei*. Dar es Salaam: Mkuki na Nyota Publishers.

National Bureau of Statistics 2009, *Tanzania Household Budget Survey – 2007. Analytical Report*. Dar es Salaam, 8 March 2009.

Sarris, Alexander and Panayotis Karfakis 2007, "Household Vulnerability", in Christiaensen, Luc and Alexander Sarris (eds), *Rural household vulnerability and insurance against commodity risk. Evidence from the United Republic of Tanzania*. FAO Commodities and Trade Technical Paper No. 10, FAO, Rome, pp. 49-70.

Shivji, Issa 2006, *Let the People Speak. Tanzania down the Road to Neo-Liberalism*. Council for the Development of Social Science Research in Africa, CODESRIA, Dakar, Senegal.

UN Special Rapporteur on the Right to Food (Olivier De Schutter) 2009, "Large-scale land acquisitions and leases: A set of core principles and measures to address the human rights challenges", 11. June.

Wangwe, Samuel 1987, "Impact of the IMF/World Bank Philosophy, the Case of Tanzania", in Havnevik, K.J. (ed), *The IMF and the World Bank in Tanzania. Conditionalities and Their Impact*. Seminar Proceedings No. 18. Uppsala: The Nordic Africa Institute.

Contributors

JUMANNE M. ABDALLAH is conducting research and teaching at Sokoine University of Agriculture in Morogoro, Tanzania. He holds a PhD in forest economics from the same university and he is engaged in a number of research projects focusing on community and participatory forestry and various aspects of forest economics in cooperation with other Tanzanian and foreign university departments.

DEBORAH FAHY BRYCESON holds a PhD from Oxford University and is currently a reader at Glasgow University. She has long experience from research on Tanzanian and Sub-Saharan issues in Tanzanian and British universities. Her research straddles a number of critical issues related to African development, among them the role of agriculture and smallholder production, rural transport, mining, HIV and AIDS and rural development, food security, the role of the IMF and the World Bank in Sub-Saharan Africa. She has published numerous books and articles in scholarly journals related to her long term research.

BRIAN COOKSEY holds a PhD in sociology and has been a researcher and teacher at universities in Britain and the University of Dar es Salaam. He has been based in Dar es Salaam since the late 1970s. He has authored books, scholarly articles and reports on various aspects of Tanzanian development, including agriculture and rural development, the impact of international assistance and, in particular, on corruption and governance issues. He established the research based organisation, TADREG, but has also worked for a number of Tanzanian research institutes, among them REPOA. Cooksey is presently an independent consultant and researcher.

JONAS EWALD is a researcher at the School of Global Studies, the University of Gothenburg. He was the co-initiator and for some time the leader of the Centre for African Studies at the same university. His research focuses mainly on Tanzania and Rwanda and on issues related to governance including democratisation, decentralisation, participation and the quality of public service delivery. He has an intimate knowledge of many Tanzanian rural regions from his wide research experience in the country.

KJELL HAVNEVIK is senior researcher at the Nordic Africa Institute and professor in development studies at the University of Agder, Norway. He has more than three decades of experience from research and higher education in Norwegian, Swedish and Tanzanian research institutes and universities. His research emphasis is on rural development, natural resource management, rural diversification, development assistance and the role of the World Bank in Tanzania and Sub-Saharan Africa. He has published a number of books and articles about various Tanzanian development issues and he led the team of researchers conducting the "Tanzanian Country Study and Aid Review", published by the University of Bergen in 1988 and the study on "African Agriculture and the World Bank", published by the Nordic Africa Institute in 2007.

AIDA C. ISINIKA is an associate professor at Sokoine University of Agriculture (SUA), Tanzania in the Institute of Continuing Education, with a mandate for teaching, research and outreach. She teaches production economics and other courses, and supervises undergraduate and graduate students in the Department of Agricultural Economics and Agribusiness and in the Institute of Development Studies. She has published and done consulting work on various aspects of development, particularly focusing on resource use efficiency. She is currently on leave from the university, coordinating the Agricultural Scale Up Initiative in Tanzania under Oxfam.

GERALD C. MONELA holds a PhD of forest economics from the University of Life Sciences in Norway. He has been the dean of the Forest Faculty at the Sokoine University of Agriculture, Tanzania and was elected vice chancellor of the same university in 2006, a position he still holds. He has wide research and teaching experience related to forest economics, community and participatory forestry, natural resource management related to forestry. Monela is a member of the board of several important Tanzanian institutions and he has been the author of many important reports and studies related to forest and natural resource management, development assistance and research organisation with a focus on Tanzania and Sub-Saharan Africa.

KHAMALDIN MUTABAZI is a lecturer at Sokoine University of Agriculture (SUA) in the Department of Agricultural Economics and Agribusiness, teaching econometrics, mathematics for economists and micro-computer data handling. He has previously worked with the International Institute of Tropical Agriculture (IITA) – Tanzania as a regional scientist. He has published various papers on a range of developmental issues, particularly focusing on institutional aspects of the environment – land and agricultural water management, and micro-level climate change adaptation economics which are still his areas of current research interest.

JARLE SIMENSEN is professor emeritus in African history at the University of Oslo. He has long experience from teaching and researching African history with a focus on West and East Africa. He has over the years been teaching and supervising a number of students at NTNU, Trondheim. He is the author of several books and journal articles addressing African issues in a historical perspective and he was also the editor of the first of three volumes on the history of Norwegian development assistance (in Norwegian) published in 2003 by Fagbokforlaget, Bergen.

RUNE SKARSTEIN is associate professor of economics at the Norwegian University of Science and Technology (NTNU). He has long experience of research and education related to problems of economic underdevelopment, with special emphasis on Tanzania. He has also conducted research on India, Latin America and global issues. He is the most outstanding Norwegian researcher in the field of political economy. He is the author and editor of several important books and journal articles dealing with economic (under-)development. His latest book was published in Norway in 2008, *Ökonomi på en annen måte* (Economics – an alternative perspective), Abstrakt forlag (publishers), Oslo.

SAMUEL WANGWE is currently an independent consultant based in Dar es Salaam and also an advisor to the Tanzanian government. He holds a PhD from the University of Dar es Salaam. He is professor of economics and dean at the same university and during the 1990s he was a co-initiator and the first director of the Economic and Social Research Forum, ESRF, in Dar es Salaam. Samuel Wangwe has been on the board of many important Tanzanian organisations and institutions. He has published a number of books on various aspects of Tanzanian and African development related to industrial development, financial matters, poverty and rural development, structural adjustment and macro-economic management. He is as well the author of many important reports and studies commissioned by governments in Africa and beyond, donors and international financial institutions.

Conference Participants

FAMILY NAME	FIRST NAME	COUNTRY	INSTITUTION
Andersson	Gun-Britt	France	Swedish Ambassador to OECD, Paris
Andersson	Ingrid	Sweden	The Nordic Africa Institute
Arora-Jonsson	Seema	Sweden	Uppsala University
Bakari	Mohammed	Tanzania	Department of Political Science, University of Dar es Salaam
Bjällås	Åsa	Sweden	Sida, Stockholm
Boesen	Jannik	Denmark	DIIS, Copenhagen
Brandström	Per	Sweden	Uppsala University, Department of Anthropology
Bryceson	Ian	Norway	UMB, Ås
Cadstedt	Jenny	Sweden	Stockholm University
Chiwona-Karltun	Linley	Sweden	Swedish University of Agriculture, Uppsala
Cooksey	Brian	Tanzania	REPOA, Dar es Salaam
Duveskog	Deborah	Sweden	Swedish University of Agriculture, Uppsala
Enfors	Elin	Sweden	Stockholm University
Ewald	Jonas	Sweden	Göteborg University
Faaland	Just	Norway	Chr. Michelsen, Bergen
Fogelberg	Karin	Sweden	Orgut, Stockholm
Friis Hansen	Esbern	Denmark	DIIS, Copenhagen
Giertz	Per	Sweden	Orgut, Stockholm
Hansson	Oloph	Sweden	Svetan, Stockholm
Hansson	Göte	Sweden	Lund University
Haram	Liv	Sweden	The Nordic Africa Institute
Hasu	Päivi	Sweden	The Nordic Africa Institute
Havnevik	Kjell	Sweden	The Nordic Africa Institute
Hårsmar Stockholm	Mats	Sweden	Ministry for Foreign Affairs,
Isinika	Aida	Tanzania	Sokoine University of Agriculture, Morogoro

Jerve	Alf Morten	Norway	Chr. Michelsen Institute, Bergen
Jämtin	Carin	Sweden	Ministry for Foreign Affairs, Stockholm
Kopone3	Juhani	Finland	Helsinki University
Kronberg	Marianne	Sweden	Sida, Stockholm
Lange	Siri	Norway	Chr. Michelsen, Bergen
Melber	Henning	Sweden	The Nordic Africa Institute
Monela	Gerald	Tanzania	Sokoine University of Agriculture, Morogoro
Odén	Bertil	Sweden	Sida, Stockholm
Otto	Opira	Sweden	Swedish University of Agriculture, Uppsala
Pettersson	Torbjörn	Tanzania	Swedish Embassy, Dar es Salaam
Reuterswärd	Karin	Sweden	Stockholm University
Rudebeck	Lars	Sweden	Uppsala University
Rylander	Sten	Sweden	Ministry for Foreign Affairs, Stockholm
Sandström	Emil	Sweden	Swedish Agriculture University, Uppsala
Simensen	Jarle	Norway	University of Oslo, Department of History
Skarstein	Rune	Norway	NTNU, Trondheim
Ståhl	Michael	Sweden	International Foundation for Science, Stockholm
Stödberg	Ann	Sweden	Sida, Stockholm
Wangwe	Samuel	Tanzania	ESRF, Dar es Salaam
Winbo	Karolina	Sweden	The Nordic Africa Institute
Winkel	Klaus	Denmark	Danida, Copenhagen until July 2004
Wohlgemuth	Lennart	Sweden	The Nordic Africa Institute
Östberg	Wilhelm	Sweden	Stockholm University